SOLUTIONS TO CRITICAL
BEHAVIORAL ISSUES IN THE CLASSROOM

Also Available

*Handbook of Evidence-Based Practices
for Emotional and Behavioral Disorders:
Applications in Schools*
Edited by Hill M. Walker and Frank M. Gresham

*Safe and Healthy Schools, Second Edition:
Practical Prevention Strategies*
Jeffrey R. Sprague and Hill M. Walker

SOLUTIONS
TO CRITICAL
BEHAVIORAL
ISSUES
IN THE
CLASSROOM

Hill M. Walker

THE GUILFORD PRESS
New York London

Printed in the United States of America

This book is printed on acid-free paper.

Last digit is print number: 9 8 7 6 5 4 3 2 1

The author has checked with sources believed to be reliable in his efforts
to provide information that is complete and generally in accord with the
standards of practice that are accepted at the time of publication. However,
in view of the possibility of human error or changes in behavioral, mental
health, or medical sciences, neither the author, nor the editor and publisher,
nor any other party who has been involved in the preparation or publication
of this work warrants that the information contained herein is in every
respect accurate or complete, and they are not responsible for any errors or
omissions or the results obtained from the use of such information. Readers
are encouraged to confirm the information contained in this book with other
sources.

Library of Congress Cataloging-in-Publication Data is available
from the publisher.

ISBN 978-1-4625-4920-7 (paperback)
ISBN 978-1-4265-5120-0 (hardcover)

To Janet Eaton-Walker, my soulmate of six decades and revered high school language arts, reading, and Spanish teacher

About the Author

Hill M. Walker, PhD, is Emeritus Professor of Special Education and Co-Director of the Institute on Violence and Destructive Behavior at the University of Oregon. He is also Senior Research Scientist at the Oregon Research Institute. Dr. Walker has focused his career on conducting research to better understand, identify, and remediate the behavioral challenges experienced by at-risk students in grades K–12, with a specialization in preschoolers and elementary students. He has 235 publications, including 20 books, and is a recipient of the Kauffman–Hallahan–Pullen Distinguished Researcher Award from the Council for Exceptional Children and the Research Award from the National Center for School Mental Health, among other honors.

Preface

TO THE READER

The main goal of this book is to provide direct guidance for teachers on solving critical classroom behavioral issues. Credible resource information is given on effective strategies for (1) enhancing adaptive student behavior that is congruent with teacher classroom expectations, and (2) reducing and eliminating maladaptive forms of behavior that research shows are uniformly rejected by teachers (Kerr & Zigmond, 1986; Walker, 1986, 1995). General and special education teachers are viewed as the ultimate end users of the book, but behavioral specialists, positive behavioral interventions and supports (PBIS) coaches, school psychologists, school counselors, and social workers who work with and support teachers should also find the material helpful in consulting with teachers on challenging behavior issues.

This book is somewhat unusual in that it is similar in principle to the *Physicians' Desk Reference* (PDR). Just as the PDR enhances a physician's practice by providing easily accessible diagnostic and treatment information, problems that are a common part of a teacher's daily responsibility are identified and recommended strategies and solutions are provided—rather than leaving it to the reader to decide which strategy best fits a particular target behavior or problem. I hope this teachers' desk reference enhances teachers' overall quality of classroom life and results in better and easier management of the classroom.

This resource book grew out of my career over the past 50 years as an applied researcher with students who have school-related behavior problems and are often emotionally challenged (e.g., anxiety, self-control issues, explosive temperaments). In the vast majority of cases, these children and youth are not well prepared to meet the basic demands of schooling, such as cooperating with others, being motivated to learn, having good study skills, respecting the teacher's authority, or being able to handle frustration. Neither teachers nor schools cause these students to behave inappropriately, but the histories, beliefs, and attitudes of these students, when combined with necessary attempts to manage their behavior, often fuel the development of conflicts with teachers, peers, and other school staff.

The challenges presented by students with school-related behavior problems develop over time and have become common occurrences in today's schools. Such problems often go unsolved, leading to a lower quality of school life for students and teachers, accompanied by potential long-term problems in development. Teacher stress and burnout can be traced to a lack of success in coping with these problems. Though these behavioral challenges vary substantially in their intensity and frequency, they are a common experience for teachers and students in school education settings.

Teachers today are under constant pressure from the public to help parents socialize children and youth to achieve school success and educational attainment. The burdens and stresses that teachers experience in this regard are enormous. The COVID-19 pandemic has illustrated just how difficult the job of teaching can be. I hope the material in this book will assist teachers in managing classrooms of a broad range of students, many of whom come from dire personal circumstances and are under substantial stress themselves. Teaching remains a vital profession, is an important pathway for helping students succeed, and is a major positive influence on our collective quality of life.

The strategies and solutions presented in this book are applicable primarily to students in kindergarten through grade 6 or 7. I have been especially focused on the goal of assisting students in getting off to the best start possible in their school careers and achieving school success, which can act much like a vaccine in preventing later problems in adolescence (Hawkins, Catalano, Kosterman, Abbott, & Hill, 1999).

This book is based on three information sources: (1) my direct experiences over more than 50 years in conducting empirical research and development work with students having challenging behavior; (2) implementing classroom and playground interventions to solve difficult management problems, along with the many takeaway lessons gleaned from the successes and failures of these efforts; and (3) continuous review of reported findings and best practices that enhance the ability of teachers and other school personnel to assist students who are difficult to teach and manage.

As mentioned, I have organized the core content of the book (i.e., Parts I and II) so that strategies are directly applied to specific target behaviors rather than presenting a series of strategies for generalized application in school settings, as is the case with most other resource books on this topic.

This provides credible information and direction regarding the match of intervention technique(s) to a specific target behavior. It is my hope that this approach provides greater efficacy and ease in applying these principles in what are often challenging classroom situations.

Throughout the book, I have attempted to base its core content on the impressive advances in schooling effectiveness practices that have developed over the past two decades. These advances have been compiled and are reflected in the work of Kathleen Lane and her colleagues and in the work of Sandra Chafouleas and her colleagues (see Lane, Menzies, Oakes, & Kalberg, 2020; Chafouleas, Johnson, Riley-Tillman, & Iovino, 2021). My goal herein is to present these strategies in a way that allows their feasible application in the classroom and larger school environment.

CONTENT RATIONALE AND EVIDENCE BASE

In the 1980s I did some research on the reintegration of students with moderate to severe behavior problems into general education settings following their brief assignment to a specialized classroom setting. As part of this work, my colleagues and I developed some instruments for assessing the behavioral expectations of regular and special education teachers to guide the reintegration process (Hersh & Walker, 1983; Walker & Rankin, 1983; Walker, 1986). The goal was to maximize the fit or match between a teacher's expectations and a student's behavior.

These instruments have been widely adopted in classroom research by others and their results have been confirmed in numerous reported studies (Kerr & Zigmond, 1986; Kauffman, Lloyd, & McGee, 1989; Lane, Pierson, & Givner, 2003, 2004). Teacher behavioral expectations of students are very important. Empirical studies show that teacher expectations of students influence not only teacher–student interactions but what students learn and how they behave (Good, 1987; Johnson, Wildy, & Shand, 2019). Further, the quality of teacher–student interactions provides a model for how peers should treat each other in social exchanges. My colleagues and I developed a national data base of 1,000 K–12 general and special education teachers who used these instruments in their classrooms. The results of this survey helped define the content foundation for this book.

These instruments allowed us to identify the highest-rated or most-preferred adaptive behaviors (out of 56 rated behaviors) and the highest-rated maladaptive or most-unacceptable behaviors (out of 51 rated behaviors). Surveyed teachers were asked to rate each of 56 adaptive behaviors as to how important they were to a successful adjustment in their classrooms. They also rated 51 maladaptive behaviors as to how tolerated or unacceptable they were.

Our survey results showed that the adaptive student behaviors teachers typically prefer to see in their students define the ideal student who *complies promptly with teacher directions, is organized and motivated to learn, follows rules, ignores peer distractions while working, and has good self-control and study skills.* These teacher-identified social behaviors are facilitative of student academic performance and positive classroom adjustment. They are referred to as *academic enablers* and are very important to most teachers. As noted, their display influences how teachers view and interact with their students (DiPerna, 2005). In contrast, the highest-rated (i.e., least-tolerated) maladaptive behaviors severely disrupt the teacher–student relationship—not to mention the classroom. They include the student who *defies the teacher, does not follow teacher-imposed rules, ignores teacher warnings or reprimands, is insubordinate, has tantrums, destroys classmates' property, and is physically aggressive with others* (Hersh & Walker, 1983; Walker, 1986).

These results align very closely with my own experiences in conducting universal screening of K–7 students as well as implementing classroom and playground interventions in schools over the past five decades (Walker, 1995, 2014). The highest-rated items addressed by the chapters in Part I of this book reflect teacher concerns regarding students who do not engage in expected teacher behaviors at normative or sufficient frequencies. In contrast, the highest-rated items addressed by the chapters in Part II, on maladaptive behaviors, reflect teacher concerns about critical behavioral events that do not depend on frequency of occurrence for their salience: It is the severity or seriousness of these that drive teachers' concerns. Students can present a behavioral challenge if they engage in teacher-preferred behaviors too infrequently and a relatively greater challenge if they display unacceptable behaviors too often.

There is evidence that students who are low on their adaptive behavioral profiles and high on their maladaptive behavioral profiles are not seen as likeable by their teachers and can inadvertently experience reduced academic support in the process of instruction (Brophy & Evertson, 1981; Brophy & Good, 1986). For example, the research of Brophy and Good and their colleagues shows that low-expectation students are often provided with fewer opportunities to respond, fewer prompts and cues, reduced corrections, and limited second chances as well as less praise and more criticism of their performance (Good, 1987; Johnson et al., 2019). In stark contrast, the teachers' reactions to their high-expectation students were the opposite.

This differential treatment of low- versus high-expectation students over time can contribute to a lack of school success that is often associated with later school failure and dropout. Given the negative relationship that often exists between teachers and challenging students, this finding is not surprising. The failure to meet teacher behavioral expectations can have serious long-term developmental consequences and speaks to the urgency of addressing this need as soon as possible in a student's career.

HOW THIS BOOK IS ORGANIZED

Part I focuses on the specific types of student behavior that teachers find desirable and acceptable, while Part II focuses on those they find undesirable and highly unacceptable. I call these behaviors a *teacher dream list* (acceptable and preferred) and a *teacher nightmare list* (unacceptable and not tolerated). Many teachers are unsuccessful in coping with students who fail to meet these behavioral expectations and, as noted, suffer stress and burnout as a result.

Effective use of the material in this book requires a basic familiarity with best practices in classroom behavior management. Part III of this book provides this information, which is focused on (1) effective strategies for increasing desirable behavior; (2) effective strategies for reducing and eliminating undesirable behavior; and (3) effective strategies for sustaining behavioral gains over time and across settings. For readers who are unfamiliar with behavioral intervention techniques and strategies for managing student behavior, I recommend reviewing the material in Part III before reading Parts I and II.

Four appendices are provided to further enhance and illustrate the book's content. Appendix 1 provides a copy of the short form of the SBS Inventory, which is a tool I have used to identify the behavioral standards and expectations of teachers in general education settings. It is especially useful in reintegrating students with challenging behavior into mainstream classrooms. In Appendix 2 I have provided a brief annotated bibliography of some additional evidence-based resources that may be of special interest to related services personnel charged with addressing larger schoolwide issues and health-related or chronic problems that often go beyond common classroom challenges (i.e., school safety of students and staff, coping with explosive students, schoolwide screening systems and intervention approaches and frameworks for supporting and delivering evidence-based practices, creation of a nurturing school culture, and strategies for linking assessment to intervention). These recommended resources are important in terms of their potential for making schools more positive, effective, and safer. Appendix 3 contains a handout that teachers can share with parents on how to debrief effectively with their children about the school day. Finally, Appendix 4 addresses the issue of unrecognized and undiagnosed child psychiatric disorders that can co-occur with the problem behaviors of Part II of this volume. These disorders have the potential to reduce the efficacy of the behavior change strategies described in Part II.

Part I: Appropriate Behavior

Part I contains six chapters, each addressing one of the six highest teacher-preferred student behaviors from our survey and presented in a standard format that includes:

- Definition, key features, and examples of the target behavior
- Causal influences and antecedent conditions
- Recommended generic strategies and implementation guidelines for addressing the target behavior (i.e., solving the problem)
- Considerations in solving the problem (e.g. what to expect, trouble-shooting, etc.)

Case studies are provided throughout the narrative to illustrate important principles and strategies. Figures and lists are also provided to set off and highlight important material at key points.

These six chapters are arranged in ascending order of complexity—the behaviors addressed range from simpler to more complex in terms of their likely resistance to or difficulty in being solved. For example, a tendency to not comply with teacher directives is much less resistant to change than a tendency to express frustration and anger when not getting one's way. Similarly, damaging others' property and possessions is less difficult to deal with than stealing, cheating, and lying.

Part II: Inappropriate Behavior

Part II also contains six chapters, each addressing one of the six most unacceptable student behaviors as indicated by surveyed K–12 teachers. The same organizational format is used as in Part I.

The unacceptable behaviors listed in Part II are considered critical events—that is, they can do a lot of damage when they occur, may require long periods for recovery, and their severity and impact do not depend on how often they occur. In a sense, they function as infrequent "behavioral earthquakes" in this regard. Critical events are high-intensity forms of behavior that can prompt destructive, escalated teacher–student conflicts, and severely disrupt the teaching–learning process (e.g., stealing, defying the teacher, damaging others' property, or having tantrums). They create strong resentments and continue to impact teacher behavior over the long term toward students who display them. Further, if a teacher is unsuccessful in dealing with these behavioral challenges, it weakens their authority in the eyes of the other students.

In cases of severe teacher defiance or threats to others' safety, it is very important that school staff be enlisted to address any forms of behavior where teachers or peers risk harm from their occurrence. A room-clear strategy is commonly required to get things initially under control and reestablish classroom order in these situations. Appropriate administrative actions should follow use of such a procedure for an out-of-control student.

Some of the behaviors listed above for both Part I and Part II of the book are best dealt with on a case-by-case basis, while others are better dealt with as universal or classwide interventions and then through individual student follow-up. For example, compliance with teacher directives, producing acceptable quality work given one's skill level, stealing or cheating, and having tantrums primarily require individualized strategies. Behaviors such as following established classroom rules, cooperating in small-group activities, and having normal interactions with peers without becoming hostile or angry are probably best taught initially on a classwide basis and then individually as necessary. Studies and expert opinion show that individualized interventions are more effective when applied in well-managed classrooms with a positive climate (Hawken, Crone, Bundock, & Horner, 2021).

Part III: Principles and Techniques of Behavioral Technology

The material in Part III is divided into three chapters that deal respectively with how to increase desirable behavior, how to decrease undesirable behavior, and how to sustain achieved behavior change over time. Techniques described under each of these areas are as follows: increasing behavior—teacher praise, reinforcement procedures, shaping, modeling plus reinforcement, verbal feedback, self-monitoring/self-control, contingency contracting, and social skills training; decreasing behavior—debriefing behavioral alternatives, redirecting behavior or performance, stimulus change, time out, and cost contingency or fines; and maintaining achieved gains—implementing a low-cost variation of the intervention that produced improvement, booster "shots", fading, substituting praise for points, and the role of special peer helpers. A common format is used across the behavior management techniques as follows: definition and examples, guidelines for correct application, and issues to consider when implementing.

Acknowledgments

There are a number of individuals who deserve credit for their contributions to the development of this volume.

- Guilford Senior Editor Rochelle Serwator served very skillfully, as did professional editor Anna Bristow, who provided superb edits, comments, and suggestions on the narrative.
- Steve Forness offered numerous substantive contributions and ideas for enhancing the book's content as well as advice and support throughout the book's development.
- Wendy Oakes provided a superb review of the chapter content and made the book's content more relevant and understandable.
- Thanks are due to Michael Bullis, Andy Frey, Ray Hull, and Chris Murray, who read and provided important feedback on key sections of the book.

Contents

**PART III. STRATEGIES FOR INCREASING DESIRABLE BEHAVIOR,
DECREASING UNDESIRABLE BEHAVIOR, AND SUSTAINING
ACHIEVED BEHAVIOR CHANGE OVER TIME**

Strategies for Solving Problems with Students Who Do Not Meet Teacher Expectations for Appropriate Classroom Behavior

Enhancing Student Compliance with Teacher Requests and Directives

Noncompliance (NC) with adult requests and directives is a very common occurrence with children and youth. It often results from inadvertent errors in the way the adult directive or command is given and/or the child's lack of understanding of what he or she is being asked to do. Compliance with adult requests and directives is one of the most important skills a young child can learn: It enables emotional growth, learning, and adjustment in many areas and sets a pattern that determines whether relationships with adults become positive and cooperative or negative and challenging.

NC AS A CHARACTERISTIC BEHAVIOR PATTERN

Many experts consider NC a gateway behavior that often leads to other forms of maladaptive behavior if not corrected (e.g., teacher–student conflict, poor classroom adjustment, weak achievement, disrupted peer relations, and ultimately school failure and dropout; McMahon & Forehand, 2005). Although NC has its origins in early childhood, it can last a lifetime and do untold damage to relationships of all kinds. Unfortunately, many children bring a well-established pattern of NC with them to the start of their school careers, having had it inadvertently strengthened at home by parents' handling of the child's refusing directives and requests. In these circumstances, some children adopt NC early on as a characteristic behavior pattern. It is very important that NC be addressed early and consistently by teachers (as well as parents) if it is a characteristic behavior pattern so as to prevent its disruption of the teaching–learning process.

DEFINITION, KEY FEATURES, AND EXAMPLES OF NC

While NC can obviously refer to refusal of directives by parents, peers, or other social agents, it is used here in relation to the teacher and classroom setting. As noted in the Preface, prompt compliance with teacher directives was rated as the most important student behavior of the 56 adaptive behaviors included in our K–12 1,000-teacher survey.

NC is defined as a student not responding to or defying a specific teacher directive. It can occur under the following circumstances: (1) no response is given; (2) no response is given within a reasonable time period (usually 5 or 10 seconds); or (3) some alternative, unrequested response is substituted for the requested behavior. It also occurs when a student fails to meet a prespecified performance standard that he or she is capable of achieving (Schoen, 1986; Morgan & Jenson, 1988). Further, some students will refuse to comply by attempting to renegotiate the nature or conditions of the teacher directive. Commands can be directed toward individuals or groups of students.

Alpha and Beta Commands

The likelihood of a student's compliance with a specific request has a great deal to do with the nature and timing of the directive. There are two major types of commands, *alpha* and *beta*, as distinguished by McMahon and Forehand (2005) in their classic work on NC.

Alpha commands are clear, direct, and specific in nature. They are to the point, do not involve excessive verbalization, and allow a reasonable time for child response. The following are some examples of alpha commands: "Sarah, I want you to pick up your room after dinner"; "Class, I need your full attention before starting this activity"; "Jose, please go to the office and see about your unexcused absence." Directives stated in this form are likely to result in student compliance.

Beta commands are characterized by excessive verbalizations and often do not specify a criterion for compliance. They can be cast in the form of lectures, are often full of criticism that can cause student resentment, and reflect adult frustration and anger. The following are examples of beta commands: "Otis, I get so tired of repeating directions because of your poor listening skills. You should learn to pay better attention when I'm speaking. Now what don't you understand?"; "Fred, your room is always such a mess. Why don't you clean it up instead of waiting for me to do it?";

"Jamey, let me know when you're ready to begin the task. I wish you were better organized and interested in your schoolwork."

How Many Commands Do Teachers Typically Give?

Golly (1994) conducted a study of commands and students' NC with their teachers' directives in grades 1 and 2. Forty general education teachers and their classrooms participated in the study and the author conducted two 30-minute observation sessions in each classroom where all teacher directives and student responses were systematically coded. The number of commands given across teachers for the two 30-minute sessions combined ranged from 1 to 163! These findings replicated those in a study reported by Strain, Lambert, Kerr, Stagg, and Lenkner (1983), who found a range of 12 to 150 commands delivered in a 1-hour period across 19 teachers. These results clearly show a very broad range in the number of teacher commands given.

In the Golly (1994) study, teachers delivered an average of 59% alpha commands and 41% beta commands. Students complied with 83% of all teacher commands; compliance rates for alpha commands were 88% and 76% for beta commands. As this study showed, the likelihood of a student complying with alpha commands is usually greater than for beta commands. In addition, beta commands are negative in tone and may be perceived as punishing by the student, while alpha commands are much easier to give and do not carry the risk of creating emotional resentment by the student.

TYPES OF NC

There are four types of recognized NC (Kuczynski, Kochanska, Radke-Yarrow, & Girnius-Brown, 1987): passive NC, simple refusal, direct defiance, and negotiation. Each is described in Figure 1.1.

As children develop and mature, simple refusal and negotiation tend to increase and direct defiance and passive NC tend to decrease. These latter two forms of NC are more characteristic of students with challenging behavior patterns, while the first two are considered more mature and sophisticated forms of NC (Walker & Sylwester, 1998).

INITIATING VERSUS TERMINATING COMMANDS

Teacher directives can also be coded as initiating versus terminating. Use of these types of directives are essential in managing a classroom of students. *Initiating commands* are a call to action and *terminating commands* call

Passive Noncompliance. In this form of NC, the individual resists performing the requested behavior but does not overtly refuse to do so. Ignoring the directive, resistant body language, or pretending not to hear or understand are common expressions of passive noncompliance. The directive may not be acknowledged and may need to be repeated to elicit compliance.

Simple Refusal. With this NC form, the request or directive is neither acknowledged nor complied with. It is a simple act of refusal normally unaccompanied by emotion or overt anger that uses such expressions of refusal as "No," "Sorry, I can't," or "I'm not doing that." As a rule, a reason for the refusal is not volunteered.

Direct Defiance. This type of noncompliance can be severe in its intensity and threatening to the teacher's authority. It refers to NC that is characterized by student anger, hostility, insubordination, and potentially threats or intimidation of the teacher. Direct defiance usually occurs when a directive is given to a student who is in an agitated state and escalates a simple teacher directive into a hostile situation. This can quickly devolve into a power struggle where neither teacher nor student backs down. The resulting escalated, negative interaction can be very damaging to the teacher–student relationship, disrupts the classroom, and often requires a room clear to get the situation under control. Such escalated interactions are dealt with in greater detail later on in this chapter.

Negotiation. This is considered a more sophisticated form of NC and is a tactic used by skilled students to avoid direct compliance with teacher directives. In negotiation, the student or child attempts to redefine and renegotiate the directive. An excuse or reason for the refusal is typically offered such as "I can't do it right now but will later," "I couldn't get my homework in on time since I misplaced it," "I'd like to substitute my extra-credit work for doing this assignment—they're about the same thing." When my son was about 3 or 4 years old, I yelled at him for not picking up his toys before our dinner guests arrived as I had told him. "Seth, I told you to get your toys all picked up pronto, but here you are still working on your Legos. So get to it!" "Dad, I can't do it." "Why not?" Seth answered, "I'm too nervous!" Seth knew it would be good to explain his noncompliance but he just needed to work on his reasons!

FIGURE 1.1. Characteristics of the four types of NC.

for stopping an action. Initiating commands are more often used to manage students engaged in academic activities, while terminating commands more often occur in managing students who are not following classroom rules or are displaying challenging behavior. Whenever possible it is better to manage a difficult situation with initiating rather than terminating commands, if feasible. For example, say that one student (Jason) is trying to divert another student's attention away from the class assignment by engaging him (Bryan) in conversation. One option is to reprimand Jason by telling him to stop disturbing Bryan; another would be to say, "Jason, I'd like you to focus on completing your assignment now." It is important to note the tone of this command. It does not send a punishing message in

TABLE 1.1. Examples of Initiating and Terminating Teacher Commands

	Initiating command	Terminating command
Academic content	"Jenny, please help me collect the class assignments." "Class, take out your math books and turn to today's assignment on p. 119."	"William, I want you to stop working on the word problems now." "Your small discussion is too loud. I'd like you to tone it down some."
Nonacademic content	"Randall, it would be good if you began your work now." "Maria, I'd like you to help me to record attendance today."	"Priscilla, Janice doesn't need you to show her how to get on the internet. Please stop trying to assist her." "Jeremiah, your humming is disturbing those around you. Please stop."

spite of Jason's behavior. Even terminating commands should be delivered in a firm but neutral or polite tone and never be used to communicate adult anger.

Table 1.1 presents some examples of initiating and terminating commands delivered within academic and nonacademic contexts.

CAUSAL INFLUENCES AND ANTECEDENT CONDITIONS OF NC

It is often puzzling why some children are much more noncompliant than classmates upon entering school. In some cases, it has to do with the nature of the child's preschool environment and the family's parenting style: Students who are initially noncompliant with teacher directives are likely bringing with them a behavior pattern they have found to be effective at home. The following are some common errors that parents make in delivering commands.

1. More beta than alpha commands are given by parents in managing the child's behavior.
2. Too many commands, directives, and prompts are given, leading to only occasional compliance.
3. Parents do not follow through and ensure that their directives are complied with.
4. Parents allow their child to intimidate them out of insisting on compliance with their commands.

5. The child's family has a pattern of poor and infrequent communication.
6. The child's activities are often unsupervised by parents.
7. The child learns that ignoring or not complying with parent commands results in increased attention, although often negative in tone.
8. The child does not receive praise or parental approval for compliance.

The stage is set for teacher–student conflict when a student who is unused to complying with adult directives participates in ordinary classroom activities that rely heavily upon the teacher's directives with expected student compliance.

CASE STUDY: THE NC TEACHER TRAP

A colleague and I conducted a classroom observational study in an elementary school general education classroom. Over a 2-week period, each of the teacher's interactions with her three most challenging students and three least challenging students were recorded (Walker & Buckley, 1973). For each teacher–student interaction, all teacher commands and student responses to them were systematically coded and recorded according to prespecified definitional criteria. The study results were strikingly different for the two groups of students:

- A clear majority of the teacher's time and attention was directed to the three most challenging students and a large percentage of it was negative in nature.
- Nearly all of the teacher's interactions with the three least challenging students were positive.
- The three least challenging students complied with the teacher's commands nearly 100% of the time, with student compliance occurring on the first issue of the directive in nearly all cases.
- As expected, a substantial proportion of the teacher's interactions with the three most challenging students was directed to their negative behavior.
- The three most challenging students occasionally complied with the teacher's initial command or directive but usually student compliance did not occur until the second, third or even fourth reissue of the command.

This situation produced an intermittent, unpredictable schedule of student compliance that led the teacher to give a very high rate of prompts and directives (mostly ineffective) in order to achieve compliance by the three most challenging students. This pattern was observed for each one of the three most challenging students. Further, this process took up huge amounts of the teacher's time, handed control of the teacher–student interactions over to the student, and was highly frustrating for the teacher.

This was a most unfortunate outcome of good intentions gone awry! By trying to direct student behavior as a necessary part of instructing and managing the classroom, the teacher fell into the trap of inadvertently reinforcing and strengthening the most challenging students' NC. The teacher was unaware of the extent to which her rate of issuing commands was under the control of her students' intermittent compliance until she was debriefed about it. This study validates the principle that the attention from adults that students' maladaptive behavior produces can serve to actually strengthen rather than reduce or eliminate it.

RECOMMENDED STRATEGIES FOR IMPROVING COMPLIANCE WITH TEACHER DIRECTIVES

As with most approaches to enhancing student behavior and performance, prevention and intervention strategies play an important role and should be coordinated with each other. This is especially true regarding compliance with teacher directives. There are some things that can be done before a directive is delivered (*antecedents*) that affect compliance, and some things that can be done after delivery (*consequences*). Antecedents include establishing a positive classroom climate and following best practice guidelines in delivering directives. Consequences include avoiding confrontations with students, using proactive coping strategies, debriefing strategies, and implementing coordinated home–school interventions to teach and improve compliance rates for chronically noncompliant students.

Antecedent Strategies (Prevention)

Research has shown that a positive classroom climate is associated with a number of positive outcomes, including laying the foundation for positive teacher–student interactions (Weimer, 2009). Schools with positive school climates also tend to be safer and more effective (Gottfredson & Gottfredson, 2001), with reduced teacher–student and peer-to-peer conflict and a reduced need for teacher directives to manage student behavior. Having to use fewer directives to manage a classroom improves teacher efficacy and reduces stress. Young (2014) has provided a roadmap for how to create a positive classroom.

Figure 1.2 contains a series of recommended steps for establishing and sustaining a positive classroom climate. The investments necessary to establish positive school climate are well worth the effort in terms of the returns in academic performance, student behavior and self-efficacy,

1. Establish a climate for the classroom that is positive, inclusive, and supportive of all students, regardless of their behavioral and academic characteristics.
2. Be aware that adults can unconsciously form and behaviorally express negative impressions of low-performing, uncooperative students to which the students are quite sensitive. The teacher should communicate a positive regard for such students and give them the benefit of the doubt whenever possible.
3. Establish and maintain high expectations in achievement and behavior for all students.
4. Develop and reinforce classroom norms for positive behavior and kindness toward others.
5. Promote positive peer relationships and nurture positive relationships with each student.
6. Create a structured learning context where students know what is expected of them and how they can access needed assistance in solving academic tasks.
7. Hold the length of transitions between academic periods to a minimum.
8. Use cooperative learning strategies that allow diverse groups of students to interact, problem solve, and develop skills in working together.
9. Teach anger management along with conflict avoidance and resolution strategies.
10. Ensure that academic programming and task difficulty for low-performing students are geared to their skill levels.
11. Teach students how to be appropriately assertive (i.e., to disagree or resist others' demands without being hostile).
12. Use difficult situations to develop and practice student self-control.
13. Find ways to praise and encourage low-performing students at the same or higher rate than for higher-performing students.
14. Try to avoid criticizing, verbally punishing, or arguing with any student, especially low-performing students.

FIGURE 1.2. Recommended steps for establishing a positive classroom climate.

avoidance of teacher burnout, attendance, emotional well-being, and improved self-esteem. Creating a positive school climate can be a very powerful universal intervention that all schools should consider striving for. According to the available evidence, one of the best approaches for this involves the widely known and adopted positive behavioral interventions and supports (PBIS) program—developed by Rob Horner, George Sugai, and their associates (2005)—a framework for interventions that is easy to implement and highly effective. A primary focus of PBIS is to create a positive school and classroom climate by teaching three values: *be safe, be responsible, and be respectful.* This schoolwide approach has been adopted by thousands of schools and districts in the United States.

Another very powerful approach to creating a positive school climate is provided by Sprague and Golly (2004) and called the BEST program. This professional development program designed for administrators and teachers illustrates how to create and maintain a positive school culture that facilitates achievement and the healthy development of students in a safe environment that is conducive to learning. The BEST program shows how to teach behavioral expectations effectively and emphasizes the five universal principles of positive behavior support for managing classrooms: being respectful, modeling positive behaviors, having clear expectations, maintaining routines, and dealing with chronic misbehaviors.

Rules and Guidelines for Delivering Teacher Directives Effectively

Over the past 30 years, extensive research by a broad range of investigators has documented effective ways of directing child or student behavior that maximize the likelihood of compliance. This research has been reviewed and its results described in several venues by myself and my colleagues (Walker, Ramsey & Gresham, 2003–2004, 2004; Walker & Sylwester, 1998; Walker & Walker, 1991). The following is a list of these rules and guidelines based on these research findings.

1. Use alpha commands to direct student behavior, never beta commands.
2. Use only as many commands as needed in order to teach and manage the classroom effectively. As a rule, student NC increases as the number of commands increase.
3. Limit and/or avoid the use of terminating commands in favor of initiating commands whenever possible.
4. Give only one command at a time. If a series of separate tasks is involved, give distinct commands for each task.
5. Be specific and direct. Get the student's attention, establish eye contact, and describe what is desired in a firm tone using alpha command language that is easily understood.
6. Allow a reasonable time (at least 5–10 seconds) for the student to respond to the command.
7. Do not repeat the command more than once if the student does not initially comply. Instead, use some other consequence or action to deal with the NC (e.g., ask the student to indicate what the problem is, tell the student to let you know when he or she is ready to respond, remove the student from the situation).
8. Give commands to an individual student in close proximity rather than from a distance (e.g., across the room). In directing and especially in redirecting individual student behavior, give direction from about 3 feet or closer.
9. Obtain student attention and make eye contact before issuing a directive.

10. Use a matter-of-fact and unemotional tone of voice (if seeking to terminate a student action, try not to show anger or use warnings and threats).
11. Provide behavior-specific praise and approval for student compliance as appropriate.

Use of the above strategies will prevent the development of many potential NC problems in most classrooms. The next section discusses intervention strategies and steps that can be used to enhance compliance with teacher directives after they have been delivered.

Consequation Strategies (Intervention)

These strategies are most useful in the aftermath of a student's failure to comply with teacher directives, whether immediate, short term, or chronic. They are nonpunitive, positive, and supportive of the student. *Important note:* It is obviously important to have a positive relationship with each individual student with whom that's possible. The better this relationship, the more likely it is students will be cooperative and will seek to comply with teacher directives.

Proactive Coping Strategies

Recommended strategies for coping more effectively with student refusal of teacher directives include avoiding confrontations that seek to force the student's hand and establish the teacher's authority, follow-up debriefing strategies for coping with NC having differing underlying causes, and involving parents in a home–school strategy to enhance compliance with teacher directives at home and in school.

Figure 1.3 illustrates what should not be done in responding to student refusal of a teacher directive—especially with students who have behavioral challenges. The situation in Figure 1.3 plays out daily in thousands of classrooms. Often it requires a room clear to reestablish order. A room clear refers to a situation where it is necessary to temporarily vacate a classroom due to the destructive and sometimes dangerous behavior of an out-of-control student, leaving only the student and the teacher in the room. This procedure removes the student's audience of classmates and allows the teacher to debrief with the student about the situation. If instead the teacher decides to engage with and correct the student in front of classmates, it can sometimes devolve into a "lose–lose" interaction for the teacher. That is, in the unlikely event that the teacher prevails in this situation, she or he will have created a resentful student who will likely seek social revenge against the teacher in the future. If the student prevails

1. The student has a history of presenting behavioral challenges and is sitting in class in a highly agitated state, which may or may not be noticeable.
2. The teacher makes a class assignment and provides instruction for same.
3. The student ignores the directive to begin and refuses to engage.
4. The teacher notices and confronts the student about the refusal.
5. The student questions, argues with, and/or defies the teacher.
6. The teacher reprimands the student and demands compliance.
7. The student explodes and confronts the teacher, escalating the situation out of the teacher's control.

FIGURE 1.3. Trying to force a student's hand on compliance.

instead, the teacher's authority and ability to manage the class will be weakened in the eyes of classmates.

If an individual student ignores or refuses a specific teacher directive, the teacher should approach the student, using neutral to positive body language, and repeat the command—but *only once,* and offer assistance as appropriate. If the student is still unresponsive, the teacher should leave the student alone and allow him or her to deal with the situation. It should be made clear that such resistance will not result in escape or avoidance of the assignment. The teacher should communicate the following to the student:

1. The student can't control the situation by arguing with the teacher or by asking provocative questions. (*Note:* Teachers should not argue with or respond to the student's questions. In most cases this fails to resolve the situation and leads to a worsening situation.)
2. When the student settles down and is ready to work, the teacher should provide any needed assistance.
3. The student will not be able to reduce or avoid the assigned work by using delaying tactics.

If this procedure does not appear to work, a more formal debriefing process should be scheduled to further deal with the situation (see next the section).

Debriefing

In well-managed classrooms, most teacher directives are usually given to the entire classroom. Inevitably, in this situation an individual student will occasionally not respond to the directive either by ignoring it or by active refusal. It is important to try and understand the reason(s) underlying a student's refusal in order to develop a solution. There are at least three possible reasons for a student's ignoring and/or direct refusal of a teacher directive. These are the following.

1. The student doesn't know how to fulfill the requirements of the directive.
2. The student is emotionally upset and/or agitated.
3. The student is habitually unmotivated to complete schoolwork.

Reasons 1 and 3 usually result in the student ignoring the directive, whereas opposition and insubordination often underlie Reason 2. A debriefing strategy can be used to deal with each of these situations.

For Reason 1, as soon as possible after the refusal occurs and the teacher has initially dealt with it, a private debriefing session should be scheduled with the student to develop a solution. The session should focus on why the refusal is occurring and how to get to a different place in responding to commands. For Reason 1, determine that the student clearly understands the directive and is capable of doing what the directive asks. Answers to the following questions should be sought in the debriefing discussion:

1. "Do you understand what I want you to do?"
2. "Do you think you can complete the assignment?" (If the answer is no, ask why.)
3. "How can I help you in doing what I asked you to do?"
4. "Do you have enough time to do the tasks I assign?"
5. "You should always raise your hand if you don't understand something or need help. OK?"

For Reason 2, the focus should be on what's driving the student's active refusal. If the student is habitually insubordinate and oppositional, it's likely the cause lies outside the classroom and centers on problems taking directives from adults generally. Antisocial, aggressive students have particular problems in this regard; such students often do not have positive relationships with adults, stemming from their family backgrounds (Patterson, Reid, & Dishion, 1992). Questions to ask in this debriefing session include:

1. "'Do you have an idea why you have trouble complying with my requests and directions to the class? I want you to succeed in my class."
2. "Do you know how important it is for you to do what your teachers ask? It's how teachers teach and students learn. If you don't do what teachers ask of you, you won't be able to have success in school. Both your parents and I want you to be successful in school."
3. "Can you think of ways I can better support you in responding to my requests? You should ask me for help whenever you need it."
4. "Can we make an agreement where you try and comply with more

of my requests and I give you more time and space to do so? I think things will improve if we meet each other halfway on this."

For Reason 3, it is important to try and understand the factors underlying the lack of interest in school. Unmotivated students are one of the greatest challenges teachers face due to their general unresponsiveness. The questions in a debriefing session might look like this:

1. "I notice you don't respond to some of my directives to the class. Can you tell me why?"
2. If the student responds with "I'm just not interested in school," the teacher can ask why that is.
3. The student should know that schooling is very important to being successful in life. "I want you to do well in school. Do you mind if I talk to your parents about how we could get you more involved in your schoolwork and put more focus on your interests?" (For this type of student, teaching the parents how to debrief with the student each day about what was good at school would be highly recommended.)

ENLISTING PARENT SUPPORT IN A HOME-SCHOOL STRATEGY TO ENHANCE STUDENT COMPLIANCE

For students who have chronic problems with teacher commands, one of the best things parents and teachers can do is work together to resolve this common problem. This can be done in two main ways: by using best practices in delivering directives, and by monitoring and motivating the child to comply with them. Both parents and teachers should use best practice guidelines in delivering directives at home and school. Guidelines for teachers were provided earlier. A similar list of guidelines for use by parents at home is provided in Figure 1.4.

DESIGN OF A BEST-PRACTICE INTERVENTION TO IMPROVE STUDENT COMPLIANCE AT SCHOOL

If a child is exposed to similar, effective guidelines for delivery of commands at home and school, the odds improve that desirable results overall will be achieved. Similarly, if the child receives praise and approval for compliance with directives at both home and school, the likelihood of positive results is further enhanced. Finally, to strengthen things even more, it would be helpful to set up a monitoring program regarding compliance at school to track the student's compliance so it can be used as a means

1. Use only direct, specific, and clear commands that focus on only one request at a time. Avoid lecturing the child as part of the command's delivery.
2. Whenever possible, give four or five initiating (starting) commands to each terminating (stopping) command.
3. Children should receive praise and approval following satisfactory compliance with a command.
4. Make only one request or directive at a time.
5. Use clear, precise language the child can understand and repeat as necessary for understanding.
6. Ensure that the child can do what is being asked.
7. Do not reissue the command more than once.
8. Do not allow yourself to be drawn into arguments about the command.

FIGURE 1.4. Guidelines for Parents in Giving Commands. Based on Forehand and McMahon (1981), Morgan and Jenson (1988), and Walker and Walker (1991). From *Solutions to Critical Behavioral Issues in the Classroom* by Hill M. Walker. Copyright © 2023 The Guilford Press. Permission to photocopy this material is granted to purchasers of this book for personal use or use with students (see copyright page for details). Purchasers can download enlarged versions of this material (see the box at the end of the table of contents).

of providing home-based incentives to improve compliance. A simple procedure can accomplish this task. Use the Good Day Card (Figure 1.5) to have the teacher rate how well the student did on compliance with teacher directives on a daily basis. Have the student take the card home daily to share with parents.

A teacher and parent meeting should be scheduled to describe the collaboration and obtain the parent's approval and participation. It should be explained that tracking the student's compliance at school and sharing that information with parents may improve the compliance rate. Parents should keep track of the daily ratings for each day of the week, and if the initial weekly total is 15 or more, a special privilege should be arranged at home to reinforce the student's efforts. This process should be repeated weekly as the student's behavior improves, with a gradual raising of the criterion for a special privilege. The following fictional case study shows how this homeschool intervention could work.

CASE STUDY: IMPROVING BILLY'S COMPLIANCE AT SCHOOL

Billy is a fourth-grade student in Ms. Atwood's general education classroom. He has a history of not responding to Ms. Atwood's directives to the class from time to time. Billy is an active student and his NC seems to come in spurts with no particular pattern evident. From time to time, Ms. Atwood has to use terminating commands with him to redirect and refocus his behavior as he is so resistant to her.

Student Name _____

Date _____

Period(s) Covered _____

Instructions: Please rate on the scale below how well the student did in complying with your directives today. Circle the number that best reflects your estimate.

Didn't Comply at All	Complied Some of the Time	Complied Most of the Time	Complied All of the Time
1	2	3	4

Teacher Comments:

FIGURE 1.5. Good Day Card for monitoring student compliance. From *Solutions to Critical Behavioral Issues in the Classroom* by Hill M. Walker. Copyright © 2023 The Guilford Press. Permission to photocopy this material is granted to purchasers of this book for personal use or use with students (see copyright page for details). Purchasers can download enlarged versions of this material (see the box at the end of the table of contents).

Ms. Atwood has mentioned to Billy's parents that his school performance would improve if he were more willing to follow her directives. Recently his NC has gotten worse and is starting to be noticed by his classmates, which concerns Ms. Atwood. She contacts Billy's parents and schedules a meeting with them about Billy's school performance and behavior. In preparing for this meeting, Ms. Atwood makes a copy of the Guidelines for Parents in Giving Commands and the Good Day Card. The meeting unfolds as follows.

Ms. ATWOOD: Thank you for meeting today. I want Billy to succeed in my class and his refusals to follow class directives and commands are interfering with his schoolwork. Do you know of any reasons why this seems to be happening?

MRS. CONGER (Billy's mom): Well, he doesn't always do what we ask him at home either. Usually, he'll come around if we pester him enough about it. I wish he would comply quicker when we make a request.

MR. CONGER (Billy's dad): There's no physical or mental condition that we know of that would explain it.

Ms. ATWOOD: Thank you for that information. It's very helpful. I think it might be a key to understanding why Billy ignores and occasionally refuses my directives. It works like this. Sometimes young children learn that by refusing to comply with a request from an adult, they can garner more attention (even though negative) by not complying than by complying. This is especially true of children for whom adult attention is powerful. That may be the case with Billy. Do you think this is a possibility? (*Both parents agree that this might be true with Billy.*) I have a suggestion about how we could work together to improve the situation with Billy at school.

Ms. Atwood goes on to explain the intervention and covers the Guidelines for Parents in Giving Commands, the Good Day Card, and why monitoring Billy's compliance is essential. She also explains the importance of reducing the amount of attention Billy gets from refusing directives and requests at home, and how to set up and manage a weekly special home privilege when he earns the required number of points. Billy's parents agree to give the intervention a try.

Ms. Atwood: Great! I look forward to working with you to make this work for Billy. I will call you several times a week to check in and deal with any potential problems. Please contact me at any time if you have problems, questions, or issues.

The intervention worked beautifully for Billy. It turns out that the excess attention he was getting at home for his NC was spilling over into his school behavior. His parents reduced their pestering and negative attention, replacing it with praise and approval for compliance. Combined with the other elements of the intervention, Billy immediately began to improve his compliance rate.

An important point about this intervention is that parents are an invaluable resource in assisting educators with improving their child's overall behavior and school performance. This is especially relevant for chronic NC, which often begins within and is sustained by the family and home setting.

CONSIDERATIONS IN SOLVING COMPLIANCE PROBLEMS

Implementing the best practice guidelines and recommendations of this chapter should lead to substantial improvement in the compliance rates for most students with occasional or chronic problems in this area. However, from time to time one may encounter a student for whom nothing works. In such cases, referral to the school's related services personnel (school psychologist or counselor) or to the schoolwide assistance team would be a logical next step. Some cautions are provided below for consideration in addressing compliance problems.

- Students should not learn that being noncompliant has incentive value for them—for example, ignoring or refusing teacher directives will produce benefits such as escape from assigned tasks, more teacher attention, or access to additional longer-term incentives via temporary interventions used to address the problem of NC.
- Student refusal, depending upon how the teacher reacts to it, can be a pathway to teacher defiance, insubordination, and severe conflict.
- Whenever possible, enlist parent support in addressing chronic NC.
- Students with challenging behavior are very sensitive to public reprimands from adults for their NC or for challenging behavior in general. Such communication should be delivered as privately as possible or in a separate meeting if necessary.

CHAPTER 1 TAKEAWAYS

- Never argue with a student about his or her lack of compliance with a directive.
- Never try to force the student's hand to achieve compliance.
- Strive to use only alpha commands rather than beta commands to direct or redirect students.
- Restrict terminating commands to the maximum extent possible.
- Deliver only one directive at a time.
- Repeat the command only once after an ignore or refusal.
- Use the smallest number of directives necessary to teach and manage the classroom.
- Look for the reasons underlying the student's NC.
- Use a combination of prevention and intervention strategies to address compliance issues.
- Strive to develop a positive relationship with students who display chronic NC.

CHAPTER 2

Improving Student Completion of Seatwork Assignments According to Instructions

The ability to engage in independent seatwork (ISW) and to complete assigned work satisfactorily under such conditions is an important skill demanded of all students within inclusive classrooms. Rock and Thread (2009) note that approximately 30% of instructional time in general education classrooms involves ISW, and other experts say that it can range up to as much as 70% of available instructional time. ISW is frequently used in reading and math subject areas and provides students the important opportunity to practice new tasks within them.

In many classrooms ISW serves both instructional and management functions. In terms of instruction, it provides an opportunity for students to practice mastery of newly presented material. Rosenshine (2012) classifies it as one of his 17 principles of effective instruction that all teachers should know, and notes that students should be carefully prepared to fully take advantage of such independent practice. ISW can also be a valuable management tool by allowing the teacher to provide needed individualized assistance for students who require it or to work with small student groups focused on a particular task or activity (Anderson, Brubaker, Alleman-Brooks, & Duffy, 1985). Thus, ISW simultaneously serves the skill mastery needs of students and the teaching-management needs of teachers and is an essential tool of effective classrooms. In addition, there is a close connection between independent study skills and appropriate student behavior with higher levels of each strengthening the other.

DEFINITION, KEY FEATURES, AND EXAMPLES OF SEATWORK

The ability to perform ISW is a critical academic skill. ISW is part of a constellation of what are called "academic enablers"—nonacademic skills that complement, support, and allow successful performance. These include social skills, study skills, motivation, ability to focus attention and concentrate, task engagement, and so forth. Academic success depends not only upon academic skill proficiency but upon display of these enablers as well. The strength of these enablers can hinder or improve academic success according to how they are displayed by students (DiPerna & Elliott, 2002).

ISW is defined as a period of time during a planned lesson in which students work independently either alone or as part of a small group (two or more students). There are two types of ISW: active and passive. Examples of active ISW are solving math story problems on one's own or two students playing a vocabulary flash card game. Passive ISW is silent reading or studying instructions for doing a task.

In order to do ISW successfully, a student must have mastered some required subskills, including the ability to focus and sustain attention, the ability to self-manage one's behavior, being able to monitor one's academic progress, having the motivation to engage in ISW, and being able to display self-control. These subskills are also called behavioral indicators of the target skill and teachers familiar with the student can easily rate their presence or absence (Walker, Marquez, et al., 2015). Breaking larger study skills down into their component subskills as above is done via a discrete categorization process (Kazdin, 1989). It is very important for the ISW to accurately reflect the student's instructional level.

Causal Influences and Antecedent Conditions of ISW

There are a number of factors that influence how well students can manage ISW. Students with challenging behavior, cognitive processing disorders, and those who are overactive and distractible typically all suffer in performing ISW (Oliver, Wehby, & Reschly, 2011). Students with challenging behavior and disorders are especially vulnerable in this regard. Such students are often not taught school success skills at home and bring weak behavioral repertoires to the teaching–learning process. Many are not capable of performing ISW successfully without elaborate teacher assistance. These students, as a rule, would need to be directly taught the subskills that enable ISW (e.g., focusing attention, being organized, being motivated).

Other students do not possess the required ISW subskills in sufficient strength to perform ISW effectively or are not sufficiently prepared and supported by their teachers in order to do so. For those students who have weak study skills, it may be helpful to use the subskills checklist in Figure 2.1 to determine a student's ISW readiness and to estimate how much teacher assistance they will need during ISW periods.

The attention subskill is the most critical to ISW success. A typical student is academically engaged about 80% of the time during seatwork and teacher-led instructional activities (Walker, Severson, & Feil, 2015). Students who are well below this threshold will likely not be successful in doing ISW without some prior training and practice in focusing their attention.

I have successfully used a simple kitchen egg timer procedure with students who have very short attention spans during one-to-one seatwork-type situations. Typically, three sessions were scheduled with six trials in each one, with each session taking approximately 8–10 minutes total to complete. The egg timer was set and reset according to the schedule of successive trials (in seconds) that averaged approximately 60 seconds over the six trials in each session. The purpose of this exercise was to further develop and expand the student's attention span, which can directly impact the student's ability to engage in ISW.

- Session 1: 30, 40, 70, 50, 60, 70; average length = 53 seconds
- Session 2: 60, 80, 50, 70, 60, 60; average length = 60 seconds
- Session 3: 70, 80, 60, 80, 60, 70; average length = 70 seconds

The egg timer was reset as soon as each trial was over and the student was awarded praise and a point if he or she maintained focused attention uninterrupted throughout the trial. Accumulated points were exchanged for a preferred activity or privilege either at home or school. This simple procedure was highly effective in lengthening students' attention spans as well as improving their ability to focus and concentrate.

RECOMMENDED STRATEGIES FOR IMPROVING ISW PERFORMANCE

One can find a number of strategies and tips for improving ISW in the educational literature. They can be grouped under three headings or topics as follows: (1) preparation, (2) monitoring and assisting the student as needed, and (3) providing academic corrections with feedback and praise. There are things the teacher can do before, during, and after the ISW period to increase the likelihood of student success. Some suggestions for this have been provided by Anderson et al. (1985), Evertson & Smithey (2000), and Good (1983).

Instructions: Place a check next to any subskill in which the student is deficient.

1. Student is motivated to engage in ISW. _____
2. Student can focus and sustain his or her attention. _____
3. Student can self-monitor progress. _____
4. Student can self-manage performance. _____
5. Student has adequate self-control. _____
6. Student can organize required materials. _____

FIGURE 2.1. ISW subskills checklist. From *Solutions to Critical Behavioral Issues in the Classroom* by Hill M. Walker. Copyright © 2023 The Guilford Press. Permission to photocopy this material is granted to purchasers of this book for personal use or use with students (see copyright page for details). Purchasers can download enlarged versions of this material (see the box at the end of the table of contents).

ISW Preparation

Use your knowledge of your student and the checklist in Figure 2.1 as tools to help make this determination. Some other tips for preparing students include the following:

1. Keep assignments short.
2. Break academic tasks into smaller units if necessary.
3. Give clear, concise, step-by-step instructions and ensure the student understands them.
4. Assist the student in getting started.
5. Set up a procedure for seeking help. Explain the importance of ISW to the student as a means to practice mastery of new skills and information presented in class.

Providing Academic Corrections with Feedback and Praise

Observe the student frequently during the ISW period for signs of struggle and frustration with the assigned task. Support the student's attempts at problem solving with feedback, praise, and approval. The challenge is to strike a balance between supporting the student's attempts at ISW and avoiding frustration and discouragement.

The student's work should be collected, corrected, and used as a basis for grading. In providing performance feedback, descriptive praise should be used that specifies exactly what the student is being praised for. Some additional recommended ISW strategies include the following (Kaimuki Middle School, 2018):

1. Set clear expectations for work time.
2. Provide backup assignments for early finishers.
3. Emphasize goal setting and self-checking of progress toward same.
4. Choose goals for time on task, productivity, and/or accuracy as appropriate.
5. Structure class periods to intersperse ISW at various points during or following teacher-led instruction.
6. Review assigned activities for ISW.
7. Prioritize tasks to be completed.
8. Create a to-do list to help guide students' time allocation.
9. Arrange the classroom so teacher has easy access to individual ISW student(s).
10. Have a supportive peer sit next to the student.
11. Help the student organize materials and unclutter desk.
12. Signal the student if off task for more than 10–15 seconds.
13. Have student begin seatwork task with you assisting.

The following case study describes a student (Jacob) who needs the benefits of ISW (practice time and individualized assistance) but who struggled to engage in it successfully.

CASE STUDY: ISW

Jacob is enrolled in Ms. Anderson's fourth-grade general education class. He has a mild learning disability and a diagnosis of ADHD. Jacob has a high activity level and tends to be impulsive. He is a low-performing student and has ongoing problems with reading and difficulties with math. Jacob was rated as deficient in all six subskills on the ISW checklist but Ms. Anderson decided to work with him on them gradually over time.

Jacob's profile on the *Diagnostic Indicators of Emerging Literacy Skills* (DIBELS) reading assessment procedure in first grade indicated that he would have problems in achieving the necessary benchmarks to ensure his adequate progress in developing reading skills and reading proficiency (*Diagnostic Indicators of Emerging Literacy Skills*, 2018). His chronic problems in focusing his attention enabled his tendency to be easily distracted from academic tasks. Meeting the ordinary demands of schooling has been a challenge for him from the beginning of first grade and is holding back his school progress.

Ms. Anderson designed an individualized program to help Jacob with his seatwork. She began with a one-to-one program to help him with his attention and focusing problems. She and Jacob practiced for 10–15 minutes per day using a kitchen egg timer, praise, and a point system. Each time Jacob sustained his attention without being distracted for an interval, he would earn praise and a point from Ms. Anderson—which he liked. Over about a week, Jacob's continuous attention span expanded to over a minute, which helped him greatly with his seatwork assignment. His parents provided a special privilege or activity at home whenever he did well in his attention sessions.

Ms. Anderson broke Jacob's seatwork assignment into smaller units. She arranged them in the order in which they should be done and discussed with Jacob how much time each unit should take to complete. She gave Jacob a small green card to place on the corner of his desk when he needed her help. She arranged for a supportive, academically skilled classmate to sit near Jacob and answer his questions when asked.

With these sources of support, Jacob began to slowly show progress in his ability to do his seatwork with success. His percent of academic engaged time improved from 45 to 60%, his rate of task completion improved substantially, and his frequency of errors decreased on his assigned tasks. Ms. Anderson encouraged him to try and work as independently as he could but not to struggle with something that caused frustration without asking for help. She communicated regularly with Jacob's parents about his schoolwork and improved performance; they were pleased with his progress and motivation to do well.

CONSIDERATIONS IN IMPROVING ISW ACCORDING TO INSTRUCTIONS

There are several key issues that should be considered regarding ISW. First, it is very important to establish a procedure where the student can easily make their assistance needs known to the teacher. As noted earlier, use of a colored card placed on the corner of the student's desk is an easy way to accomplish this but it requires the teacher to monitor the student carefully. Second, ISW provides an excellent opportunity for academic low-performers to access needed practice, teacher feedback, and assistance. Third, ISW can be used to form small student groups who share the same skill deficits or have common specialized instructional needs. Finally, it provides a platform for peer tutoring by matching more-skilled with less-skilled students; peer tutoring has proven effectiveness and is popular with both students and teachers (Ginsburg-Block, & Rohrbeck, 2006; Kunsch, Jitendra, & Sood, 2007). Peer tutoring can be adapted for use with small groups and for whole classrooms of students (see Chapter 3).

CHAPTER 2 TAKEAWAYS

- ISW is an important tool in establishing effective classroom instruction.
- ISW allows distribution of limited instructional resources to diverse groups of students with varying skill levels.

- For students in general, ISW is a recommended option for affording practice opportunities following teacher-led presentation of new material.

- ISW meets the instructional needs of students while facilitating teachers' flexibility in managing the classroom.

- Low-performing/low-skilled students benefit from extra teacher assistance, support, and attention during ISW periods.

CHAPTER 3

Motivating Students to Produce Academic Work of Acceptable Quality for Their Skill Level

Students who do not perform up to their skill and ability levels are often characterized as poorly motivated. Teachers frequently complain that the unmotivated student is one of the most frustrating challenges they have to deal with. Students who achieve well below their skill and ability levels are often viewed as wasting their educational opportunities and the teacher's time. Such students are characterized as having a low need for achievement (N-Ach). This includes an individual's desire for significant achievement, the mastering of skills, having self-control and discipline, and subscribing to high standards in one's schoolwork. Individuals with a high N-Ach engage in prolonged, intense, and repeated efforts to accomplish something difficult. The works of David McClelland (1961, 1987) popularized N-Ach, and this concept has received broad acceptance as a useful means of characterizing student motivation.

DEFINITION, KEY FEATURES, AND EXAMPLES OF STUDENT MOTIVATION

The achievement motive has been the subject of numerous scholarly works and research over the past three decades. Critical features of N-Ach include setting standards, competing with peers and self, having a quest for excellence, having hope for success, taking moderate risks, desire for constant feedback on performance, and a preference for autonomy and independence. Students with high N-Ach have been described as motivated, driven, and as having grit. Low-motivation students are the polar opposite and have lower levels on these attributes.

There are two primary sources of student motivation: intrinsic and extrinsic. Intrinsic motivation means that students are motivated by a genuine interest in academic subject matter and feel it has relevance to their lives. In contrast, extrinsic motivation is driven by external factors such as grades, parent and teacher expectations, or preparing for a career. Maximal performance is most likely achieved through a combination of these two types of motivation. However, some experts argue that for complex tasks requiring creativity and persistence, extrinsic rewards and consequences can diminish and hamper motivation. Having pride in one's academic work and achievement is associated with high standards for the quality of one's schoolwork. Teacher and parent approval are likely by-products of such pride.

Research shows that students who fully engage in schooling and are attached to the schooling process tend to be protected from a number of later negative developmental outcomes. School success is highly protective against later delinquency, violent offenses, heavy drinking, sexually transmitted diseases, teen pregnancy, school misbehavior, low achievement, and school failure and dropout (Hawkins et al., 1999). Low-motivation students are more likely to miss out on these protective influences.

CAUSAL INFLUENCES AND ANTECEDENT CONDITIONS OF LOW STUDENT MOTIVATION

There is a broad range of individual attributes, experiences, attitudes, and emotional factors that can account for low student motivation. This can be divided into internal and external factors, whose collective impact can disrupt and weaken a student's desire to do well on schoolwork and achieve school success.

Internal factors include such things as a student's general self-concept (including academic self-concept), other priorities that can compete for attention with schoolwork, emotional problems (e.g., depressed mood), fear of failure, a tendency to make negative social comparisons with accomplished classmates, a failure to see the relevance of schoolwork to their lives, a low need for achievement, and modeling negative family attitudes toward the importance of schooling (i.e., attitudes toward schooling tend to become more negative as a student progresses through the grades). External factors refer to experiences the student has that weaken and disrupt motivation. These can include learning disabilities and processing deficits that make schoolwork challenging, absence of a supportive classroom climate, experiencing frequent failures, schoolwork that is either too difficult or too easy, lack of family support for school achievement, performance expectations that are too high, trauma in the student's life that disrupts motivation and N-Ach, and need for assistance that is not adequately addressed.

These examples illustrate just how complex the causes of low student motivation can be: It is easy to detect but very difficult to successfully change. Having a family background where parents are open to teaching school success skills, developing habits of persistence and pride in one's work, and developing positive attitudes toward the value of schooling are very important and set the stage for school success.

RECOMMENDED STRATEGIES FOR REDUCING LOW STUDENT MOTIVATION

There is a wide range of suggested techniques for addressing low student motivation. Due to the multiplicity of possible factors accounting for low motivation, there have been few studies that validate actual correspondence between causal factors and intervention strategies that can reduce it. Most of these strategies are based on trial and error, commonsense professional speculation, and anecdotal experience in dealing with low motivation. It is important for school staff to do all that is feasible to impact this persistent problem even though numerous underlying causes of low student motivation may be due to factors outside the classroom and school. In spite of this, teachers may be able to help motivate the student to achieve and better engage with schooling.

Priming Strategies for Enhancing Student Responsiveness to Motivation Enhancement Approaches

Priming strategies are used to help make students more responsive to and interested in schooling. These strategies may be useful for students with low motivation as well as those who are generally at risk of school failure and weak school success.

The 2 × 10 Strategy

One strategy in this category is the 2 × 10 strategy, enhancing the teacher–student relationship through mentoring, advocacy, and debriefing, and creating a supportive classroom environment. There is extensive commentary in professional literature on the merits of this strategy, and it offers an excellent way for a teacher to make a positive connection with an at-risk student who struggles in the classroom (McKibben, 2014). The teacher finds a time of day to briefly chat with the student for 2 minutes for 10 straight days. The subject during these chats is whatever topic the student wants to talk about (it does not need to be about schoolwork). This special teacher attention can be quite flattering and demonstrates a genuine interest in the student. The 2 × 10 strategy can serve as a useful screening device to find out what is going on in the student's life that might impact school performance, but its major purpose is to help the student view school more positively and hopefully to more fully engage in it.

Enhancing the Teacher-Student Relationship through Mentoring, Advocacy, and Debriefing

A number of schools have implemented teacher mentoring programs where teachers are assigned to at-risk students in order to better meet their individualized needs. Teachers are expected to offer mentoring, general advocacy, and specialized assistance with behavioral and academic challenges a student may be facing. Debriefing with a student about struggles with schooling may reveal emotional problems that hamper motivation, performance, and adjustment. In such cases, a referral to the school counselor or psychologist would be a viable strategy, as teachers should generally not try to solve such problems.

Creating a Supportive Classroom Environment

Many low-motivation students do not perceive the classroom as a supportive setting where they feel comfortable and are socially accepted. Often these problems result from lack of exposure to peers and unfamiliarity. The teacher of a well-managed classroom may have only limited ability to impact this issue, but communicating acceptance of the student and involving him or her in joint tasks and small-group activities with classmates can do much to alleviate such problems and help the student feel more positive about schooling.

These priming strategies are highly recommended for students with low motivation. They set the stage for direct intervention strategies, some of which are briefly described in the next section.

There are both academic and social–emotional strategies that can be implemented to enhance a low-motivation student's struggles and challenges.

Direct Intervention Strategies for Addressing Low-Motivation Students' Academic Performance

Direct intervention approaches are focused on how to improve student motivation levels. The following strategies directly target improving the performance of low-motivation students.

Discipline Problem Solver Series Recommendations for Low-Motivation Students

The Discipline Problem Solver series (Shore, 2003) is an excellent resource that includes a unit on unmotivated students and what can be done to motivate them. Shore recommends using a debriefing strategy with this type of student to try and convince them that increased effort will result in more success with academic tasks, and to identify the contexts, situations, and conditions that the student is responsive to that can be used for motivational purposes.

Shore also notes that the unmotivated student is often demoralized and discouraged by repeated failure at academic tasks. Interrupting this cycle of failure is critical and can be accomplished by breaking assignments into more manageable pieces, making the beginning of an assignment easy, and correcting mistakes without criticizing the student. Providing approval and descriptive praise for progress is essential to building student confidence and helping students sustain effort. It is important to remember the following:

- Allow the student to have choices in assignments and/or how to approach them.
- If feasible, incorporate the student's interests into the lesson.
- Relate the content of lessons to real life whenever possible.
- Focus on the student's individual progress rather than making comparisons with that of peers.

Classwide Flashcard Practice Drills

Because the unmotivated student often suffers from social isolation due to not fitting in and a lack of peer contact or exposure, it is a good idea to involve him or her in regularly scheduled vocabulary or spelling flashcard drills with classmates. These drills can involve either selected classmates or the entire classroom where students take turns with a different peer each time. This process can seed associations or relationships that might not otherwise occur.

Classwide and Individualized Peer Tutoring

Classwide peer tutoring (CWPT; Greenwood, Carta, & Hall, 1988; Greenwood, Maheady, & Delquadri, 2002; Kunsch et al., 2007) is a method for individualizing instruction in ways that enhance student participation in the teaching–learning process. It is a highly recommended strategy for improving both the academic and the social engagement of low-motivation students.

With CWPT, students are organized into pairs and assigned an instructional task. During the session one student takes the role of a tutor and one is tutored and then they exchange roles. Both students and teachers have found CWPT to be a very popular and effective strategy; it provides the opportunity for students to practice and master what they are learning while simultaneously enhancing social exposure to and interactions with each classmate. For example, decades of research show that students acquire literacy skills at a faster rate, retain more, and make greater social competence gains with CWPT than they do with a range of other instructional methods (Greenwood, 1997). The use of CWPT also reduces the need for specialized instructional services and supports.

Peer tutoring can also be used as a one-to-one strategy where a low-motivation student would be paired with a more academically skilled student or students on a continuing basis. This could improve the tutee's motivation, enhance academic progress, and provide a basis for social mentoring and the development of potential friendships.

CASE STUDY: ADDRESSING THE NEEDS OF A LOW-MOTIVATION STUDENT

The following account is based on true events. Rodrigo was a member of a migrant family who followed the harvests of seasonal crops such as beans, corn, and peas in Oregon's Willamette Valley. In any given year, Rodrigo could be enrolled in as many as four or five different schools, requiring him to adjust to different teachers and a whole new set of peers each time. These disruptions to Rodrigo's educational experience negatively affected his interest in schooling and severely limited his academic progress. Rodrigo was quite discouraged about school and felt he did not fit in with the schools in which he had been enrolled.

When Rodrigo was a freshman in high school, he was assigned to a reading lab for low readers. The lab was run by Ms. Fletcher, a reading expert who was very skilled at working with students like Rodrigo. She introduced him to a direct instruction program in reading that is highly effective and especially so for older students who are low readers. This program is phonics based and relies upon principles of direct instruction. Rodrigo responded very positively to this approach and to Ms. Fletcher's teaching. He began making excellent progress in mastering written symbols and their corresponding sounds, as well as the rules of language.

One day Rodrigo's parents stormed into the high school's front office and wanted to know what was going on in Ms. Fletcher's classroom. They explained it was time for them to move on to the next harvest site and Rodrigo had announced he wasn't going. When asked why, he said he didn't want to leave because of Ms. Fletcher. The reason was simple: For the first time in his life, Rodrigo was learning to read and he loved it!

This reading program and Ms. Fletcher's personal interest and support had a profound effect on Rodrigo's schooling and life. It was a real success story of how the performance of a student with low motivation and achievement can have his school experience turned around. The individualizing of instruction, personal interest, mentoring, and provision of support can sometimes work wonders in reengaging low-motivation students.

CONSIDERATIONS IN IMPROVING THE MOTIVATION AND PERFORMANCE OF LOW-MOTIVATION STUDENTS

Due to the multiple causal factors of low student motivation that operate primarily outside the school setting (e.g., trauma, lack of family support), it is not usually possible to positively impact them based on what happens at school. Thus, expectations for changing a student's motivation should be modest. Nevertheless, teacher implementation of solutions at school may improve the situation somewhat and should be initiated when feasible. If possible, the support of a low-motivation student's family in improving school motivation and engagement is very important if it can be achieved.

Low-motivation students are often aware of and emotionally sensitive to their reduced interest in school and to their lower performance relative to peers. Accommodating this sensitivity in trying to motivate a student is important to their self-perception in these attempts.

Building up the student's self-esteem and confidence is an important part of any effort to address this challenge. Taking a personal interest in the student and mentoring and advocating for her or him is extremely important. How a teacher interacts with an individual student is carefully noted by peers and influences how they view the student's status.

Thoughtful instructional programming and care in the selection of academic tasks are also steps that should be structured to maximize the student's achievement and school success. For example, breaking tasks down into smaller units and making the initial part of the task easier are good ways to more easily engage low-motivation students and prevent discouragement.

CHAPTER 3 TAKEAWAYS

- The low-motivation student who achieves below his or her ability level is one of the greatest frustrations for teachers and is also one of the most challenging problems to impact successfully by educators.

- Many of these students simply do not view school as a way forward in their lives and are marking time until they can leave it.

- Students who engage with the schooling process are protected from a host of later negative developmental outcomes.

- Low-motivation students often fall in the category of low-expectation students and do not receive the same academic opportunities and benefits as high-expectation students during the teaching–learning process.

- Enhancing the low-motivation student's social support through positive teacher interactions, mentoring, and advocacy, as well as increased peer support, can help these students see the classroom and school as a more welcoming place.

- Since no single strategy is likely to work for all low-motivation students, a variety of strategies and approaches should be tried.

Teaching Students to Have Positive Interactions/Conversations with Peers

Having positive peer relations is very important to a student's social and emotional well-being as well as to their social status within their peer group. Behaviorally at-risk students who are oppositional and antisocial tend to carry high levels of anger that can spill over into their peer interactions and verbal exchanges. Students with a habit of being irritable, agitated, and hostile toward peers tend to be avoided and are often excluded from peer-controlled activities. This can disrupt not only peer relations but also the climate of the classroom—especially during small-group instructional activities.

How students communicate and interact with each other also partially determines their classmates' view of them: Being perceived by peers as perpetually negative instead of neutral or positive harms their social status. Research has shown that negative social status resulting in social rejection by peers serves as a long-term risk factor for a host of negative developmental outcomes, including school failure and dropout, delinquency, and appearance on community service registers in adulthood (Newcomb, Bukowski, & Patee, 1993).

The purpose of this chapter is to address this very important dimension of a student's social and emotional development. Teaching students about the value of social relationships and how to forge positive ones will have enduring benefits in their school and nonschool careers.

DEFINITION, KEY FEATURES, AND EXAMPLES
OF NEGATIVE INTERACTIONS AND CONVERSATIONS

Interactions are defined as social exchanges among two or more individuals, in which verbal behavior or conversations occur. There are three critical features or components to an interaction: (1) an initiation that starts it; (2) an answer or response to the initiation; and (3) following an initiation and response, continuation of the social exchange until it naturally ends. Anger and hostility can be expressed within any of these components by any party to the interaction.

Negative initiations are not uncommon among peers. For example, peers often try to start an interaction by shoving the person they are initiating to or calling them a name such as, "Hey, stupid!" This type of behavior is more common among boys. Girls typically show more subtlety in this regard, using initiating remarks designed to hurt, embarrass, or humiliate: "Melany, did you forget to fully dress this morning?" or "You can't hang out with us when your hair looks like that!" Actions of this type are referred to as relational aggression and can lead to social isolation and rejection of the peer to whom they are directed (Delaney, Frey, & Walker, 2015). Responses to negative initiations like these are sometimes met with no response or with answers and responses that are equally negative in tone, leading to a hostile social exchange. It is very important to teach students who characteristically behave this way positive social exchange strategies and to understand the damage they can inflict on themselves and others.

CAUSAL INFLUENCES AND ANTECEDENT CONDITIONS OF HOSTILITY IN SOCIAL INTERACTIONS AND CONVERSATIONS

Similar to low student motivation, there can be multiple different reasons for anger and hostility in ongoing social and verbal exchanges with peers. Students who carry high levels of agitation are more likely to respond negatively than positively to peer initiations no matter their form or shape. Students who suffer from social isolation often don't have the skills or confidence to respond to social bids from peers when they do occur. In such cases, the student avoids social exchanges or is nonresponsive when an exchange is initiated by a peer. Further, antisocial and aggressive students who are used to forcing others to get their way tend to turn ongoing social exchanges negative when they resort to coercion or attempted manipulation during the interaction. This usually has the effect of short-circuiting the interaction. Finally, students who are targets of bullying and mean-spirited teasing tend to avoid responding to social bids out of fear of humiliation if they do, and students who harass and bully selected peers are often rejected by their peer group.

More often than not, it is the initiator of the social bid who displays anger and hostility and plays the role of victimizer during the interaction. Often, the target of the social bid plays the role of victim during the interaction and copes with it via avoidance and by being unresponsive. However, the exception to this rule is the highly agitated student who is engaged by a peer in a way that provides a trigger for anger or hostility. Such students are referred to both as victims and as victimizers.

Addressing this common problem requires attending to issues of self-awareness and self-control, and providing brief social skills training. The most likely targets of these actions would be highly agitated, challenging students who display antisocial and aggressive behavior in their peer relations. Recommended strategies for targeting these intervention areas are discussed in the next section.

RECOMMENDED STRATEGIES FOR TEACHING STUDENTS HOW TO INTERACT WITHOUT ANGER AND HOSTILITY

Students for whom normal social interactions and conversations are a challenge usually suffer from one or more of the following: a lack of self-awareness as to how their behavior is perceived and the impact it has on others; an absence of self-control to manage intense emotions such as agitation, frustration, and disappointment; and social skills deficits that cause their social bids and responses to be awkward, inappropriate, and not well received by peers.

Solving this common problem is not an easy task. A combination of debriefing and social skills training, along with monitoring and reinforcement are recommended for responding to this problem. A brief discussion of each follows.

Debriefing

This strategy is recommended for helping a student to become more aware of their behavior and to understand how different it is from what is normal or expected. Being aware of the negative impact their behavior can have on peer relationships is important in providing a basis for changing it. A one-on-one session with the student should be scheduled. The following script might prove useful to the teacher in structuring this session. It deals with arguing but could also apply to students who tend to be socially negative, insulting, or abrupt during their interactions with peers.

> "I've noticed that you often argue with peers when you interact with them. Are you aware that instead of just talking with them you are prone to arguing? What do you think causes you to do this and how do you think your peers react to it? *[Teacher and student discuss student answer(s) to this question. Student likely may not be aware that he or she is perceived as arguing and thus would not have an idea about its impact.]*

"Do you know the difference between discussing, or just chatting about something versus arguing? In arguing, there is usually anger and sometimes hostility with one person insisting they are right and the other is wrong. Most people do not like situations such as this and tend to avoid them. So, to make and keep friends, you should discuss rather than argue. *[Teacher and student discuss further and the teacher answers student's questions. Teacher encourages student to try discussing rather than arguing whenever possible.]*

"When you have a disagreement with a peer, it's much better to try and resolve it through discussion rather than argument. Solving a disagreement this way requires each side to do some 'give and take' and it usually works out better than arguing.

"Remember, If you want to have more positive interactions with peers and be more accepted by them, you should argue less and discuss more. Using the skills we practiced, why don't you give it a try?"

Social Skills Training

Obviously, students vary tremendously in their social skills. Students may become negative and/or hostile in peer interactions simply because they do not know how to properly initiate to others, respond to social bids, or sustain an interaction over time through normal give and take. Table 4.1

TABLE 4.1. Steps for Interactions with Peers

Initiating an interaction	Responding to an initiation (answering)	Continuing the interaction
1. Wait until the person isn't busy or talking to someone else.	1. Be positive.	1. Make small talk.
2. Get their attention.	2. Show you are interested in spending some time talking.	2. Share information about interests, likes, and dislikes.
3. Make eye contact, smile, and greet them.	3. Invite him or her to share an activity, if feasible.	3. Get to know each other.
4. Act friendly.	4. Do not ignore, walk away, refuse to talk, or say something mean.	4. Extend invitation(s).
5. Start a conversation.		5. Wait till the interaction comes to a natural end.
		6. Agree to meet again.

presents some general steps for how to positively approach, respond to, and continue an interaction with others.

For students who carry high levels of agitation and anger, and appear to be socially unskilled, teaching and regularly reviewing steps can be highly beneficial.

Rules for Joining a Group of Peers Involved in an Ongoing Activity

A social task that many students have trouble with is joining already formed groups of peers. Walker and his colleagues have studied elementary-aged students regarding how they try to join their peers during an ongoing activity (Irvin & Walker, 1993; Irvin et al., 1992). Direct observations and focus-group interviews of peers indicate that entry into the group is more likely if the following steps are followed:

1. Approach the group, observe the activity, and listen carefully to what is being said.
2. Don't make uninvited comments about the activity.
3. Hover and wait patiently for an invitation to join the activity.
4. If an invitation does not occur, wait for a break in the activity and say you'd like to join.
5. Offer your ideas for the activity but only when called on to do so.

Monitoring and Reinforcement

The consequences of engaging in the above social skills obviously are supplied by peers primarily within free-play settings. Thus, teachers have a very limited ability to influence them directly as they occur. However, it is important for the teacher to carefully monitor the student's performance on a regular basis. Using a one-on-one debriefing procedure, the teacher should monitor the student's self-evaluation of how their peer conversations and interactions went on selected days. Doing so once or twice per week would probably suffice unless the student is having serious difficulties. You can use the form in Figure 4.1 for this purpose.

The student's responses to these questions can be very revealing of how their peer relationships are faring. Students should be praised and approved of for being forthright as well as for making progress in becoming more positive.

CASE STUDY: DEALING WITH AN ANGRY, HOSTILE STUDENT

William Ferguson, known to his peers and classmates as "Willie," was a perpetually angry, unhappy student enrolled in Ms. Pritchard's third-grade class.

Student Name _____ Teacher _____

1. How many conversations with peers today? ____ 1 to 5 ____ 6 to 10 ____ more than 10.

Comments:

2. How positive were they? ____ mostly positive ____ some positive and some negative ____ mostly negative.

Comments:

3. How did you handle the negative conversations?

4. What did you learn about yourself from today's conversations?

FIGURE 4.1. Student Self Evaluation Form for Daily Peer Conversations and Interaction. From *Solutions to Critical Behavioral Issues in the Classroom* by Hill M. Walker. Copyright © 2023 The Guilford Press. Permission to photocopy this material is granted to purchasers of this book for personal use or use with students (see copyright page for details). Purchasers can download enlarged versions of this material (see the box at the end of the table of contents).

Though appearing to be sad and keeping to himself, his nickname among peers was "crabapple" because of how he reacted to frustration and to approaches from peers.

Willie came from an unhappy, abusive home life. His father was an alcoholic who had spent time in prison; he was physically and emotionally abusive of family members, and especially cruel when drinking. Willie confided to the school counselor about his father's abuse when he was referred by Ms. Pritchard to child protection, as required by law, because of her concerns about some bruises and red welts on his head and neck. Due to the emotional chaos and abuse of his family life, Willie's teacher wondered if the family could benefit from a connection to community mental health that could provide support and coping strategies for dealing with the family's stressors that so negatively affected Willie.

Willie's peers were unaware of his family background and were not sympathetic to his anger and hostility. When he was negative, they tended to either respond in kind or avoid him. Ms. Pritchard took note of how Willie's behavior was affecting his peer relationships and scheduled a private meeting with him. She asked him if he realized how negative he was being with peers and how it affected his relationships. Generally, he was largely unaware of how severe the problem had become.

Ms. Pritchard asked Willie if he would be interested in learning how to be more positive with peers to help him to have more friends. He said he was willing to give it a try. She indicated he would need to learn how to start, answer, and continue interactions in a more positive way and that she would teach him how to do it. Ms. Pritchard scheduled some daily 15- to 20-minute sessions to teach Willie these strategies. She reviewed the key steps he needed to take when approaching others (e.g., make eye contact, act friendly), when responding to approaches by peers (e.g., smile, show you are interested), and to continue the interaction (e.g., share interests). Above all, she urged Willie to try and focus on staying positive and not to lose his temper with peers. If he felt himself getting angry for any reason when interacting, he should stop, take several deep breaths, and decide whether he needed to say or do anything about the reason for his anger. As a rule, she told him that it would be better to say or do nothing in this situation and to refocus on staying positive or at least neutral so the interaction could continue. Ms. Pritchard said they should try out several things to see how Willie would respond in this situation. She told Willie, "Say I approach you and we start talking and I laugh at something you say but you didn't mean it to be funny. Or when we are talking I don't agree about something you said, and you don't like the way I handle the disagreement. What would you say or do?" In the first instance, Willie said he wouldn't say or do anything, for which Ms. Pritchard praised him. In the second instance, Willie said it would be OK for his peer not to agree even though he still thought the peer was wrong, for which Ms. Pritchard also praised him.

As Willie began learning the steps involved in forging positive peer interactions and conversations, he was given opportunities to apply them on the playground during recess—an essential step in mastery. Ms. Pritchard set up a process where two classmates were recruited as special helpers each day to help Willie get access to peer-controlled activities at recess, to model positive behavior for him, and to facilitate his peer interactions. The special helpers were given extra credit for their efforts.

Ms. Pritchard set up a monitoring and review process to help Willie gauge his progress in becoming more positive with peers. She scheduled a brief meeting at the end of each day to review his behavior and used a form for this purpose similar to the one in Figure 4.1. From time to time she asked Willie's special helpers to also say how well they thought things were going.

As expected, Willie initially struggled in learning how to control his temper and anger during peer interactions. However, he was able to gradually improve his self-control over time. As Willie became less hostile and more positive with peers, they responded in kind. He showed this same pattern in his positive attempts in starting, answering, and continuing peer interactions and conversations. Some days were good and some not so good in Willie's view. The special helpers generally confirmed the accuracy of his reports. Ms. Pritchard was pleased with Willie's overall efforts and progress and continued to approve of and frequently praise him for both. Willie is expected to gain friends and share more peer activities as this program is continued.

CONSIDERATIONS WHEN TEACHING STUDENTS TO HAVE NORMAL INTERACTIONS AND CONVERSATIONS WITHOUT BECOMING ANGRY OR HOSTILE

Students like Willie, who are socially unskilled and have anger management problems, are at risk for social isolation and disrupted peer relations. It is important to help them overcome the challenges that deprive them of friendships and positive peer relationships. Failure in one's peer relationships is a risk factor for both negative developmental outcomes and lack of school success (Hawkins et al., 1999).

Efforts to intervene in this area require some tact and should be conducted as privately as possible. Peers are acutely aware of each other's behavioral characteristics and social status. Interventions should be designed to increase a problem student's social status rather than diminishing it through a positive intervention that inadvertently stigmatizes a vulnerable student.

A two-pronged intervention is recommended for such students—one to deal with anger management problems and one designed to improve social skills in starting, answering, and continuing positive peer interactions. Per the above, a self-control strategy is recommended for the anger and hostility, and a social skills training procedure is recommended to improve social skills and social status. Both interventions should be carefully monitored to determine their impact on peer interactions.

While any student with these behavioral challenges could potentially benefit from this combined intervention approach, it is recommended that it be applied only to the most severe cases wherein a student's social status and peer difficulties are broadly known by classmates. To reemphasize, students with mild difficulties in these two areas might have them highlighted rather than diminished by participation in an intervention that would attract the attention of peers. If a number of students share these problems within a classroom, a classwide universal approach to addressing them might be more appropriate.

CHAPTER 4 TAKEAWAYS

■ The combination of anger and hostility with peer-related social skills deficits can do extensive damage to a student's social status and peer relationships.

■ Anger and hostility, along with deficits in knowing how to conduct positive interactions, should be targeted in assisting students who suffer from these conditions. Separate intervention procedures should be used to address each problem.

■ Left unaddressed, severe anger and hostility will further isolate students from their peers and disrupt their overall school adjustment; long term, they may also negatively impact development.

■ The combination of anger and hostility as well as social skills deficits should be addressed with direct intervention procedures for only the most severely affected students. Universal interventions in these areas should be used to address such problems for students in general.

CHAPTER 5

Developing Students' Ability to Follow Classroom Rules and Behavioral Expectations

Organizational rules are commonly used to direct the behavior of individuals or groups toward some desired end or result. Schools and teachers are charged with educating all students. Thus, they must have rules in place to manage every student individually as well as groups of students. This can be a challenging task, as today's students bring a diverse array of family histories, experiences, beliefs, and attitudes to the schooling process. Due to their backgrounds, many students are not well prepared to meet the ordinary demands and routines of schooling, while others have negative attitudes about schooling that interfere with their ability to achieve school success. In spite of this, all students are expected to learn, master, and follow the necessary rules and expectations that make instruction and management of the classroom possible.

One of the most important tasks for teachers is to identify, define, communicate, teach, and reinforce following these rules that create success in the classroom. The more teachers invest in this process, the more manageable and teachable the classroom becomes. The material in this chapter addresses this task.

DEFINITION, KEY FEATURES, AND EXAMPLES OF CLASSROOM RULES AND BEHAVIORAL EXPECTATIONS

In typical usage, rules refer to the things students should or should not do in the classroom and the school at large. Rules can be positively or negatively stated such as "walk when in the hallways" versus "no running in the halls," or "focus on your own work" versus "don't disturb others when they are working." Too often, rules are expressed as a list of things students are *not* allowed to do and lead to a negative mindset about them among students. On the other hand, behavioral expectations usually state the desired behavior positively, such as "show kindness to others during class and free-time periods," "apologize and try to correct mistakes when you hurt others' feelings," or "ask for help when you don't understand the teacher's instructions for a task." When rules are stated positively, they are essentially interchangeable with behavioral expectations. While some teachers rely on negatively stated rules beginning with "no" or "don't," this is not recommended.

Research suggests that students are more likely to comply when rules and expectations are positively stated. It also helps to specify what the student is expected to do when developing classroom rules and expectations. In the above example, the alternative to "no running in the halls" could be "walk slowly, take your time, and leave room for others." The desired behavior in response to asking for help might be "raise your hand and wait patiently until the teacher calls on you."

Examples of Classroom Rules

One of the most crucial features regarding rules and expectations is not to have so many that they overwhelm students. The PBIS program (Horner et al., 2005) contains three core values that guide student behavior and that all students are expected to learn and master: Be safe, be respectful, and be responsible. These are very broad values that can translate into a large number of supportive behavioral indicators; these core values are easy to remember as shorthand for students, signifying a number of positive actions.

Sprague and Golly (2012) have defined each of these values as follows: (1) *Be safe* means stay free from harm; (2) *Be respectful* means be polite, cooperative, and concerned about others; and (3) *Be responsible* means you are dependable, trustworthy, and make positive choices. These authors have developed detailed strategies and lesson plans for communicating and teaching these expectations as well as identifying the supporting behavioral indicators of each core value. In addition to directly teaching behavioral expectations, they can be strengthened through such simple strategies as modeling, use of behavior-specific praise, and precorrections.

Another option in identifying classroom rules and expectations is to select a list of no more than five to seven that govern classroom management and instruction. Walker (1986, 1995) has compiled such a list, based on years of mainstream research, that has become popular among educators. These expectations are listed in Figure 5.1 and define the ideal profile for succeeding academically.

Students who can display this general behavioral profile will be accepted by most teachers, will have positive teacher–student instructional interactions, and are likely to achieve school success. This list would have to be adapted considerably depending on the grade level and developmental status of the students being taught. But these teacher-preferred behaviors may be useful as a starting point in developing rules and expectations in cooperation with students.

CAUSAL INFLUENCES AND ANTECEDENT CONDITIONS AFFECTING STUDENT ACCEPTANCE OF SCHOOL RULES

The way in which an individual learns a rule can influence how realistic the rule is for him or her. Rules are learned in two main ways: (1) through direct experience of their consequences as when a rule is followed (pleasant) or not followed (aversive), and (2) indirectly through being taught the rule by others such as a parent or by watching what happens when others do or do not follow an established rule. The first method is called learning a rule by *contingency shaping*—by directly experiencing the consequences of either following or not following it. For example, when a child breaks a rule by touching a hot stove, the parental rejoinder is sometimes "Taught you a lesson, didn't it?" The second method of learning rules is called *rule governed,* where the rule is learned indirectly through antecedent conditions. That is, by being taught the rule via verbal instructions one's behavior is directed toward some desired end or goal absent having to experience the consequence directly. For example, a parent's prompt to a young child

- Comply promptly.
- Follow rules.
- Control anger.
- Make assistance needs known appropriately.
- Produce acceptable quality work.
- Work independently.
- Adjust to different instructional routines.
- Respond to teacher corrections.
- Listen carefully to teacher.

FIGURE 5.1. Teacher-preferred student behavioral expectations.

to wear a coat when it's cold outside can avoid discomfort and possibly catching a cold.

Experts often argue that contingency-shaped rule-learning is more meaningful and rules learned this way are more likely to be followed by the individual in the future. This may or may not be true but it is clear this method cannot be relied upon by organizations to teach essential rules governing safety or responsible behavior. Use of verbal antecedents and instructions in teaching rules is very efficient, since the consequences can be described and illustrated without needing to be experienced by those governed by them. Students are more likely to follow rules that are stated positively rather than negatively (Sprague & Golly, 2012). As described later in this chapter, classroom rules should be taught in the same way as academic content, using group and individualized instructional procedures.

Other factors that can influence how rules are perceived and reacted to are a student's history with being taught rules at home and in other settings; the extent to which parents support their child's participation in organizations that rely upon rule-governed behavior, such as scouts, 4-H clubs, boys' and girls' clubs, and the like; and a student's attitude toward rules of conduct generally. Given the diverse range of student backgrounds in today's schools, it is inevitable that students will vary in how accepting they are of classroom rules. Some students will actively resist rules of conduct that constrain their behavior, and might need extra or individualized assistance in accepting and following essential rules. The following case study profiles such a student.

CASE STUDY: ASHLEY, THE RULE BREAKER

Sometimes teachers have to deal with a student, or several students, who will not accept and comply with rules that apply to all their classmates. Ashley Scott, a bright, talented fourth-grade girl in Ms. Rodriguez's class, was such a student. Ashley displayed a high level of agitation in her interactions with others and was quick to find fault with others in any social situation. She had a difficult temperament, causing many in her social network to misinterpret her intentions as self-serving when in fact they often were not. In spite of this, Ashley was socially powerful and influential among her peers, and used relational aggression tactics to socially isolate and punish classmates who disapproved of her.

Ashley's parents had high social status in the community and were financially well-off. They were frequent critics of school policies and practices, well-known to school administrative staff, and often modeled negative attitudes toward schooling that Ashley adopted. In prior years involving teacher conflicts with Ashley, the school administration often sided with Ashley's parents, and teachers felt they were not adequately supported. Partly as a result, Ashley displayed a noticeable lack of respect for school staff in general and for Ms. Rodriguez in particular. Other students were aware of Ashley's lack of respect and it negatively affected their view of Ms. Rodriguez.

At the beginning of the school year, Ms. Rodriguez scheduled several class periods to have students participate in developing classroom rules and expectations. Ashley proved highly disruptive of this process, frequently challenging the appropriateness of the rules her teacher was asking the class to consider. It became so disruptive at one point that Ashley had to be excused from the class discussion of rules. The class and Ms. Rodriguez ultimately agreed on a set of six core rules that would govern student conduct and academic performance for the year.

Ashley's behavior made it clear that she did not accept the agreed-upon rules. Over time, Ashley tended to be a disruptive influence in almost any small-group activity in which she was involved. She frequently disturbed classmates who were trying to work and insisted on talking with classmates during work times instead of during free time. Despite many efforts by Ms. Rodriguez to correct and redirect Ashley's problem behavior—including debriefing, prompts, reminders, and praise—it finally became too much and Ms. Rodriguez made a disciplinary referral to the principal's office. A parent–teacher conference was scheduled, which was led by the principal and school counselor and attended by Ms. Rodriguez. It was a minor disaster, devolving into a shouting match with the parents blaming the school and in particular Ms. Rodriguez for the situation. A decision was reached that the situation with Ashley and her teacher had become unworkable, and Ashley's parents grudgingly agreed to a process being started to transfer Ashley to a different fourth-grade teacher.

Sometimes factors combine to produce students who display intractable problems that prove resistant to even the best behavior-management attempts. This exact scenario seemed to characterize the situation with Ashley. The school was left with very few choices for resolving the situation satisfactorily. A change of placement that would afford Ashley a fresh start seemed to be the best available option.

RECOMMENDED STRATEGIES FOR IDENTIFYING, COMMUNICATING, TEACHING, AND REINFORCING RULES AND EXPECTATIONS

Identifying and Communicating Classroom Rules with Students

There are two general approaches or options for identifying and communicating classroom rules and expectations. Option one is to select specific behaviors from a list such as that in Figure 5.1. Option two is to choose a small number of core values, as in the PBIS approach, and then identify the specific behavioral indicators that support each core value. It has not been established that either approach is superior to the other—it is matter of teacher preference. For teachers who prefer a more academic focus for classroom rules, option one is probably best; for teachers who want a more dual focus between academic and social–emotional dimensions, option two is probably best.

Option One

The teacher lists the nine student behaviors in Figure 5.1 on the board and initiates a class discussion about which are most important in the classroom. The task is to select the five to seven most important rules for helping students be successful. In cooperation with the teacher, students rank the rules in order of importance and then select the top-ranked behaviors to govern the classroom for the school year.

The teacher instructions for this task could be as follows:

> "Class, I want us to discuss and decide on a list of behaviors today that can help you be successful and will serve as our classroom rules. It's important for you to help develop them as they will govern how the class operates for the school year. Let's discuss why each one is important and choose the five that we want."

The teacher orders the list according to the behaviors' importance based on this discussion. If the teacher prefers an instructional or academic focus to the class rules/expectations, the discussion can be shaped in that direction.

Option Two

This option uses an approach similar to PBIS (i.e., a small number of core values with identified supporting behavioral indicators of each value), such as Sprague and Golly's (2012). Figure 5.2 lists two broad core values with accompanying supporting behaviors for each. They are based on the view that there are two core dimensions of school success: being a good student and getting along with others. I have included the specific supportive, teachable behavioral indicators under each core dimension.

It helps to remind students that these two core dimensions are the two jobs they need to do well in order to achieve school success. The information in Figure 5.2 should be written on the board and a discussion initiated with the class about how the listed behaviors can help them be successful academically and in getting along with others. The following teacher narrative is suggested:

> "Class, I have listed on the board the two jobs students have in order to achieve success in school. Some ways you can do this are listed under

Be a Good Student	Get Along with Others
1. Be organized and prepared for class.	1. Be positive with your teacher and peers.
2. Work hard and do your best work.	2. Be helpful.
3. Listen to teacher and follow directions.	3. Cooperate.
4. Accept feedback and correct errors.	4. Show kindness to classmates.
5. Ask for help if you need it.	5. Apologize and try to make amends.

FIGURE 5.2. Core dimensions of school success with sample supportive behaviors.

each job. I want you to tell me how you think each way listed could be helpful. How about the first item under 'Being a Good Student'?"

The teacher continues on until the two lists are discussed.

By developing rules and behavioral expectations in collaboration with students and showing their importance, teachers can do a great deal to help all students be successful in their schooling and enhance classroom positivity. As noted earlier in the chapter, students generally will have greater ownership of rules and expectations that they are involved in developing.

IDENTIFYING RULES AND EXPECTATIONS FOR SCHOOL AREAS OTHER THAN THE CLASSROOM

This book is focused primarily on the teacher and classroom. However, when it comes to setting rules and behavioral expectations for the school as a whole, you will likely be asked to participate. Many schools choose to identify rules for student behavior within different settings or contexts in the school. For example, Sprague and Golly (2012) identified rules and expectations for the following school contexts: common areas, cafeteria, playground, bus stops, hallways, and bathrooms. They created a matrix that listed the three core PBIS core values across the top and the contexts down the side. Then behavioral indicators were included in each row/column square of the matrix. For example, the "being safe on the playground" square in their matrix includes the behavioral indicator of "uses playground equipment safely and correctly"; the square for "being respectful in the cafeteria" was "allow anyone to sit next to you," and the square for "being responsible in common areas" includes "follow school rules and be honest." One can easily add other school areas (auditorium, gym, etc.), core values, and behavioral indicators to the matrix (e.g., "being respectful in the gym" is indicated by "take your turn and use equipment properly").

It is easy to see how this matrix process could get carried away depending on the number of school areas, core values, and behavioral indicators added. While very helpful as an organizer, it is not possible to cover all or even most possible situations using this approach. As in many cases, economy is a good thing to strive for.

TEACHING AND REINFORCING RULES AND EXPECTATIONS

It is important to reinforce the rules and expectations to strengthen them after they have been developed and communicated to students. Review each rule or behavioral indicator and discuss with students why it's important to school success. Discuss with your students examples as well as nonexamples of each rule or behavioral indicator so they can clearly understand the difference. Role-play or demonstrate the contrast for students as appropriate.

The rules/expectations should be reviewed with the class at least three times a week until they become second nature to students. When individual students are following a rule, they should receive call-out praise noting this event so all students can hear. A teacher option would be to monitor how well the class as a whole does daily and assign a daily 1–5 rating, where 5 is perfect and 1 is unsatisfactory. If 80% of available points are earned by the end of the week, a brief free-time class activity could be provided.

For students such as Ashley in the above case study, a combined debriefing and frequent praise strategy might be considered. Understanding the basis for a student's resistance can sometimes be uncovered through debriefing. Providing support for the student and praise of their attempts at rule following could be helpful, as would a daily 1–5 rating from the teacher.

CONSIDERATIONS IN HELPING STUDENTS LEARN TO FOLLOW CLASSROOM RULES AND EXPECTATIONS

The key point to remember about rules and expectations is not to have so many that students are overwhelmed and can't keep them all in mind. Shorthand core values that are then translated into behavioral indicators may make it easier for students to accept, remember, and follow them (e.g., be a good student and get along with others). They should always be stated positively and students should have a clear idea about positive and negative examples of them. It may be an easier management task for the teacher if there is a consistent set of general rules across classrooms that are similar in content. On this point, if a school has adopted the PBIS framework schoolwide, it may be best to use the three core PBIS values as a basis for developing behavioral indicators as opposed to creating a set of individual classroom rules and then developing behavioral indicators for each.

CHAPTER 5 TAKEAWAYS

- Communicate the rules and expectations in shorthand form.

- State them positively.

- Teach the rules/expectations in the same way as you would academic content.

- Identify multiple behavioral indicators that support each core rule or expectation.

- Once developed, post the rules and expectations prominently in the classroom.

- Review the rules and expectations with the class at least weekly.

- Develop a structured plan for teaching and strengthening the rules once they are developed.

Helping Students Cope with Disappointment, Frustration, and Failure

Our schools now have many angry, frustrated, and discouraged students. Their lives are full of struggles and disappointments, leading to a range of negative emotions that can be difficult to manage. When students come from home environments where coercive tactics are modeled for them, they can learn that the use of these tactics is necessary to reach their social goals (Patterson, 1982; Patterson, Reid, & Dishion, 1992), and they can carry high levels of agitation. They bring these tactics to their schooling and apply them to interactions with school staff and peers. Thus, behaviors that are learned at home may not serve children well as they participate in larger social contexts such as school. When these tactics do not work as intended and the student fails to get his or her way, reactions can range from discouragement and depression, to sulking, to an intensified display of coercion. In such cases, their school success is placed in jeopardy and their mental health may be as well. The recent Surgeon General's report (Office of the Surgeon General, 2021) on children's mental health brings these concerns to the public eye as a national emergency. This chapter is focused on helping these students cope with not getting their way and teaching them acceptable alternatives when their approach does not work.

DEFINITION, KEY FEATURES, AND EXAMPLES OF COPING WITH NOT GETTING ONE'S WAY

All students have individual goals they want to achieve—for example, being included in peer activities, being accepted by classmates, securing teacher approval, getting good grades, or being selected for a sports team.

Executive function refers to the cognitive processes that are necessary for success in achieving one's goals. Skills such as planning, flexible thinking, self-monitoring and self-control, evaluation of situations, working memory, and ability to organize are all examples of executive function (Zelazo, Blair, & Willoughby, 2016). Some experts have identified up to 12 executive function skills or processes. These skills allow you to select, plan, act, assess, self-regulate, self-manage, and analyze events and situations in pursuing your goals. They are often the difference between success and failure.

Even if highly motivated and skilled in these executive functions, pursuing personal goals always carries some social or emotional risk of failure, and students should plan for its possibility. However, many do not have the skills to cope effectively with such failure and instead pout, sulk, complain, apply coercive pressures, and/or do not consider alternatives to their failed strategy. Healthy responses in this situation would be to try to analyze why the strategy failed and to develop alternatives that have a better chance of working.

These executive functions are sometimes grouped under the rubric or framework of emotional intelligence as opposed to genetic endowment. They are skills that can be taught and learned by most students. The field of social–emotional learning (SEL) has developed instructional approaches to this task and emphasizes both academic and social–emotional competence. The SEL approach (see *https://casel.org/fundamentals-of-sel*) includes five broad competence areas: self-awareness, self-management, social awareness, relationship skills, and responsible decision making (Weissberg, Durlak, Domitrovich, & Gullotta, 2015). Skills in these areas obviously would be helpful to students as antecedents in coping with failure and in its prevention.

CAUSAL INFLUENCES AND ANTECEDENT CONDITIONS OF STUDENTS' INABILITY TO COPE WITH FAILURE

Students learn coping strategies through having them modeled by parents or taught directly to them, and by observing coping strategies and their effects as used by others. Observational learning is very important: The family situation is a powerful socializing influence in this regard, and it can also be highly influential for a student to observe how peers handle failure and disappointment.

Many students come from backgrounds where they have limited opportunities for this type of learning, have no experience with executive functions in dealing with difficult situations, or they do not receive needed supports from caregivers to deal emotionally with failure. The result can be emotional outbursts born of frustration and a failure to accept reality, or—more seriously—an expectancy of failure as in the case of students with low self-esteem. Such students are often angry, view the world as unfair, and do not have healthy responses to failure such as generating alternatives through problem solving. Alternatively, they may be depressed and view school as a punishing environment where they don't belong. Students with psychiatric disorders such as depression, anxiety disorders, and attention-deficit/hyperactivity disorder may be especially prone to this social isolation risk (Forness, Walker, & Kavale, 2003).

RECOMMENDED STRATEGIES FOR HELPING STUDENTS COPE WITH FAILURE

How a student responds to failure is primarily influenced by their parents and family situation. But when teachers see an individual student who is frustrated and struggling to cope with disappointment, they may be able to help the student by being supportive and empathetic, and encouraging him or her to view the situation as an opportunity for growth and improvement. Providing experiences that allow the student to build confidence from seeing their success is a great antidote to feeling discouraged. Breaking through the "expectation of failure" is a critical step in this regard. The following case study illustrates how a discouraged student can be encouraged and supported by a teacher.

CASE STUDY: JAIME, AN ANGRY, DISCOURAGED STUDENT WITH LOW SELF-ESTEEM

Jaime was a fifth-grade student enrolled in Mr. Fletcher's classroom. He had a slight learning disability, reflected in language and math difficulties, that caused him to struggle with schoolwork. He seemed to have low self-esteem, was reluctant to try new tasks, and had a general expectancy that his efforts would result in failure. He was often irritable and some peers called him a grouch. When Jaime did not do well on a task or assignment his frustration sometimes resulted in tears, which caused teasing by classmates. His parents were fully aware of his difficulties and did their best to support his schoolwork, but their attempts to help Jaime have a more positive outlook were limited.

Mr. Fletcher asked Jaime's parents if they objected to him referring Jaime to a social skills group conducted weekly by the school's counselor. He said Jaime seemed discouraged with schoolwork much of the time and that this might help his outlook toward himself and others. His parents approved the referral and asked how they might assist with Jaime's participation.

The counselor's social skills group consisted of three boys and two girls in addition to Jaime. They learned about relationship skills for interacting with peers and adults such as initiating to others, responding to initiations from others, and continuing an interaction over time. The counselor verbally described each relationship skill and provided positive examples and negative nonexamples of them so group members could understand the difference(s) in how to apply them correctly. Students took turns role playing each of the relationship skills in pairs and then switched roles. The role playing was followed by a discussion of what went right and what went wrong and how each instance could have been improved or corrected.

The counselor also presented challenging situations such as how to join an ongoing peer group activity at recess without getting rejected and the students were asked to offer their suggestions for joining strategies that might work. Then research evidence on this topic was also presented, which is to observe the activity quietly, don't make comments or ask questions of the group, and wait for an invitation or for a natural break in the activity before asking to join.

The counselor also presented a strategy for the small group's analysis that required the use of some selected executive functions. This strategy is called *triple A* for assess, act, and amend. She explained that when you're dealing with a new situation, you need to first assess it, which means you evaluate the situation and consider why, how, and whether you want to become involved in it. If you decide to get involved, you act according to your best guess. After you act, you then evaluate or analyze the situation to see if you need to make any changes in how you act (amend your actions). The group discussed different situations presented by the counselor for their analysis. This exercise required the following executive function skills: flexible, adaptable thinking; problem solving to develop alternatives; evaluation of situations; planning; self-monitoring; and working memory. It took the students time to get the hang of the triple A strategy but they eventually grew to like it and saw how it could help them in their relationships and more generally.

Finally, the counselor presented Rule #1 to the group: *Be polite and cooperative with others.* She explained that using this rule at school and in their daily lives would make things better for them in many ways and would help them make friends, be more accepted with peers, result in teacher approval, and be more likely to succeed in school.

Jaime wasn't sure about the social skills group initially but grew to like it and looked forward to his weekly meetings. He and Mr. Fletcher had regular debriefings about what he was learning and how it might improve his liking of school (which clearly seemed to be occurring). Mr. Fletcher set up a daily monitoring system for Jaime's use of Rule #1. He earned praise and points that he could exchange at home for special privileges.

This case study illustrates how a teacher's interest and concern combined with participation in a small-group activity can lead to improvements in a discouraged student's quality of life at school. Mr. Fletcher provided much-needed emotional support and encouragement. Jaime's participation in the social skills group of fellow students taught him about relationship skills and how to better negotiate the social landscape of school. The techniques and strategies in this case study should be considered by schools in helping students like Jaime. (See Chapter 4 on how to teach social interaction rules and skills to students so they can have positive conversations.)

The idea for students like Jaime is to experience as much success as possible to reduce their expectancy of failure, but also to learn from failures and develop healthy responses to them. The following are some suggested strategies for helping discouraged students cope with failure.

- Monitor discouraged students constantly for incidents of failure.
- Offer emotional support and debriefing about the incidents.
- Help students develop alternatives that might have caused things to turn out differently.
- Encourage students to view failure as a growth and improvement opportunity.
- Arrange as many success experiences for students as possible.
- Adapt academic tasks as needed to maximize students' success.
- Provide frequent praise and approval for students' efforts.
- Enlist parental support in efforts to mitigate the emotional impact of failure.

CONSIDERATIONS IN HELPING STUDENTS WITH LOW SELF-ESTEEM COPE WITH DISAPPOINTMENT, FRUSTRATION, AND FAILURE

Students with low self-esteem often have unmet mental health needs that lower their quality of life and put them at risk. Since those students who do receive mental health services access them through their schools in 75% of cases, it is essential that school staff be sensitive to their needs. There are some things teachers can do to facilitate meeting the needs of vulnerable children and youth in school. They include the following:

1. Make a referral of a distressed student to the school counselor or the school psychologist serving the school who would be able to determine if the student should be referred to an outside agency.
2. Advocate for a mentorship program where vulnerable students could be assigned to teacher mentors who would support and advocate for them.
3. Help establish a confidential student crisis hotline such as Youthline in Oregon and Safe2Tell in Colorado.
4. Implement strategies for helping students cope with loneliness, which many of today's students suffer from.

For the last item in the list above, I recommend a recently published book, *Lonely Kids in a Connected World: What Teachers Can Do* (Fad & Campos, 2021), which provides a compendium of strategies teachers can consider to help students cope with loneliness.

Social connections are extremely important to students' mental health and emotional well-being. Depression among today's children and youth, which can be exacerbated by loneliness, has long been of concern as a potential correlate of suicide. Depression has also been detected among children as young as preschool, indicating how pervasive this disorder has emerged (Luby, 2013). Forness, Walker, and Kavale (1983) have provided an analysis of drug treatment options that can enhance the school performance of students with psychiatric disorders who are at risk of social isolation. Teachers who have concerns about such students should consider facilitating access to mental health treatments for this student population.

CHAPTER 6 TAKEAWAYS

- Far too many students in today's schools have a low quality of school life.
- Many students are discouraged by the circumstances of their lives.
- Most discouraged students do not have healthy responses to failure.
- Schools are limited in how they can assist such students.
- The emotional support of teachers and peers is critical.

PART II

Strategies for Teaching Students How to Avoid and Reduce Challenging Behavior

Teaching Students to Avoid Damaging Others' Property and Possessions

One of the basic rights all individuals have is for their personal space, property, and possessions to be respected by others. When this right is violated without a valid reason, the victim feels a sense of violation, betrayal, and exploitation: Such action shows a fundamental lack of respect.

This basic right extends to the classroom and school setting where an individual student is most likely to experience this treatment at the hands of peers. Aside from being a display of hostility to the victimized student, this action may be viewed and subtly approved of by certain peers. It is an act of intimidation and bullying and may be highly disruptive to the classroom atmosphere depending upon how it plays out. Such behavior is often sustained by the pleasure destructive students achieve from inflicting damage on others and the social status that results from approving peers.

DEFINITION, KEY FEATURES, AND EXAMPLES OF DAMAGING OTHERS' PROPERTY AND POSSESSIONS

Destructive behavior toward others' property and possessions can be defined as a form of personal vandalism. Traditionally, vandalism is thought of as destructive acts against buildings or other forms of property, for example graffiti. However, one can identify three types of vandalism that occur in schools. First there is covert vandalism, which is very common and involves the stealth destruction of public or private property. Second, there is deliberate destruction of others' property or possessions, which is individualized, personal, and usually overt in nature. Finally, destruction of one's own effects is a self-directed form of aggression and can be a clear sign of emotional problems.

In the classroom, destructive behavior can take the form of actions that deface valued possessions such as notebooks and desks or taking a cell phone and refusing to return it while seeking embarrassing personal information that may be stored on the phone. As a rule, the more vigorous the protest, the greater the reinforcing value of the destructiveness.

CAUSAL INFLUENCES AND ANTECEDENT CONDITIONS OF STUDENTS' TENDENCIES TO DAMAGE OTHERS' PROPERTY AND POSSESSIONS

There are numerous possible reasons that prompt personal vandalism, ranging from envy or greed, to seeking revenge and getting even for something, upsetting someone you don't like or respect, attention seeking, achieving greater social status and peer approval, or simple malicious mischief. Other causes or antecedents for this type of behavior can be that it is a learned behavior pattern within an external setting or context where destructive behavior has not been subject to sanctions by adults and the child learns he or she can engage in it with impunity.

As students mature into upper elementary and middle school, these events occur less often as the consequences for them can be more severe. However, personal vandalism is a serious violation of social norms and should be dealt with directly. Often teacher involvement and/or administrative support is required to resolve situations involving destruction of possessions. Our research shows that teachers strongly object to the display of this behavior (Hersh & Walker, 1983; Walker, 1986).

RECOMMENDED STRATEGIES FOR REDUCING AND ELIMINATING DESTRUCTIVENESS TOWARD OTHERS

Destructiveness toward others is a classic example of how a restorative discipline (RD) approach can be effective in addressing a serious relationship issue. RD is derived from restorative justice used in the criminal justice system to deter offenses by requiring offenders to assume responsibility for restoring and repairing the damage caused by a criminal act. The central idea of RD is to build positive school climates by restoring and repairing damaged relationships (involving peers as well as staff) to their prior status: the five R's of RD are relationships, respect, responsibility, repair, and reintegration. RD emphasizes student involvement in resolving problems, social engagement versus punishment, and is an alternative to punishing suspensions and sanctions. It does not focus on violations of school or classroom rules and is not effective for use in this context.

As a rule, RD is adopted by a whole school but its principles can also easily be applied to the individual classroom; it has proven to be popular as an alternative for schools to use in dealing with peer-to-peer and peer-to-staff conflicts. Schools that adopt this disciplinary approach can expect a steep decline in suspensions and expulsions. The RD process usually involves a small group of students (including the offending student) who participate in a restorative circle coordinated by a staff member. This is similar to student courts that are sometimes used in high schools. The group process focuses on the following issues.

1. Understanding the issues of the problem situation and getting to the root of the problem
2. Respecting each member's contributions
3. Determining accountability
4. Mutual trust of group members
5. Deciding how restitution and repair will work
6. Reintegration or returning to conditions prior to the event's occurrence

It is very important that all participating students have a clear idea of the way a circle should be conducted. The specific steps or protocol for conducting a restorative problem-solving session follows below:

1. A restorative circle is established to evaluate the situation and resolve it. Four to five students are recruited to participate in the circle, including the victim and offending student.

2. A problem-solving anchor is used to determine the severity of the situation and the approach used to solve it. The behavior or action prompting formation of a circle is coded as either "a big deal" or "no big deal." A big deal would be a report of a fight, an injury, or a physical threat. A "no big deal" would be one student calling another an obscene name, a dispute on the playground over a game, or a student being teased. Situations coded as the latter can be potentially resolved in many instances among the involved students without adult engagement or conducting a circle.

3. A teacher or other staff member (e.g., school counselor or behavioral coach) conducts and leads the session. The session leader's tasks are to (a) maintain a problem-solving focus, (b) get to the root of the problem, (c) establish accountability but ensure that blame is not assigned, (d) ensure that all circle members have a chance to contribute, (e) facilitate a consensus decision, and (f) encourage circle members in the use of affective

statements (i.e., communicating personal feelings about the situation) to express their views.

4. Circle members develop a consensus-based restore and repair solution to resolve the situation, with optional behavioral contracting if necessary.

5. A follow-up session is planned as needed.

One of the strong benefits of this process is that it allows the offending student to see how peers view the incident and its behavioral implications. Destructive students rarely appreciate the gravity of their actions or their true impact on others. The following case study illustrates how a teacher and classmates dealt with a destructive classroom situation involving two peers.

CASE STUDY: JEREMIAH'S ATTACK ON JAMIE AND HIS POSSESSIONS

Jeremiah was enrolled in Mr. Bates's fourth-grade class and had a history of problem behavior starting at the beginning of his school career. He was very oppositional and resisted necessary rules as a matter of course. There had been many conflicts between Jeremiah and both his classmates and his teachers in previous grades. His reputation preceded him and did not serve him well. His peers expected him to behave badly even when he wasn't intending to do so, causing Jeremiah to complain that he was not being treated fairly.

Tension and problems had existed for some time between Jeremiah and Jamie, a classmate. Jeremiah had taken a dislike to Jamie from the moment they first met and Jeremiah taunted Jamie with mean-spirited teasing whenever the occasion allowed. Jeremiah was the more aggressive of the two, was larger in size than Jamie, and purposely intimidated Jamie with threats of physical harm. In spite of this treatment, Jamie did not complain to his teacher about Jeremiah's behavior.

One of Jamie's prized possessions was a leather-bound notebook that he'd received for his birthday. One day in class, while Mr. Bates was not looking, Jeremiah walked over to Jamie's desk, took out a pocketknife, and defaced the leather cover of the notebook. Jamie was dumbfounded with Jeremiah's act and protested loudly to Jeremiah and the teacher. Mr. Bates severely reprimanded Jeremiah for such a vicious act of deliberate destructiveness. It was clear that Jeremiah's goal was to inflict emotional pain on Jamie regardless of the consequences to himself.

Mr. Bates filled out a behavioral referral about the incident and sent it to the principal's office. As the school had recently adopted an RD approach to handling relationship problems such as this, a decision was made to create an RD circle to deal with it. Mr. Bates was charged with setting up and leading the circle's problem solving of the incident. He selected three of his students to form the circle, along with Jeremiah and Jamie. The group's discussion went as follows.

MR. BATES: I called this circle to get to the root of the problem between Jeremiah and Jamie, to find out why this happened, and to develop a restore and repair plan to deal with it going forward. Thanks for your willingness to participate in resolving this problem. Jamie, in your own words, please tell us what happened.

JAMIE: Jeremiah has been picking on me ever since we first met and I've done nothing to make him do that. Cutting the cover on my notebook was just the latest thing he's done to hurt my feelings. My parents gave me that notebook for my birthday and were furious when I told them what happened. They threatened to meet with Jeremiah's parents about it and complained to the principal's office.

MR. BATES: Jeremiah, can you tell us why you damaged Jamie's notebook?

JEREMIAH: He always thinks he's better than everyone else. I wanted to show him what I thought of him.

MR. BATES: Do you think this was the right way to show your disapproval? What do the rest of you think? (*Each classmate says Jeremiah should not have shown his disapproval in this way and needs to find ways to control his anger.*) Jeremiah, how would you feel if one of your classmates did to you what you did to Jamie?

JEREMIAH: I guess I wouldn't like it very much.

MR. BATES: One of our school rules is that we should respect others. Jeremiah, do you think cutting Jamie's notebook cover was an act of respect?

JEREMIAH: I guess not. (*All their classmates agree.*)

MR. BATES: So how do we make amends and repair the damage that was done? Jamie, what do you think?

JAMIE: He could start with an apology and promise not to do anything like that again! I'm tired of his teasing and bullying.

MR. BATES: Does anyone else have suggestions? (*One peer suggests Jeremiah see the school counselor about learning how to control his anger. Another says Jeremiah and Jamie should try to become friends and share time together at recess.*)

JAMIE: My parents want Jeremiah to replace my damaged notebook with a new one.

MR. BATES: These all sound like reasonable suggestions. Jeremiah, you should know that what you did is not acceptable in school. You should never treat anyone in this manner. There are many ways to deal with your dislike of a person other than destroying or defacing their possessions. This school will not tolerate such behavior. I want you to apologize to Jamie and learn to interact with him in a more positive manner. I will check in from time to time to see how you and he are doing. Thanks to all of you for your help.

This case study provides one example of how an RD approach to relationship problems in school can be dealt with more constructively than via suspension or expulsion. The RD process requires publicly confronting one's behavior along with its effect on others and making amends in an effort to restore the situation. The use of punishing sanctions in the above case would likely not have been as effective going forward. RD strategies are used in subsequent chapters to show how diverse peer relations problems can be resolved. As noted earlier, however, they are less appropriate for dealing with violations of school rules that are not relationship based. Normal classroom and administration procedures should be used to deal with rule violations.

CHAPTER 7 TAKEAWAYS

- The overt destruction and damage to a student's property or possessions is a clear gesture of dislike and lack of respect, and severely damages the relationship between victim and victimizer.

- When the destruction or damage is done covertly, it communicates a similar message of dislike and disrespect.

- Immediate steps need to be taken to restore and repair the situation to the extent possible.

- RD procedures should be strongly considered for dealing proactively with student conflicts.

CHAPTER 8

Reducing Insubordination and Enhancing Students' Respect for the Teacher

Insubordination is the most frequent cause of office discipline referrals (ODRs) that occur in grades K–7 and is often prompted by a student's refusal to abide by a teacher's direction, request, or command (Gion, McIntosh, & Horner, 2014). The student's refusal is frequently accompanied by a clear lack of respect for and/or defiance of the teacher's authority. These acts are highly disruptive and cannot be tolerated by a classroom teacher if they wish to still maintain control of the classroom. If such incidents are of sufficient intensity, they may require a "room clear" to restore classroom order. Far and away, the best strategy is to prevent their occurrence. When that is not possible, the strategies discussed herein can limit their damaging effects.

At the elementary level, teacher defiance and disrespect account for 36% of all minor ODRs to the principal's office. At the middle school level, this figure is 37%. With major ODRs, approximately 27% and 23%, respectively, of elementary and middle school referrals are accounted for by more serious acts of defiance or disrespect (Gion et al., 2014). This type of insubordination in the classroom can pose a real threat to the teacher's effectiveness, weakening their authority and making the classroom much more difficult to teach and manage. Whenever possible, as noted above, it is best to prevent acts of insubordination in order to limit their damaging effects. If severe insubordination results in a major ODR, it is likely that some degree of damage to the teacher–student relationship has already occurred.

In addition to the risks that insubordination and teacher defiance pose to students, the teacher, and the classroom environment, there is a further serious risk concerning the destructive influence of implicit bias that operates below conscious awareness and that can be embedded in differential teacher expectations, which, in turn, can become behaviorally expressed toward certain students. The research of Brophy and Good (1970), for example, shows that teachers tend to provide high-expectation students in their classroom with more positive responses and treatment generally than they do low-expectation students in the same classroom. Such implicit bias, based upon ethnicity, race, or gender, can lead to inappropriate ODRs, discriminatory discipline, and negative behavioral treatment of students—particularly from Black and Latino backgrounds. This bias in disciplinary policy and practice has been well established in our schools for a number of years and has risen to an urgent national priority partly through the efforts of the civil rights divisions of the U.S. Department of Education and National Institute of Justice (2014, 2018; Raffaele-Mendez & Knoff, 2003; Anderson, Ritter, & Boyd, 2015).

Over the past two decades, Skiba and his colleagues have made substantive contributions to our collective understanding of how teacher reactions to student behavior, perceived as provocative, can reflect an implicit bias regarding students from minority ethnic and racial backgrounds (see Skiba, Michael, Carrol-Nardo, & Peterson, 2002; Skiba et al., 2011). This bias can register in a number of unfortunate ways but most importantly in (1) teacher–student interactions and in (2) teacher-initiated ODRs. The consequences of this bias can thus lead to reduced student achievement, hostile teacher–student interactions, and unfair victimization through repeated discriminatory, disciplinary actions.

For example, Skiba et al. (2011), in a seminal study, reviewed office discipline referrals in 364 elementary and middle schools and found that (1) students from Black families were 2.19 (elementary school) to 3.78 (middle school) times more likely to be referred to the school office for problem behavior as their White peers were and (2) students from Black and Latino families were more likely than their White peers to receive expulsion or out of school suspension as disciplinary consequences for the same or similar behavior. Like the failed wars on crime and drugs, these zero tolerance policies of schools regarding disciplinary infractions have not improved student behavior or school safety. But they have deprived students of needed development and school achievement opportunities and have also contributed to negative developmental outcomes in adolescence for students with minority status (American Psychological Association Task Force, 2008; Skiba, Arredondo, & Williams, 2014; Skiba & Losen, 2015–2016; Walker, Colvin, & Ramsey, 1995).

Researchers have cited some important work as part of a national initiative regarding steps that schools and teachers can take to address this longstanding and recurring problem (Gregory, Bell, & Pollock, 2016). These steps emphasize the following school policies and practices:

- Build positive teacher–student relationships at every opportunity.
- Ensure academic rigor while setting high expectations for *all* students.
- Engage in culturally relevant and responsive teaching by integrating students' racial, ethnic, and gender identities into curricula and school events.
- Create bias-free classrooms and respectful school environments.

If implemented conscientiously by schools, these measures could go a long way toward addressing this critically important priority. As part of this effort, teachers should make every effort to be aware of implicit bias in the expectations they may hold for diverse groups of students and to ensure they are not reflected in their individual student interactions and referral practices (Gregory, Hafen, et al., 2016)

DEFINITION, KEY FEATURES, AND EXAMPLES OF INSUBORDINATION

Insubordination is defined as defiance of authority. It may be defined as a refusal to follow or comply with a directive from someone in a position of authority, such as a teacher, and is often accompanied by a lack of respect. An example would be as follows:

TEACHER: Billy, I just gave the class instructions for our math assignment. You aren't getting ready. Were you listening? Should I repeat them for you?

STUDENT: I don't like math, and I'm not doing this dumb assignment.

TEACHER: Can I assist you? Is there something about it you don't understand or do you need some extra time?

STUDENT: No! I don't need any help from you. I hate this class.

TEACHER: If you are going to stay in my class, you have to complete your schoolwork.

(*Billy blows up and storms out of the classroom.*)

This situation plays out in many classrooms daily, and it's one where the teacher has few options. Teacher defiance has emerged as a very serious obstacle to teaching and learning in today's schools as disruptive behavior continues to trend upward in our public schools (Brooks, 2022).

In teaching and managing classrooms, there is a wide range of student behaviors that prompt ODRs for teacher defiance. School records contain ODRs for numerous serious offenses, including blatant disrespect and defiance, bullying of peers, cheating, cell phone use in class, theft, missing detention, leaving class without permission, violation of hall passes, obscene language/gestures, fighting, threats toward peers or teachers, possession of weapons, verbal abuse, vandalism, and having smoking materials. However, these school records also contain ODRs for many minor offenses (e.g., possession of prohibited items such as gum, passing notes, failure to be prepared for class, being minimally disruptive, having minor conflicts with peers, etc.) that could be better handled by other means than referral to the principal's office. Based on these results, it is clear that insubordination serves as a catchall device and is a substantially overused reason for ODRs.

It is recommended that school faculties discuss and come to agreement on operational definitions of concerning behaviors that result in ODRs. In this process, schools would have the opportunity to standardize behavioral criteria for referrals across classrooms and school settings that would allow communicating them to all students and staff. As a result, some of the overuse of the referral process involving very minor infractions would likely be reduced.

CAUSAL INFLUENCES AND ANTECEDENT CONDITIONS OF INSUBORDINATION

Student populations have become more diverse in their beliefs, attitudes, and behavior, and the social conflicts we see in society are spilling over into schools. Combined with the growth in negative attitudes toward schooling as students progress through school grades, it is unsurprising that teacher–student conflicts have emerged as a major barrier to teaching and learning (Versova & Mala, 2016). As a rule, teachers do not receive specific instruction on how to respond as effectively as possible to student defiance. As noted throughout this book, doing what comes naturally (i.e., trying to establish authority by repeating and escalating the directive's intensity) is exactly the wrong thing to do!

The frequency and types of student behavior prompting ODRs for insubordination vary substantially within and across school contexts. The decision to refer a student to the principal's office is an important one. An appropriate referral can allow a student to be disciplined fairly for their actions and initiates a pathway for restoration and access to specialized services that the student may need. Student defiance and insubordination are likely when an individual student is confronted by the teacher for the following offenses:

- Blatant disrespect/defiance
- Bullying

- Violation of hall pass
- Theft
- Leaving class without permission
- Obscene language/gestures
- Fighting
- Making threats
- Having weapons at school
- Verbal abuse
- Vandalism
- Having alcohol, tobacco, or drugs

A referral to the principal's office for any of these offenses should occur regardless of whether the student becomes insubordinate when confronted about them. Minimally disruptive behavior that interferes with the teaching–learning process, such as not being prepared for classwork, possession of prohibited items, ignoring deadlines, and so forth, should be addressed on an in-class basis whenever possible.

ODRs also vary by gender, time of year, and location within the school. Boys are much more likely to have insubordination referrals than are girls (Gion et al., 2014). Carefully reviewing overall ODRs and especially insubordination ODRs provides keys for understanding what's going on within a school's operation and the kind of school climate that exists. The next section presents strategies for preventing and coping with teacher defiance and disrespect so that damage to the teacher–student relationship can be minimized.

RECOMMENDED STRATEGIES FOR ENHANCING POSITIVE TEACHER-STUDENT RELATIONSHIPS AND REDUCING INSUBORDINATION

A two-pronged strategy is recommended for dealing with insubordination toward teachers. One is classwide and focuses on prevention; the other is individualized and focuses on both preventing and managing teacher–student conflicts that can result in insubordination. At a classwide level, there are two frameworks recommended for creating a positive classroom climate. One is the PBIS program (Horner et al., 2005) mentioned in Chapter 1, and the other is the everyday restorative practices (ERP) curriculum. Each is described below.

Classwide Prevention of Insubordination Incidents

Creating a positive classroom climate where students are encouraged to behave responsibly and to respect themselves, classmates, and the teacher is extremely important in reducing insubordination. There are many teaching–learning opportunities for both academic outcomes and social–emotional development afforded by this kind of classroom ecology. A calm, well-run classroom of this type can also prevent problems in later school grades. For example, an intriguing longitudinal study of child aggression was reported by Kellam, Ling, Merisca, and Brown (1998) that provides evidence for this observation. The researchers found that aggressive boys who were enrolled in chaotic first-grade classrooms had much higher rates of aggression years later in middle school than boys who were enrolled in first-grade classrooms that were not chaotic.

The PBIS framework is suitable for use in elementary, middle, and high school, and is a proven intervention approach for addressing problem behavior (Nocera, Hillbread, & Nocera, 2014; Horner et al., 2005); it has been adopted by thousands of U.S. schools over the past two decades. It teaches three core values: *be safe, be respectful, and be responsible.*

Within PBIS schools, in addition to managing core values and behavioral indicators based on them, a detailed reactive plan is provided so that ODR data can be used with confidence in decision making. This reactive plan names and defines major and minor problem behaviors for the school and how they are to be addressed, providing guidance for what teachers should be expected to manage in the classroom and guidance on how to decide when an ODR is needed. It is very important for teachers to try and prevent ODRs by intervening in the classroom before making an ODR, whenever feasible.

The ERP curriculum is a highly recommended resource for building a positive classroom climate within middle schools. It presents research and instruction on restorative practices such as kindness, empathy, repair of behavioral mistakes, and other social skills that contribute to school safety and positive school climate. Students and teachers are guided through interactive problem-solving sessions and brief cognitive exercises that systematically support personal and group behavioral changes within the school environment and beyond. The curriculum is taught as instructional content for brief periods daily over two months and includes video vignettes, PowerPoint presentations on key implementation material, and written materials. Though the ERP curricular program was originally developed and evaluated for use in high schools, further testing and revision have enabled it to be adapted for effective use in middle schools.

Steps That Teachers Can Take to Facilitate Classwide Prevention of Insubordination

There are three steps teachers can take to help build a more positive classroom climate: (1) establishing classroom rules fostering positive student behavior, (2) avoiding the display of different teacher expectations for students who excel and those who don't, and (3) communicating a genuine interest in the lives and success of all students.

For Step 1 the goal is to develop classroom rules and display behavior that facilitates positive peer interactions and reduces the risk of teacher–student conflicts. Positive teacher–student interactions help students engage in and bond with schooling, facilitate cooperation, and teach interpersonal skills via modeling and observational learning. The Committee for Children (Beland, 1999) has developed a set of classroom rules that help achieve this goal in terms of personal safety and peer relations. These values can be easily built into the generic set of classroom rules for governing student behavior throughout the school year. Research shows that schools with positive climates tend to be safer and more effective (Sprague & Walker, 2021; U.S. Secret Service National Threat Center, 2021).

Step 2 requires teachers to become aware of and avoid the negative impact of different expectations for certain types of students. Extensive research has shown that some teachers form and display different performance and behavioral expectations for students who excel versus those who are challenging to teach and manage (Brophy & Good, 1970, 1974). Per the researchers, such expectations occur naturally and are formed from the following sources: observation and comparative evaluation of student performance over time and across situations, test results, earned grades, and anecdotal records. Unfortunately, many teachers act to maximize the achievement of high-expectation students (i.e., use of praise, prompts, opportunities to respond, providing second chances to correct mistakes, etc.) and fail to do so for low-expectation students.

While not all teachers display these different expectations, Brophy and Good (1974) identified three types of teachers who do display them as reactive, proactive, and overreactive. Reactive teachers are those whose expectations are directly shaped by the contrast between low-performing versus high-performing students. Proactive teachers are aware of their expectations, keep them flexible, and modify them as changes in student performance warrants. Overreactive teachers hold strong, rigid expectations, whose display is most likely to negatively impact low-performing students. Based on this research, it is clear that the best strategy is to hold high expectations for all students regardless of their skills, performance, and perceived motivation.

Step 3 involves teachers taking an interest in students' activities, interests, and challenges, especially for low-performing and behaviorally challenged students. An excellent strategy for this purpose is the 2 × 10 strategy (discussed in Chapter 3). In this procedure, the teacher selects one student at a time and for 10 days in a row spends 2 minutes each day one-on-one, discussing whatever the student wishes to talk about. It is an excellent way to communicate a sincere interest in the student and can have numerous positive impacts on the teacher–student relationship.

Individualized Approaches to Preventing Insubordination

I recommend the following two approaches for coping with individual students who are likely to be insubordinate when their behavior is corrected or redirected by the teacher. It involves avoidance of and responding to a difficult situation.

The first approach is avoidance. Struggling students are often highly agitated, which can make them behave atypically and do things they might not do under normal circumstances. Many express their frustration and anger through body language and subtle displays of emotion. Attempting to direct such a student's behavior via an appropriate request or demand can result in a difficult situation that may escalate. If a student is showing behavioral signs of agitation, it may be best to wait and allow the student to calm down. This can be done through simple delay or by asking the student if they'd like some time before beginning an assigned academic task. The point is to not to force the situation or to teach the student that tasks can be avoided by displaying agitation but rather to avoid an unnecessary, potentially damaging confrontation. This process requires nuanced decision making and careful reading of a student's behavior.

The second approach can be used if a teacher ends up in a serious confrontation or escalated interaction with an agitated student before realizing how it began or what caused it. The following guidelines from Linsin (2011) may be helpful in managing these situations.

- Don't react naturally, which is to try and control the student and situation.
- Don't feel you have to "win" or prevail in the situation.
- Ignore student provocations.
- Don't take insults personally.
- Stay calm.
- Be deliberate and do not respond to student attempts at escalation.
- Give the student time to calm down and reflect.
- Deliver consequences well after episode has ended and the student has calmed down.
- Notify the principal's office and parents, as appropriate.

At the first opportunity, attempts should be made to debrief the situation with the student in order to develop alternatives to teacher defiance and to repair any damage to the teacher–student relationship that may have occurred. Debriefing is defined as a semi-structured interview between a teacher and student in order to review the situation and how it developed. The following are some suggested guidelines for conducting the session.

- Schedule a time and place where the debriefing can be conducted privately.
- State the purpose of the session.
- Be as supportive as the situation allows.
- Don't try to assign blame.
- Review the situation and how it developed.
- Discuss consequences to the teacher–student relationship.
- Discuss alternative ways of how the situation could have been handled differently.
- Commit to avoiding defiance and confrontations in the future.

A sample script for a hypothetical debriefing session is provided in the following case study.

CASE STUDY: DEBRIEFING AN EPISODE OF INSUBORDINATION

TEACHER: I scheduled this private session with you so we can learn from this episode and avoid another one in the future. I want us to speak frankly to each other about it. What is said here will remain between us. What do you think caused this situation between the two of us?

STUDENT: I think my teachers are more likely to blame me than help me when I don't understand an assignment or something.

TEACHER: I am sorry you feel that way as it can make you angry and discouraged. Teachers are very busy and are not always able to appreciate how each student is feeling. Now that I know you feel this way, I will make it a special point of supporting you and giving you the help you need.

Let's review what happened between us. When I gave instructions for the math assignment to the class, you seemed preoccupied and not listening. Then when you didn't understand what to do and asked for help, I thought it was because you were not listening. Is that true?

STUDENT: Maybe I didn't listen as well as I should have but I really didn't understand what you wanted us to do. So I asked you to repeat the instructions for me. You seemed irritated by my asking, which I thought was unfair. That's why I acted the way I did.

TEACHER: Nobody's perfect, and it looks like we each made a mistake! Together they led to the negative situation we had to deal with. Maybe we both overreacted a bit in what we each said.

STUDENT: I guess so.

TEACHER: Confrontations like this can be very damaging to the teacher–student relationship. They can also have bad results for both the teacher and student, so it's best to try and avoid them. I can't be a good teacher if I allow them to happen and fail to do something about it. Do you understand why?

STUDENT: Yes. You would lose the respect of the class.

TEACHER: Right. So can we think of some ways to avoid these situations?

STUDENT: Maybe I can listen better and not be so quick to blame my teachers.

TEACHER: That sounds very good! And I will try and be more tuned in to you and your feelings and give you the benefit of the doubt when I'm not sure about your behavior.

STUDENT: I've never had someone tell me they'll give me the benefit of the doubt. Thank you for that!

TEACHER: Thank you for what you said today. I think we will do much better in the future, and giving each other the benefit of the doubt will help a lot! Remember—if you're unsure about something, just ask me and I'll try to support you.

Unfortunately, it is not likely that each attempted debriefing session would work out as well as this example. However, approaching a student in such a proactive, nonaccusatory manner to problem-solve the insubordination episode could do a great deal toward repairing damage and restoring the teacher–student relationship. This postconfrontation strategy is highly recommended.

CHAPTER 8 TAKEAWAYS

- Insubordination occurs when a teacher corrects or redirects a student's behavior and the student reacts with defiance.

- Insubordination is the most frequent ODR that teachers make for student misbehavior.

- Depending on the student's reaction, insubordination ODRs can occur when teachers attempt to redirect even minor forms of problem behavior.

- When insubordination is ignored or tolerated, the teacher's ability to teach and manage the classroom is weakened.

- When students challenge teacher authority and display a clear and public lack of respect, teachers are justified in reporting their concerns via ODRs and other means of communicating this information to the school's leadership.

CHAPTER 9

Teaching Students Not to Have Tantrums When Unable to Get Their Way

Tantrums are a natural by-product of the normal development process where infants and toddlers learn to communicate their needs and desires. Until they develop the necessary language and communication skills, children tend to rely upon tantrum-like behavior to resist what they don't want as well as to communicate what they do want that isn't immediately accessible. The "terrible twos" refers to the developmental period where a child's behavior in this regard reaches an apex and they begin saying no frequently to adult requests and demands. Some children can learn to have a meltdown when denied a request. If not dealt with effectively, out of control tantrums that turn into meltdowns can have a devastating impact on a child's schooling and social acceptance by peers.

The frequency with which preschool children are suspended and expelled from preschool settings has become shocking, depriving large numbers of vulnerable children the benefits of early education (Gilliam & Shahar, 2006). Research by the Foundation for Child Development reports that preschoolers are expelled at three times the rate of K–12 children and youth. Preschool-age boys are four times as likely to be expelled as are preschool girls. Black children are expelled at nearly twice the rate as Latino and White children, and five times more often than Asian American children. These rates are very discouraging and preschool programs are being urged to find alternative means to discipline preschoolers other than through exclusionary means. At the same time, these rates reflect disturbing trends in how unprepared children are to achieve success upon entering preschool.

This chapter is focused on coping with children who bring a pattern of tantrums with them to their schooling in order to achieve their desires and social goals. Teaching them alternative strategies and self-control is of critical importance, as there are both short-term and long-term disadvantages of disruptions to one's schooling in preschool and the early grades.

DEFINITION, KEY FEATURES, AND EXAMPLES OF TANTRUMS

A tantrum is considered to be a form of communication to an adult about the child's need or desire for something—such as getting their way or relief from an aversive situation—that is being frustrated. It is very much a matter of wanting something that is not happening or not wanting something that is. The child expresses anger and disappointment through crying, screaming, holding their breath, or displaying explosive behavior. A severe form of tantrum is referred to as a *meltdown*, which is a total absence of self-control and may result in property destruction and possible injury.

Most attempts at controlling a child's behavior while in this emotional state are fruitless. It is much better to wait for the tantrum to subside before trying to reason with the child and to teach alternative behavior in the situation. This is especially difficult to do when in public spaces such as a grocery store.

Tantrums are often associated with oppositional defiant disorder (ODD), a recognized psychiatric disorder that affects approximately 2 to 3% of children and youth (Institute of Medicine, 2009), and children who display tantrums at severe levels are referred to as having the "explosive child" syndrome. ODD is a highly disruptive disorder that is marked by negative, hostile, and defiant behavior toward authority figures lasting for at least 6 months. Additional behavioral characteristics of ODD include blaming others and revenge seeking. However, it is not particularly marked by aggression toward others or damage to their possessions as is the case with antisocial, bullying children and youth.

The inappropriate response of parents to a child's noncompliance can inadvertently set the stage for a permanent pattern of oppositional behavior. The roots of such behavior in PreK, kindergarten, and the early primary grades can often be traced back to parental mistakes where the child learns that noncompliance and tantrums produce increases in adult attention and in some cases access to what prompted the tantrum when the parent relents or gives in to the child's demand(s).

Fortunately, tantrums begin to decline in frequency by age 4 in most children and rarely occur by the age of 8. However, preschool and early grade-school teachers need to be prepared for coping with tantrums that can morph into meltdowns and even physical assaults on teachers. The high rate of suspensions and expulsions of preschool children is likely a result of a combination of severe noncompliance and explosive tantrums or meltdowns that are highly disruptive of the preschool setting.

CAUSAL INFLUENCES AND ANTECEDENT CONDITIONS OF TANTRUMS

Children often learn to manipulate adult behavior by having or threatening to have a tantrum. Tantrums emerge from two paths. Early on in a child's development, a tantrum can have a largely biological origin that results from a prolonged period of exposure to unpleasant conditions such as hunger or a wet diaper. This type of behavior is considered respondent in nature and usually stops when the aversive condition is terminated. As the child matures, this type of tantrum becomes unnecessary through improved language and communication skills.

However, some children learn to use tantrums instrumentally as a means to get what they want. The tantrum typically stops once their need or wish is granted. Thus, the child is positively reinforced for having a tantrum and the parent is negatively reinforced through termination of the tantrum when the child gets what he or she wants. When this sequence occurs, the tantrum is considered a form of learned operant behavior where the child acts on the surrounding environment to achieve their goal(s).

Unfortunately, this is a common situation for many families. It can result in a characteristic, long-term pattern of learned behavior (tantrums) for a child who then generalizes the behavior to adults in preschool settings (e.g., teachers). Children who have limited impulse control, are oppositional, and have a difficult time managing or controlling their emotions are especially vulnerable in this regard. Children who successfully use tantrums to get what they want are likely to have a very difficult time adjusting to the ordinary demands of schooling (e.g., cooperating with others, working on assigned tasks, waiting one's turn, following teacher directions).

A number of experts have attributed the substantial increase in explosive meltdowns in schools, which often require room clears to reestablish classroom order, to the changed policies and administrative practices regarding antisocial students who have severe forms of challenging behavior. The press to educate the great majority of today's students within general education settings has substantially broadened the diversity of behavioral characteristics with which teachers must cope. Much of this increased behavioral diversity comes in the form of challenging behavior and a lack of respect for school authority that can increase the level of classroom disruption.

It is important for children and youth to be aware of their emotions and their impact on self and others. Teachers, whenever possible, should use naturally occurring situations to teach them how to label and better understand strong feelings and emotions. In addition, universal screening procedures are important to help identify and assist young children who struggle with self-control and managing emotions.

RECOMMENDED STRATEGIES
FOR AVOIDING TANTRUMS IN THE CLASSROOM

Tactics for dealing with classroom tantrums are discussed below (Brooks, 2015). These tactics include steps in each of the following categories: prevention of tantrums, management of tantrums when they occur, and debriefing about the tantrum and triggering situation(s) afterward.

Prevention of Tantrums

Tantrums can range from minor to major or severe in their intensity. It goes without saying that a positive classroom climate combined with clear rules and teacher expectations can help prevent many minor problem behaviors. This applies to minor tantrums as well. However, severe tantrums require intervention beyond the classroom and teachers should not be held accountable for them. The following steps can be helpful in the prevention of minor tantrums.

1. Create a nurturing classroom atmosphere where the teacher takes an interest in each student. Use of the 2 × 10 strategy described in Chapter 3 works well for this.
2. Develop a knowledge of the circumstances that might trigger a student's tantrum when frustrated or confronted with a difficult situation. Try to minimize the difficulty for the student when feasible in these situations.
3. Select a space in the classroom, or adjacent to it, where the student can go to calm down whenever he or she is frustrated and likely to get upset. This space should allow supervision and visual contact with the student. Students should be encouraged to voluntarily use these spaces when they are upset and have a loss of self-control.
4. Consult with the child's parents regarding situations that are likely to trigger tantrums in the home setting and in similar school situations.
5. Hold discussions regularly with the entire class about the importance

of self-control, managing emotions, and learning to deal with frustration.

Management of Tantrums

As noted earlier, coping with a severe tantrum that turns into a meltdown is one of the most challenging crises confronting teachers. It holds the potential for injury to the child as well as others, not to mention its disruptive effect on the classroom. Strategies for managing minor and major tantrums are described below.

Minor Tantrums

Tantrums that are minor in their intensity are best handled by removing the child to a space in the classroom or adjacent space where they can still be supervised by the teacher. Once the child's emotions of frustration and anger have subsided, a debriefing session should be held where the trigger for the tantrum can be used as a teaching opportunity. Helping the child to develop alternatives regarding how they could have responded differently is essential. The key steps for managing minor tantrums are:

1. Do not try to manage the tantrum by ignoring it.
2. Remove the child to a calming space in the classroom and allow time for cooling down.
3. Use the incident as a teaching opportunity via debriefing.
4. Help the child develop and understand how he or she could have handled the situation differently.
5. Refer the child for counseling about the tantrum and coping with strong emotions, if needed.

Major Tantrums

Some children begin school having such severe tantrums that they suffer educationally and have their schooling put at risk. Their behavior obviously makes it difficult for teachers to instruct and manage the classroom and prevents classmates from learning and achieving as they would normally.

While mild tantrums can be managed effectively in most classrooms, the severe tantrums of the explosive child require more intensive intervention that extends to psychological and medical services delivered beyond the classroom. Teachers and school-based related-services staff, along with parents, are in the best position to jointly determine when a child needs access to medical and/or psychological treatment. A model program for the treatment of severe tantrums, called the Regional Intervention Program (RIP), is profiled in a later section of this chapter.

The following are recommended steps for dealing with major tantrums:

1. Notify the principal's office immediately.
2. Take whatever steps are necessary to prevent injury, chaos, and property destruction.
3. Do not attempt to physically restrain the child in any way.
4. Consider removal of the child from the classroom or a room clear strategy that can be implemented safely.
5. If using a room clear coping strategy, ensure there is an appropriate place for classmates to congregate as a group.
6. Notify parents and schedule a parent–school conference to review the situation and discuss next steps.
7. Refer child to the counselor or school psychologist for determination of the need for mental health services beyond the school.
8. Determine if the family needs mental health support and training in managing the child at home.

DEBRIEFING AND FOLLOW-UP

It is very important to follow up with the child after a minor tantrum and with the family after a major one. Some families are essentially held prisoner by a child who severely tantrums and may be eager to work with school and community resources to resolve the problem.

An example of a program that would likely benefit families with an explosive child is the Family Check-Up (FCU) process developed by Dishion and his colleagues, which was offered as a resource to middle school parents whose adolescent children had difficulties in school. The FCU is an ecological, school-based, and family-centered intervention (Stormshak & Dishion, 2009; Stormshak, Connell, & Dishion, 2009; Stormshak et al., 2011) that is highly effective in assisting families with disruptive behavior problems such as oppositional defiant behavior and conduct disorders. The FCU, when offered by middle schools, has proved to be very popular with families and effective in connecting them to needed family therapy and management services.

The FCU is profiled in the annotated bibliography of recommended programs in Appendix 2 (recommended for parents), along with a similar companion program, called the Classroom Check-Up, for use with teachers (Reinke, Lewis-Palmer, & Merrell, 2008).

The RIP, mentioned earlier, is specifically designed for teaching parents how to reduce and eliminate severe tantrums in their young children.

Profile of the RIP

The RIP was designed and established by John Ora and Phil Strain of Vanderbilt University, highly regarded experts in early childhood education, and is sponsored by the Tennessee Department of Mental Health.

This program is now an internationally recognized model-parenting program for children who have severely challenging tantrums and socially destructive behavior. It is designed for children who have meltdown-type tantrums associated with severe behavior disorders or who experience developmental delays under the age of 6. The program has been extensively replicated in other states and countries, including California, Connecticut, Iowa, Kentucky, Ohio, Washington, Canada, Brazil, and Venezuela.

RIP receives referrals from a range of sources, including physicians, child care centers, and social service agencies, and is no cost to the family. It requires 24 2-hour visits over approximately 7 months. The program has four treatment modules: behavioral skills training, social skills training, a model preschool classroom program, and child care/school intervention. Through exposure to these modules, participating parents develop a repertoire of important skills, including generic parenting, monitoring, shaping, skill development, and child behavior management. A cohort training model is used for helping parents with mastery of skills and to provide support and share information.

Strain and Timm (2001) have conducted long-term studies of RIP graduates and their outcomes. These researchers followed up with graduates when they were 3–9 years beyond the end of intervention. Follow-up results showed that RIP graduates complied with parental requests 82% of the time and 97% of their interactions with their parents were positive. At school these same graduates complied with teacher requests 89% of the time and were appropriately engaged in 85% of instructional periods. Other key findings included:

- All but one completed high school and a large number went to college.
- All but one were currently employed.
- During adolescence one experimented with illegal drugs and one was involved with the criminal justice system.
- None were identified as in need of special education services.
- There were no reports of any displaying aggression toward others.

In addition, parents of the participants reported that the program had transformed their lives (Walker et al., 2004).

The long-term protections suggested by these findings show that RIP can substantially improve the quality of life for parents and their children.

However, it is important to remember that for children with severe tantrums, especially those with psychiatric disorders and/or developmental delays, it will often be necessary to implement complex, multicomponent interventions similar to RIP in order to bring their oppositional behavior under reasonable control. One should search for intervention programs that are similar to RIP in design and operation, where feasible. The following case study illustrates the behavioral characteristics of young children for whom RIP has been successful.

CASE STUDY: SAM, THE HOLY TERROR

Sam was a 5-year-old kindergartner when he unexpectedly came to the attention of his teacher, Ms. Wolfe, just after the start of the school year. Neither his teacher nor the school was aware of his developmental history, which included a difficult temperament dating from birth, frequent noncompliance with parental requests, severe tantrums when not getting his way, a diagnosis of attention-deficit/hyperactivity disorder, disputes with playmates, and a general pattern of oppositional behavior. Sam's behavioral profile fit the description of the "explosive child" (Green, 2014).

During math, Ms. Wolfe was explaining the directions for an assignment. Instead of listening, Sam was playing with a toy he always carried in his pocket. Ms. Wolfe asked that he put the toy away and listen to the directions. Sam refused, after which Ms. Wolfe demanded that he turn it over to her. This caused Sam to explode with anger, calling Ms. Wolfe derogatory names and yelling at the top of his lungs. When she threatened to call the principal's office for assistance, Sam turned over the toy. Ms. Wolfe promised to return it at the end of the day. She was clearly shocked and upset by his outburst and had no reason to expect such a reaction from Sam as she didn't know his developmental history and it was only the beginning of the school year.

Though Sam's outburst was highly disruptive of the classroom, Ms. Wolfe decided to leave Sam alone and allow him to calm down, which took longer than she preferred. His classmates seemed to take the outburst and Ms. Wolfe's handling of the situation in stride and did not focus their attention on his behavior. Wisely, she did not respond to Sam's attempts to engage her in an argument when he protested his treatment but said she would discuss things with him after class.

Ms. Wolfe had a private debriefing session with Sam to review the incident and try to get to the bottom of the situation. She reminded him of the rule about listening to instructions. She got him to understand that you can't understand them if you aren't listening. Sam admitted that he should have not been playing with his toy during class time. When Ms. Wolfe asked why he did not give it to her when she asked, he said it was his favorite toy and an older, bigger student had tried to take it from him at recess. He said he was afraid he might lose it. Ms. Wolfe said he should know that she would not keep it but that if he kept playing with it in class she might have to hold it during class periods.

She asked him how he might have acted differently in the situation. Sam said he shouldn't have been playing with the toy in class and should have handed it over when she asked. Ms. Wolfe agreed and praised him for his answer. Finally, she said outbursts like his couldn't be allowed in her class and he needed to learn how to not have a tantrum when he didn't get his way. She asked if he would like to work on learning how to control his anger so he didn't get so upset. Sam said maybe.

Ms. Wolfe filled out a referral form about the incident and recommended that a conference be scheduled to inform the parents, review the incident, and see what could be done to prevent future outbursts. This conference was held and included the family, Ms. Wolfe, and the school's behavioral coach. It resulted in a joint family and school effort, led by a behavioral coach, to find a community resource for treating Sam's tantrums.

CHAPTER 9 TAKEAWAYS

- For infants and toddlers, tantrums serve as a way to communicate their needs.

- Some children learn to use tantrums instrumentally in order to manipulate their social environments and get their way.

- Children with psychiatric disorders are more prone to tantrums.

- Minor tantrums should be dealt with by teachers in the classroom; major tantrums require more than classroom intervention.

- The first rule during a major tantrum is to prevent injury to the child, classmates, or teacher.

- During a tantrum, attempts should not be made to reason with the child about the triggering event(s) or to teach the child a lesson.

Reducing Students' Aggression
in School Contexts

Aggressive behavior comes in a variety of forms or types, as students have varied ideas about how to achieve their social goals, leading to varied strategies for doing so and differences in their self-perceived effectiveness. Types of aggression include physical, verbal, mental, emotional, instrumental, reactive, and hostile, as well as accidental aggression due to misinterpretation of the behavioral intentions of another. There is no single approach that is effective across all forms of aggression and its myriad manifestations, such as bullying, spreading false rumors about others, social media abuse, or trying to arrange for the social isolation of a peer. Bullying peers begins as early as preschool and increases in salience and impact as students mature.

Often aggression and its consequences have to be dealt with on a case-by-case basis. Because it occurs primarily between and among peers, approaches for reducing aggression often go beyond the classroom and involve such interventions as PBIS or schoolwide RD, as discussed in Chapters 1 and 7, respectively. It is very important to teach students to reject aggression among their peers. As part of this teaching process, students should be reminded of the personal costs of aggression, which can include administrative sanctions, loss of friendships, and reductions in peer acceptance.

DEFINITION, KEY FEATURES, AND EXAMPLES OF AGGRESSION

Aggression can be defined as a range of acts that result in harm or damage to oneself, others, and/or objects. As a rule, it centers on harming someone else either emotionally or physically. Behavioral indicators of aggression include the following.

- Deceiving someone so they are embarrassed or humiliated
- Verbally harassing a younger child
- Damaging or taking a student's prized possession(s)
- Forcing someone to do something they don't want to do
- Telling lies about a student to harm their reputation
- Physically attacking a weaker student
- Threatening someone over the Internet

Obviously, this list could be substantially expanded, but it serves to illustrate the many and varied behavioral forms that aggression can take.

As a general rule, aggression can be divided into two broad categories: proactive and reactive. *Proactive aggression* is intentional, planned, and usually designed to achieve some sort of social goal—such as achieving dominance over an individual or inflicting verbal or physical punishment on a disliked peer. Threatening a peer with physical violence would be an example of this type of aggression. In contrast, *reactive aggression* is usually prompted by circumstances that involve an emotional response (anger, revenge) to a provocation. Retaliation to a perceived slight or offensive remark by a peer would be an example of reactive aggressive. Reactive aggression is more likely to be situational or circumstantial, while proactive is more likely to be part of a characteristic behavior pattern and more difficult to change.

Due to its locus among peers, aggression is more likely to occur in some school contexts than others. Typically, aggressive behavior does not occur in classrooms, but if it does it assumes a very subtle form. Low-supervision areas where peers have lots of unsupervised contact—such as the playground, school grounds, hallways, bus stop, bathrooms, and lunchroom—are frequent sites for aggressive behavior, particularly bullying, harassment, and intimidation. The nature of these settings, combined with limited adult supervision, makes it difficult for school staff to monitor and address such behavior effectively.

Types of Bullying

There are four manifestations of aggression that are particularly destructive and connected to the school setting. They are verbal and physical bullying, cyberbullying, harassment, and relational aggression.

Verbal and Physical Bullying

In this type of bullying, attempts are made to directly harm, intimidate, or coerce someone who is perceived as weaker or defenseless. Boys are more likely to engage in this form of bullying than girls are. Prevalence studies indicate that anywhere from 10% to approximately 33% of today's students are victimized by bullying and it has been estimated that 100,000 students miss school each day due to fears about being bullied. Thirteen percent of students admit to bullying peers, and from 1 to 12% admit to being both victimizers and victims of bullying (Sprague & Walker, 2005). Bullying has emerged as a major social toxin in our schools and has increased substantially in recent years.

Cyberbullying

This form of bullying relies on electronic communications and social media to bully others by sending messages, posting, or sharing information that is negative, harmful, false, or cruel. These messages can appear to come from multiple sources when in actuality they can be sent by a single individual. Though challenging to detect and reduce or eliminate, cyberbullying can be successfully addressed in school contexts. A meta-analysis of prevention programs by Gaffney, Ttofi, & Farrington (2019) reported that cyberbullying perpetration was reduced to 9% from 15% and cyberbullying victimization by 14–15%. Though very challenging, efforts to control and reduce cyberbullying remain worthwhile for schools in collaboration with parents and police.

Harassment

This form of aggression occurs when speech or actions are so severe that it hinders the victim's ability to function as a student, damages their well-being, and interferes with their rights. Its focus is often on personal beliefs or characteristics, such as gender, style of dress, appearance, sexual orientation, disability, race, or religion.

Social Bullying or Relational Aggression

This type of aggression refers to harm within relationships caused by covert bullying and social aggression and is focused on manipulating relationships and reputations among peers. It involves isolating a student through exclusion, making a student the subject of gossip and rumors, attempting to separate a student from a support group, and causing the alienation of friendships. Relational aggression is engaged in more frequently by girls than boys.

There is obvious overlap among these categories of bullying. For example, it is likely that an intervention for verbal bullying would also impact harassment and possibly relational aggression, as they involve the same basic process—inflicting emotional harm on the victim. However, in each case interventions should be carefully tailored to the specific manifestation(s) of aggression and its context.

CAUSAL INFLUENCES AND ANTECEDENT CONDITIONS OF STUDENT AGGRESSION

In the past decade, preschool teachers have been confronted with extreme aggression and violence from young children, such as kicking, screaming, biting, and hitting. As noted in Chapter 9, there have been numerous literature and media reports of suspension and expulsion rates for preschoolers now exceeding that of middle and high school students. The exact cause(s) of this increase in violence has not been identified, but the American Academy of Child and Adolescent Psychiatry (AACAP, 2015) has offered up a number of factors that can act as exacerbators:

- Being the victim of physical and/or sexual abuse
- Prior aggression or violent behavior
- Exposure to media violence
- Exposure to violence in the home setting
- Being the victim of bullying
- Genetic factors
- Drug and alcohol use in adolescence
- Presence of firearms in the home
- Stressful family and socioeconomic trauma (divorce, poverty, unemployment, etc.)

It is very important for families and schools to address child and youth violence—especially early in its development. As the above list of influences shows, many of the root causes are beyond the ability of schools to address. However, at the very least, schools have an obligation to clearly communicate to children, youth, and their families that this kind of behavior is unacceptable and will result in sanctions to discourage it.

As part of any school-based strategy to address this problem, students who are at risk for this type of behavior need to be identified and supported in adopting acceptable behavioral alternatives. The following warning signs were listed by AACAP (2015):

- Intense anger
- Frequent loss of temper or blowups
- Extreme irritability
- Extreme impulsiveness
- Becoming easily frustrated

When combined with a tendency to bully and harass others, students with this behavior pattern can become a serious obstacle to their own and peers' emotional adjustment in school. Long-term implications for the development of such children and youth are extremely problematic (Patterson et al., 1992). At a schoolwide level, all students should be screened and identified for these behavioral characteristics.

RECOMMENDED STRATEGIES FOR REDUCING BULLYING IN SCHOOLS
School Leadership and Teachers' Roles

There are important roles that the school administration, teachers, students, and parents can play to reduce the likelihood of bullying and harassment. Further, the school psychologist, behavioral specialist, or PBIS coach is in an ideal position to coordinate a school's response to bullying. The school's leadership should promote a lack of tolerance for bullying and harassment of students through endorsing a positive school climate and advocating kindness in social relationships with students and staff. An especially important role for school administration is providing adequate staff resources in traditional low-supervision areas of the school (e.g., hallways, playground, lunchroom, bus stop, other school grounds).

Although direct bullying and harassment rarely occur in the classroom setting, the teacher's role is especially important in reducing and preventing them through teaching anti-bullying values and helping to implement anti-bullying intervention strategies in partnership with related services professional.

Students' Roles

The following are role expectations for both the bully and the victim.

Bully

- Reject membership in antisocial or deviant peer groups that support bullying others.
- Commit to refraining from direct and indirect bullying of peers.
- Adopt kindness values and behavior that reject cruelty toward others.
- Cooperate with school staff in learning a replacement behavior pattern.
- Understand the consequences to those you bully.
- Know that chronic bullying and harassment can result in your suspension or expulsion.

Victim

- Tell the bully to stop and walk away.
- Do not engage with the bully or try to fight back.
- Ignore the bully's taunts and questions.
- Tell a responsible adult you trust about what happened.
- Inform your parents about the incident.

Parents

Parents can be effective partners with schools in putting a stop to bullying. If a school has particular problems with widespread bullying, having parents serve on a schoolwide assistance team to address it would provide a very important parental perspective. If feasible, parents of the victim(s) of bullying should be willing to work with a school staff member and the parents of a bully to resolve conflicts and prevent future incidents. Similarly, the parents of chronic bullies should be confronted, held accountable, and engaged in solving this problem, although their cooperation is by no means assured.

In terms of prevention and reducing the likelihood of bullying in a school, it goes without saying that a positive school climate will enhance the effects of many if not all anti-bullying efforts. There are three recommended strategies that can be used to achieve bullying prevention goals: implementing schoolwide anti-bullying interventions; designating the school as a student-centered, bully-free zone where the prevention of bullying is the primary goal; and teaching anti-bullying and anti-harassment values and strategies in the classroom. These strategies are briefly described in the next section.

IMPLEMENTING SCHOOLWIDE ANTI-BULLYING INTERVENTIONS

There are three well-known, evidence-based anti-bullying programs that are universal in design and recommended for adoption and schoolwide implementation. They are the Olweus Bullying Prevention Program (OBPP), the Steps to Respect® program, and the Bully-Proofing Your School (BPYS) program.

The OBPP (Olweus, 1994, 2007) addresses bullying as well as vandalism and truancy at elementary, middle, and high school levels and contributes to a positive school climate. This program is the most well-known of the anti-bullying school interventions and has been proven effective via extensive evidence-based studies conducted in Norway and the United States (Ttofi & Farrington, 2011). This program also meshes well with

PBIS, as indicated in a recent study sponsored by the National Institute of Justice (Mitchell et al., 2019).

The Steps to Respect program is designed to address bullying and related problems for children in grades 3–6. It has three levels or phases that are implemented sequentially. Widely adopted and implemented, this program is included in a number of reviews of recommended anti-bullying interventions, such as the Collaborative for Academic, Social, and Emotional Learning (CASEL), and there is strong evidence for its efficacy (Frey, Hirschstein, Schoiack Edstrom, MacKenzie, & Broderick, 2005; Brown, Low, Smith, & Haggerty, 2011).

BPYS is a comprehensive anti-bullying program with five main components: staff training, student instruction, victim support, perpetrator interventions, and collaboration with parents and families. BPYS is designed for students in grades 3–5 and is focused on reducing bullying, victimization, and school violence. It has been rated as a promising program by the CrimeSolutions unit of the U.S. National Institute of Justice (2015), and was evaluated in a study by Menard and Gropeter (2014) involving 3,497 elementary students over a 3-year implementation period. Study results included more positive perceptions of school safety and reduced bullying and related forms of problem behavior.

It should be noted that these programs are most useful in the prevention of bullying, harassment, and related forms of problem behavior. By no means will they control many specific acts of bullying on school grounds: These will need to be dealt with on a case-by-case basis.

DESIGNATING THE SCHOOL AS A BULLY-FREE ZONE

This approach has much to recommend it in terms of engaging students to prevent bullying and harassment. Getting students to take ownership of bullying prevention is one of the most positive actions a school can take for three important reasons: (1) Students are more likely to respond to anti-bullying advocacy efforts by their peers than by adults; (2) students understand that their participation in such advocacy is in their own self-interest as well as that of peers; and (3) students are the best source of information about who is being bullied or harassed and why.

Boy and girl pairs should be nominated from each grade level in the school to serve on a Stop Bullying Committee of around 10 students. The primary goal of this committee would be to plan a schoolwide anti-bullying campaign whose activities could include: developing posters for display in hallways, classrooms, and other school spaces; participating in school assemblies where anti-bullying and anti-harassment messaging is presented; and recruiting peers who can serve as volunteer defenders, friends, and advocates for students who are often the target of bullying and harassment.

A related-services staff member such as a school psychologist or behavioral specialist should be appointed as a faculty advisor for this committee.

TEACHING ANTI-BULLYING AND ANTI-HARASSMENT VALUES

Olweus and his colleagues (Olweus & Limber, 2010) have contributed a valuable schema called The Bullying Circle, where a victim is surrounded during each act of bullying by students who play roles that can either encourage or discourage such incidents. Typically, student roles that encourage bullying are referred to as henchmen, passive bullies, potential bullies, and disengaged bystander observers who don't take a stand but whose presence still encourages the bullying. Roles that discourage bullying are played by students who reject the bullying but choose not to actively intervene, and by defenders, called upstanders, who try to help and defend the victim. This schema has been very useful in helping to better understand the dynamics of bullying and as a guide for intervening effectively.

Stopping bullying, harassment, and mean-spirited behavior toward others requires two things: internalizing anti-bullying values, and making a commitment to refrain from engaging in these forms of behavior. There are numerous societal forces that work against today's students being able to do this, including family environments, societal influences, media images and messages, and the support of deviant peer groups that encourage bullying others. Schools are in a key position to teach values that discourage bullying and encourage kindness toward others. They also have the capacity to implement conflict resolution strategies and restorative discipline techniques for repairing and restoring relationships damaged by this toxic behavior. These interventions are much preferred and more effective than the use of suspensions and exclusion to control this behavior, and those should only be considered as a last resort.

Anti-Bullying and Anti-Harassment Values

The following values should be posted in the classroom and regularly discussed with students.

Reasons Why You Shouldn't Bully Others

- Every student has a right to feel safe at school: Bullying makes a student feel threatened and unsafe.
- Treat others as you would like to be treated yourself: Bullying makes students feel upset, embarrassed, disrespected, and discouraged.
- Show kindness to students you know and don't know: Bullying is a form of cruelty.

- Students want to make friends and be accepted by peers: Bullying will keep peers from being your friend.
- Being a good student and having success in school is very important: Bullying others will limit your school success.

In particular, aggressive students who are likely to bully others should be individually debriefed about these values and how to incorporate them in their daily lives. Strategies for students to use in reducing their likelihood of being bullied are listed in the next section.

STRATEGIES FOR COPING WITH BULLYING AND HARASSMENT INCIDENTS

Bullying and harassment vary in two important dimensions: severity and chronicity. How comprehensively a school responds to bullying is often determined by these two dimensions. Minor to moderate incidents or those that happen only occasionally should be dealt with by normal disciplinary strategies such as debriefing, administrative sanctions, notification of parents, and referral for counseling or detention as appropriate. In contrast, for severe or chronic bullying, an RD strategy should be set up to investigate and address the incident rather than using suspension and expulsion, unless circumstances warrant otherwise. For example, if a student's bullying or harassment behavior is both severe and chronic as well as resistant to change, then additional steps in order to address the problem include parent involvement, sanctions, and mental health services.

Mary Armstrong is a leading advocate of the application of restorative justice principles to the remediation of bullying. She is an educational consultant in the Australian National Centre Against Bullying. She was interviewed on this topic (Armstrong, 2022). Armstrong has contributed valuable contributions in the application of restorative justice concepts and principles to school bullying. This material is discussed in the next section.

RD STRATEGIES APPLIED TO BULLYING

RD strategies, introduced in Chapter 7, can be used to effectively address severe and/or chronic incidents of bullying and harassment in schools, as they focus on the repair of damage to relationships and seek to restore them to their prior condition. These strategies are based on the following assumptions: (1) When an individual harms another person, he or she also does self-harm as well as harm to the school community; (2) RD is not focused on rule breaking, which is the focus of traditional discipline, but instead upon the quality of relationships; and (3) this strategy requires that when severe relationship damage occurs via bullying or cruelty to others, it needs to be investigated and steps need to be taken to repair the damage.

To implement RD in the context of bullying, a third-party facilitator (teacher, school psychologist, counselor) brings all affected parties into a restorative circle similar to the approach used for destructiveness toward others in Chapter 7. These parties would include the victim, perpetrator, henchmen, bystanders as well as defenders, playground supervisors, and parents as appropriate and feasible. The facilitator provides a structure and a script for conducting the circle, whose deliberations move through a series of stages that seek to answer the following three questions.

1. Stage One: What happened?
2. Stage Two: Who has been affected and how?
3. Stage Three: What can we do the fix this and ensure that it does not happen again?

While RD is a recommended strategy for dealing with the most severe forms of school bullying and harassment, it is only one of many strategies for addressing this problem. The following are critical elements or considerations in applying RD to school bullying.

- The RD process is not a substitute or replacement for traditional disciplinary practices applied to rule breaking and other behavioral infractions.
- The RD process requires careful preparation and development of a structure or plan for implementation, and can be a time-consuming process.
- The restorative circle process should be facilitated by a professional trained in conducting these problem-solving circles.
- The RD process should allow offending students to clearly understand how their behavior affects others.
- The RD process should produce a follow-up and monitoring plan to see that the group's recommended solutions are being carried out.
- Addressing severe incidents of bullying should include all affected parties and never just the bully and victim.

The following case study illustrates how a school psychologist used RD to address a bullying situation.

CASE STUDY: PLAYGROUND BULLYING OF A VULNERABLE STUDENT

Nolan was a third-grade student, large for his age, who had been sanctioned numerous times by his school administration for bullying and harassment. He was part of a peer subgroup that supported his aggressive behavior toward others and sometimes participated in his acts of bullying.

One day during recess, for no apparent reason, Nolan began harassing and teasing a shy student, Geoff, by name calling, making negative comments about his appearance, and issuing threats to "beat him up" after school. Geoff, who had done nothing to provoke such treatment, asked him to stop, and when he didn't, Geoff left the playground in tears. He reported the incident to his teacher, who informed the principal's office. Because of Nolan's prior history of chronic bullying and the severity of this incident, a decision was made to convene a restorative circle to investigate the incident, try to repair the damage, help Nolan to better understand and change his behavior, and prevent future occurrences.

Ms. Murray, the school psychologist who had been trained in RD, was asked by the principal to convene and coordinate a restorative circle to resolve the issue. In order to clearly understand details of the incident and the attitudes of those involved in it before developing a script to guide the session, Ms. Murray first interviewed Nolan, Geoff, Josh (one of Nolan's henchmen), and Clay, who had defended Geoff against Nolan's bullying and harassment.

Goals for the session were: (1) to have everyone hear what happened, (2) to get Nolan to understand how his bullying and harassment affected others, (3) to make amends, and (4) to prevent future bullying. The following exchanges occurred in the session.

Ms. Murray: We're here today to find out what happened between Nolan and Geoff at recess and how to prevent this behavior in the future. Let's keep in mind that we see our school as a bully-free zone. We all need to do our part to help with this. Geoff, please tell us what happened between you and Nolan at recess and how it made you feel. (*Geoff does so and notes how ashamed he felt from his treatment by Nolan in front of peers.*)

Thank you, Geoff. Nolan, would you like to share your view of things? (*Nolan does so and doesn't try to deny what happened but has no defense for his treatment of Geoff. He shows little remorse or regret for his actions.*)

Clay, do you agree with Nolan and Geoff's accounts?

Clay: Yes, that's what happened.

Ms. Murray: Nolan, how would you feel if another student, larger and stronger than you, treated you in the same way you treated Geoff?

Nolan: I guess I wouldn't like it.

Ms. Murray: Would you expect an apology from that student? Do you think Geoff deserves an apology?

Nolan: Yeah, I would and I guess he does.

Ms. Murray: Do we all agree with this? (*Everyone present agrees.*) I think we can all agree that we shouldn't bully or harass others and instead treat them like we'd want to be treated. Nolan, do you agree with this statement? (*Nolan agrees.*) So, how can we develop a plan to keep this from happening?

CLAY: I think Nolan needs to promise not to do this in the future to Geoff or any other student. Also, he should stop hanging out with students who support these actions.

Ms. MURRAY: Nolan, what about this? Are you willing to make this pledge?

NOLAN: I guess so but I shouldn't have to give up my friends. I don't think that's fair.

JOSH: I agree with Nolan. It's not fair to ask him to give up his friends and not play with them at recess.

CLAY: If Nolan promises to stop bullying and discourages others from doing it, he should be allowed to keep his friends if he keeps his word.

Ms. MURRAY: This sounds like a reasonable option. Can we try it going forward and reserve the right to change things if needed? (*All agree to this option.*) Geoff, how does all this sit with you? Are you OK with it?

GEOFF: I guess so but I want to see what happens. If Nolan doesn't change, I want the school to do whatever is needed to get him to stop.

Ms. MURRAY: This sounds like a good plan to me. I will ask the recess supervisors to pay careful attention to Nolan and his friends to see how well they stick to this plan. Also, I will meet regularly with Geoff and Clay to see what they say about how things are going.

Ms. Murray writes a report of the session and what was decided for the principal. He was pleased with the outcome and supportive of the plan going forward. They also met with Nolan's parents to inform them of the situation and to enlist their support in reducing his bullying behavior.

CHAPTER 10 TAKEAWAYS

- Aggression is one of the most damaging acts that students inflict on each other.
- There are four manifestations of aggression that are especially problematic for schools: bullying, harassment, cyberbullying, and relational aggression.
- Numerous studies show that bullying reduction programs can produce approximately 20 to 25% improvements in bullying.
- Schoolwide anti-bullying interventions are recommended for preventing bullying and harassment.
- RD practices are recommended for dealing with severe and chronic bullying on a case-by-case basis.
- RD is focused on relationships (mainly among peers) and does not address violations of school rules as traditional discipline does.

CHAPTER 11

Coping with Teacher Defiance When Managing the Classroom Behavior of Oppositional Students

Up to this point, the chapters in this book have focused on the needs of students with either behavioral deficits or excesses that warrant teacher attention, provision of supports and assistance, or delivery of disciplinary consequences. In contrast, this chapter deals primarily with the needs of teachers who must cope daily with a range of students capable of teacher defiance, making threats, and even assault in rare cases. While there is some degree of overlap between the content of this chapter and of Chapters 7 and 10, teacher defiance is considered a more serious form of resistance and opposition than the insubordination discussed in those chapters.

Increasing numbers of today's students bring a pattern of anger, agitation, irritability, defiance, and generalized resistance to authority with them to the schooling process. These behavioral tendencies are typical of many disruptive, antisocial students and are especially characteristic of students with oppositional defiant disorder (ODD). Typically, teachers do not receive either the necessary preservice or inservice training in how to cope with these challenging students, or adequate support from their school administration when students engage in severe teacher defiance. Often classroom teachers are expected to handle these episodes without external assistance and are encouraged not to refer students responsible for them.

A great deal has been written about teacher stress and burnout, and the numbers of teachers leaving the profession. Teacher stress and burnout have been recognized internationally as a major problem for the teaching profession (Kyriacou, 1987). Between one-third and half of new public school teachers drop out of the profession within the first 5 years. The dropout rates are even higher for special education teachers who must deal with a more challenging student population (Brunsting, Srechovic, & Lane, 2014). In a Rand Corporation national survey (Doan, Greer, Schwartz, Steiner, & Woo, 2022) of public school staff, nearly one-third of teachers reported being depressed and half reported having severe stress and experiencing burnout.

Studies of this issue, as reported in the literature, typically include a long list of possible causes of teacher stress and burnout. Most prominently, they consist of unrealistic role expectations cast against overwhelming time demands, limited societal respect for their contributions, and a lack of needed administrative supports. However, nearly every list includes the stress from having to manage challenging student behavior. This chapter does not address the larger issues of teacher stress and burnout, but rather focuses on teacher efforts to better cope with students who challenge the teacher's authority and engage in severe defiance resulting from high levels of agitation, which can fuel intense teacher resistance and hostile, or even threatening teacher–student interactions.

DEFINITION, KEY FEATURES, AND EXAMPLES OF TEACHER DEFIANCE

Teacher defiance is a subset of antisocial behavior that refers to "recurrent violations of socially prescribed patterns of behavior" (Simcha-Fagen, Langer, Gersten, & Eisenberg, 1975). In the classroom, teacher defiance involves intense resistance to authority as well as challenging, confrontational behavior often accompanied by a clear lack of respect. The behavioral characteristics of the "explosive child" (Green, 2014) define the defiant student who is oppositional and highly agitated. These students have explosive temperaments accompanied by highly disruptive emotional outbursts, and many would likely qualify for a diagnosis of ODD. Major criteria used to diagnose ODD are an angry and irritable mood, argumentative and defiant behavior, and vindictiveness displayed across settings and lasting at least 6 months (American Psychiatric Association, 2013).

Episodes of teacher defiance often occur when the teacher attempts to correct or redirect the behavior of a student who is in a highly agitated mood. A simple teacher request or demand of an agitated student can spark an emotional explosion that functions, depending upon the teacher's reaction, much like a behavioral earthquake. An episode of intense teacher defiance might look like the following example.

Ms. Frazier provides class instructions for how to complete an in-class math assignment. Students begin working on the assignment—except for Freddy who is sitting quietly in his seat doing nothing. Though sullen, his severe agitation and disturbed mood are not obvious to his teacher. Ms. Frazier asks him why he isn't engaging the task and offers her assistance.

Freddy replies that he doesn't feel like doing the assignment and doesn't care about it. She tells him that in-class assignments are an important part of his grade and that he needs to do it. Freddy explodes in anger, calls her a derogatory name, and tells her to leave him alone. She tells him she has no choice but to send him to the principal's office. Freddy threatens her and storms out of the classroom.

Episodes such as this severely damage the teacher–student relationship. They clearly require intervention beyond the classroom and will also involve parents and perhaps mental health services for resolution. Suspension or expulsion would remove Freddy from the classroom and school but would likely not be effective in discouraging this behavior in the future.

CAUSAL INFLUENCES AND ANTECEDENT CONDITIONS OF TEACHER DEFIANCE

In cases of teacher defiance, the student is often in a highly agitated state caused by something that happened outside the classroom context (i.e., at home) and has an emotional outburst that is unrelated to anything happening in the classroom. In such cases, the student may be seething with anger and respond out of all proportion to the request or situation. Signs of such agitation can include a student sulking and having angry, sullen body language. Often a busy teacher does not recognize these signs until a command or behavioral redirection attempt has been issued that prompts an escalating episode between teacher and student.

How a teacher first responds to a student showing the signs of being agitated has very much to do with how the episode plays out. If the teacher engages with the student in a back-and-forth exchange (i.e., argues), it can serve as grist for the defiance mill much like ladder fuels enable the acceleration and expansion of a forest fire. Many antisocial students are masters at engaging teachers in an escalating series of phases that have increasing levels of hostility. As long as the teacher responds to student comments or provocations, the student—not the teacher—is in control of the interaction. If the student prevails in this exchange, the teacher's ability to manage the classroom is weakened. If instead the teacher prevails, the student may likely be dedicated to getting even, which holds difficult implications for the teacher–student relationship going forward. It is crucial for the teacher to disengage from this situation immediately. Doing so puts the student's provocations on extinction, terminates the interaction, and reduces the teacher's above risks as well as increasing their feelings of efficacy in addressing students' behavioral and emotional needs.

The following is a series of sequential phases, identified by Walker, Colvin, and Ramsey (1995), seen during an escalating interaction of increasing emotional intensity.

1. Calm
2. Triggering event
3. Agitation
4. Acceleration
5. Peak
6. De-escalation
7. Recovery

It is important to remember that the oppositional, agitated student may appear behaviorally calm but is anything but calm emotionally. A simple request, demand, or attempted redirection usually serves as a triggering event for an escalated interaction. If the student successfully engages the teacher in an exchange about his or her initiation, it will likely escalate rapidly into a hostile interaction that can reach a destructive peak or explosion, after which there is a de-escalation and recovery. This behavioral process plays out in thousands of classrooms daily. Many teachers are inadvertently caught up in these interactions because student agitation is so difficult to recognize prior to its behavioral expression. A useful resource on how to handle agitated students and teacher defiance is by Colvin and Scott (2015).

In its extreme form, an escalated interaction can lead to a behavioral explosion that requires a room clear or other immediate administration action(s). Threats and even attacks on teachers may be prompted by such interactions. In 2013, the American Psychological Association created a task force to investigate violence against teachers (Espelage et al., 2013). The task force surveyed 3,000 teachers in 48 states: 44% of respondents reported physical offenses of some type by students, including thrown objects, physical attacks, and showing weapons; 6% of surveyed teachers reported being the target of verbal abuse by students; and 7% reported being threatened with physical injury by their students. These are alarming findings and help define the risks that teachers experience just from performing their roles. Engaging in escalated interactions with agitated, oppositional students could, in some cases, be a risk factor for teacher safety.

RECOMMENDED STRATEGIES FOR COPING WITH AND PREVENTING TEACHER DEFIANCE

If a student is perpetually agitated with fellow students and/or the teacher, it is important to try and get at the source of the agitation. Strategies to consider in this regard might be having a private meeting first with the student, and if indicated, with parents as well to discuss the agitation. Another strategy might be to refer the student for counseling. It is important to understand the reasons for the agitation as it will continue to drive conflict with both peers and the teacher, and understanding the cause is essential for treating defiance successfully. This section discusses some suggested strategies for coping with defiance when it occurs and for its prevention.

As stated earlier (and emphasized throughout this book), Rule #1 in dealing with teacher defiance is not to continue the interaction under accelerated conditions of high emotional intensity by the student. The first step is to terminate the interaction immediately and give the student a chance to calm down rather than pressing the issue. There is no way the teacher can prevail by continuing to argue whatever the point is with the student. The rising anger and emotion effectively prevents this, as do teacher and student concerns about the risk to their status depending on the interaction's outcome.

The student should be informed that the interaction will not continue until a later point when the student has been able to calm down. No additional demands or requests should be made of the student during this recovery period. If the defiance results from the student refusing to engage in an assignment, he or she should not think that engaging in teacher defiance provides a means of escape from or avoidance of in-class assignments. Letting the student know that the assignment will still need to be completed is obviously essential.

If the teacher defiance results from a correction or behavioral redirection attempt, the student should be left alone and encouraged to calm him- or herself down. If the student insists on continuing the defiance, he or she should be removed to a quiet area outside the classroom and steps should be taken to determine what will be required to reenter the classroom. In such instances, other school staff may have to be involved in order to resolve the issue.

In either of the above scenarios a debriefing session should be scheduled to help the student explore alternatives to their defiant behavior. This should include coverage of such things as learning how to accept feedback and corrections from teachers, learning how to disagree with others without becoming hostile or insisting on their point of view, and learning how to appreciate another's point of view. The following case study illustrates how these topics can be dealt with more constructively during private, one-on-one debriefing sessions, in order to create a more positive teacher–student relationship.

CASE STUDY: THE TRIALS OF AN AGITATED STUDENT

Leonard was a fifth-grade student with a difficult temperament that greatly complicated his relationships with others. He was perpetually in conflict with peers and classmates over seemingly mundane matters. He had a reputation among school staff as a difficult, contentious student who opposed adult authority and would argue at the drop of a hat. These characteristics made his schooling especially problematic, and peers would avoid spending time with him at recess because he didn't seem to know how to make or keep friends.

Leonard's homeroom teacher, Ms. Cortez, was skilled at dealing with challenging behavior from students. She scheduled a private meeting with him and said that she'd like to improve their relationship and help him get along better with teachers and peers. She indicated that he had a lot to offer others but that his tendency to be irritated tended to put peers off and stop him from making friends. She also said arguing with teachers and opposition to classroom rules hurt his school success. Ms. Cortez asked Leonard if he would be willing to work on a plan to improve things in these two areas and he agreed.

Ms. Cortez and Leonard developed a plan for improving his peer relations that included a focus on learning how to disagree acceptably with peers. This would require understanding another's point of view, realizing that it was possible he could be wrong and a peer right about a particular issue, and controlling his tendency to escalate the disagreement to get his way. Ms. Cortez scheduled a series of short one-on-one coaching sessions where she and Leonard behaviorally rehearsed these behaviors using common playground situations. Through these role plays, Leonard began to understand how being irritable all the time was holding him back and costing him friends and playmates. He also promised to do better in his interactions with peers and classmates. Ms. Cortez suggested that they have a daily 5- or 10-minute session to review and debrief about his day and discuss how things went. Leonard looked forward to these sessions and agreed to provide a self-rating of 1–5 regarding how he did. Once a week, Ms. Cortez would call Leonard's parents and discuss his progress. Results showed a gradual improvement in Leonard's peer relations based on his self-reports and occasional reports from peers.

Ms. Cortez scheduled another private session with Leonard to deal with his agitation and defiance with her and his other teachers. She explained that his irritability was causing the same problems with teachers as with peers and it was getting in the way of his school success. She said that school rules allowed teachers to teach and students to learn. His tendency to question every rule and to argue with teachers about it had given him a reputation as a contentious student.

Ms. Cortez suggested that Leonard consider adopting a rule to guide his classroom behavior called Rule #1: Be polite and cooperative. She provided examples of how to display this rule in his interactions with teachers and other school staff. Ms. Cortez went out of her way to let Leonard know how much she thought of him and how much she wanted him to succeed. Leonard seemed flattered by her interest and efforts to help him achieve school success. A similar, daily self-rating of 1–5 was set up for Leonard but this time Ms. Cortez also gave him a rating of 1–5 based on how she thought he did in her classroom. Discussion of these new ratings, and how they agreed or disagreed, were included in the already scheduled daily debriefing for his peer relations. Ms. Cortez asked Leonard if she could send a Good Day Card (discussed in Chapter 1) home with him when he had a really good day. He agreed.

Leonard showed gradual progress in these two areas but did sometimes have setbacks and lose control of his emotions. It was difficult for him to control his irritability and to adopt a new, more positive behavior pattern. However, he continued in his efforts to do so with the support of his Ms. Cortez, his parents, and his peers.

CHAPTER 11 TAKEAWAYS

- Teachers must deal with increasing numbers of agitated students who engage in teacher defiance.

- Severe teacher defiance from very challenging students can be a risk factor for teacher safety.

- When a teacher is inadvertently pulled into an escalating interaction with an agitated student, the #1 rule is to terminate the interaction and deal with the issue after the student has calmed down.

- Severe episodes of teacher defiance require administrative intervention beyond the classroom.

- Antisocial and students with ODD often display intense resistance to teacher and adult authority.

- The source(s) of a student's severe agitation should be understood and addressed as part of any effort to prevent teacher defiance.

CHAPTER 12

Addressing Student Lying, Cheating, and Stealing at School

At an individual level, lying, cheating, and stealing are forms of covert behavior that are often sustained by a desire to maximize one's advantage at the expense of others. They are also interrelated (i.e., stealing or cheating and then lying about it when detected). These kinds of deceitful behaviors are most common among children ages 5 to 8, and their prevalence varies widely across age groups.

In prior decades, our nation's schools were extensively invested in character education, which teaches behavioral traits and values that support civic pride, caring for others, accountability, responsibility, trustworthiness, and mutual respect. A number of experts and school leaders are now calling for the reinstitution of character education in school curricula (Smarick, 2021). Many argue, and rightly so, that parents and families should have the prerogative of teaching their children values and behavioral standards. However, schools can do a great deal to support, elaborate on, and reinforce standards of behavior that can lead to the betterment of our society and improvements in human relationships. This is especially true if families are meaningfully involved in a school's efforts to teach such content.

This chapter focuses on addressing lying, cheating, and stealing when they occur at an individual level within schooling contexts and also on their prevention through the teaching of character education curricula. It should be noted that stealing was rated as the most objectionable student behavior out of 51 behaviors rated by teachers in the survey of 1,000 K–12 teachers described in the Preface. Unlike other forms of problem behavior that are appropriate for proactive, universal screening, there should be *no such screening* of students for these forms of covert behavior due to the reputational damage that could be inflicted upon targeted students. Instead, they should be dealt with on a case-by-case basis as they occur naturally and circumstances warrant corrective action.

DEFINITION, KEY FEATURES, AND EXAMPLES
OF LYING, CHEATING, AND STEALING

Lying is defined as making a false statement in order to deceive, conceal an act, avoid accountability, or protect someone (in which case the motives are altruistic). Cheating refers to acting dishonestly in order to gain an advantage, such as in a game or on a test. Stealing involves taking another person's property or possession without their permission and without intending to return it. The opposite of lying is being honest; the opposite of cheating is being responsible; and the opposite of stealing is being trustworthy. When debriefing with individual students or groups about these traits, it is helpful to promote these polar opposite values and to clarify how they are different.

Children under the age of 3 do not understand the concept of lying. Between the ages of 3 and 6 or 7, children do not lie intentionally but make up stories and tales that do not correspond with reality. Beyond this age level, lying can serve instrumental purposes, particularly if it is modeled by a parent as a way of coping with an environment. There are numerous incentives for children and youth to lie, including escaping from the consequences of one's actions, parental expectations that are too high for the child to achieve, to get a disliked peer into trouble, to protect family members from an embarrassing or vulnerable family situation, or to keep from hurting the feelings of others.

Cheating is an especially harmful behavior for teachers who strive to create and enforce fair rules for judging student performance. Cheating is a dishonest effort to achieve an unfair advantage normally unavailable to others. The pressures to excel in school are a primary driver of cheating, especially among college-bound students. Experts argue that cheating is rampant in our K–12 schools, with estimates ranging between 70 and 95% of students who admit to cheating or plagiarism. Donald McCabe, a Rutgers University professor, surveyed 24,000 students and found that 95% admitted to cheating in high school (2019). Twenty percent of students say they began cheating in first grade. Advances in technology have substantially enabled cheating through use of cell phones, graphing calculators, text messaging, and email, contributing to a huge increase in cheating within schools over past decades.

Stealing has a direct impact on others as it removes something of value from another person. Prior to age 3, children do not perceive that taking something belonging to someone else is inappropriate; they do not as yet have a conception of possession and ownership. By age 9, children should understand that stealing is wrong and should be avoided. Children who see their parents stealing without remorse during childhood have a particularly problematic life path. Stealing as an adolescent and as an adult is a very high-risk behavior that can result in serious legal consequences.

Findings in the professional literature seem to suggest that male students are more likely to engage in dishonest behavior than female students are. Further, there is some evidence that parents are more likely to model dishonest behavior in front of males than to model it in front of females. This sends a subtle message to males that dishonesty is indirectly sanctioned by their parent(s). Further, males are more likely to adopt a "win at any cost" strategy and are often more competitive in the extreme than females are (May, 2012).

CAUSAL INFLUENCES AND ANTECEDENT CONDITIONS OF LYING, CHEATING, AND STEALING

A great deal of the speculation as to why individuals lie, cheat, and steal has been focused on the usual natural incentives to do so, such as to inflict harm on others, avoid punishment, secure an unfair advantage, or take something of value belonging to someone else. A popular explanatory theory has been the cost–benefit analysis, where the odds of benefiting from something are weighed against the odds of getting caught and being punished for it. However, Dan Ariely, a psychologist in behavioral economics at Duke University, suggests that this theory does not adequately explain why people commit dishonest acts. Ariely has extensively investigated the reasons for dishonesty and asserts that the cost–benefit theory is a bad descriptor of human behavior and a poor basis for policy. He argues that most people cheat a little but tend to still view themselves as good people; however, if the dishonesty occurs too often, this self-view is no longer tenable and the dishonesty may stop. This finding is based on thousands of participants who were interviewed and surveyed on this topic and is consistent with surveys of high school students who have a positive self-view but admit to committing dishonest acts.

In an interesting and relevant development, it is important to note here that a 2012 study by Ariely and colleagues on marketplace dishonesty has recently been retracted from its National Academy of Sciences publication venue due to fraudulent data. While the theoretical work of Ariely et al.

appears credible and has been widely cited (Mazar, On, & Ariely, 2008) in TED talks, print media, and behavioral economics literature, this outcome suggests his research findings on dishonesty should be interpreted with caution.

Lies also have functional value for individuals and serve differing purposes. For example, *antisocial lies* are those intended to inflict harm through deception. In contrast, *prosocial lies* are protective in nature and are used to avoid embarrassment or to keep from hurting someone's feelings. *Self-enhancement lies* are intended to embellish one's attributes. Finally, *exaggeration lies* are often used to attract attention and impress others.

Skilled lying involves a certain cognitive awareness, sensitivity, and sophistication on the part of the liar in that perceptiveness about circumstances and social dynamics is required. Research shows that socially skilled students are the most effective at lying. They have the ability to read situations and can appear credible by controlling their emotions and body language when they know they are intentionally lying. Skilled liars often embed lies within truthful information. Lying can also be habit-forming and there is evidence that lying is self-perpetuating (Ariely, 2012; Cooper, 2021; Verigin, Meijer, & Bogaard, 2019; Zanette, Walsh, Augiment, & Lee, 2020).

The students of greatest concern are those whose dishonesty is chronic and who show no remorse (Stouthamer-Loeber, 1986). These characteristics more likely typify antisocial students, many of whom are members of a deviant peer group, whose core values support dishonesty and delinquent acts (Patterson et al., 1992; Walker, Colvin, & Ramsey, 1995; Walker, Ramsey, & Gresham, 2004). These students have failed to be socialized to rule-governed forms of behavior and respect for others. The long-term outlook for such children is very problematic (Patterson et al., 1992).

RECOMMENDED STRATEGIES FOR COPING WITH AND PREVENTING LYING, CHEATING, AND STEALING

Lying

Lying is a common occurrence among students and it often may be beyond the teacher's purview and ability to detect its occurrence. Given that, it is best not to accuse students who are suspected of lying unless there is clear evidence that a student is misrepresenting facts in order to avoid responsibility for a dishonest act. As noted earlier, some students lie to protect themselves, their families, and others from embarrassment or from potentially damaging situations. Lying in such circumstances is understandable and can be acceptable depending on the situation.

Nearly 90% of high school students say they have lied and more than

90% of lying instances are not detected by teachers or school staff. Levine, Serota, Carey, and Messer (2013) found that high school students reported an average of 4.1 lies told in the past 24 hours. Studies of adult prevalence found 60% of respondents told no lies in the past 24 hours and that half of all lies were told by 5% of respondents (Serota, Levine, & Boster, 2009). Among adults, the majority of lies seem to be told by a very small part of the population. High school students tell 60% more lies than college students and 150% more lies than adults. Thus, lying appears to decline with age and maturity.

Teachers should promote honesty in one's personal life, and students should learn that lying for personal gain carries social risks. While lying to deceive others, seek advantage, or avoid accountability negatively affects others and is very much a personal choice, it can damage one's reputation. Students who chronically lie may become known by peers as untrustworthy and be socially rejected. In such cases, it may be useful for the teacher to conduct a private debriefing session about the social costs and consequences of persistent lying. During such sessions it is important to follow guidelines on dealing with lying as promoted by psychologist Ken Shore (2018).

- Address the lie constructively and calmly.
- Indicate that you disapprove of the behavior—not the student.
- Meet with the student in private.
- Investigate the student's reasons for the lie.
- Praise the student for being honest.
- Do not punish the student for lying.
- Problem-solve alternate strategies to lying.

Two case studies on lying are presented here. The first addresses classroom lying and how the teacher constructively dealt with it. The second focuses on the long-term consequences that can result from lying in certain situations.

CASE STUDY: CASEY IS CAUGHT IN A LIE BY HIS TEACHER

Ms. Samuelson was a third-grade general education teacher who was very concerned that all her students learn to read as well as possible by the end of the school year, which is the point where students shift from learning to read to using their reading skills as a tool in learning. She gave her students considerable practice in mastering basic literacy skills as well as in learning to understand and interpret written text in order to prepare them for this critical change.

Ms. Samuelson gave her class an overnight reading assignment of a passage that she said they would review and discuss the next day. She emphasized that everyone should come prepared to participate in the exercise. During class the next day, she asked students to raise their hand if they had read the passage. Nearly all students did so, including Casey, who had not read it but was fully capable of doing so. When he was asked a question about the story, it was clear Casey had not read the passage as he had indicated, since he could not answer the question. He was quite embarrassed, as all the other students realized he had been caught in a lie. Ms. Samuelson called on another student with the same question but did not say anything to Casey about the lie in front of the class.

After the period was over, Ms. Samuelson called Casey up to her desk to talk about the incident. Ms. Samuelson made it clear she was not going to punish Casey for his failure to do the assignment and then claiming he had. The following exchange then occurred.

Ms. Samuelson: Casey, can you tell me why you weren't able to read the passage?

Casey: When I got home, my little brother had had a bike accident. We took him to the doctor to see about it and I totally forgot about the assignment.

Ms. Samuelson: Things like that happen and sometimes it causes us to forget what we're supposed to do. But it would have been much better if you had just told the truth rather than trying to get away with a lie. I would have understood and so would have your classmates. You also could have told me about it before class. As it is, you were embarrassed in front of the class.

Casey: You're right. I should have just said why I forgot to read it.

Ms. Samuelson: Good. You simply could have said you forgot because you were so upset and concerned about your little brother. It's best to be honest even when the truth can hurt. I hope you will remember this lesson in the future. Thanks for your understanding.

The following case study illustrates the personal costs of chronic lying as a lifestyle choice.

CASE STUDY: LONG-TERM COSTS OF LYING AS A HABIT

Frederick was raised in a family where lying and deception were characteristic occurrences. He grew up watching his parents engage in dishonesty and deception of other people as well as organizations (e.g., tax fraud) for personal benefit and gain. One could say that lying in his household was a lifestyle choice given its frequency. Frederick was of course influenced by this atmosphere and pattern of behavior. As soon as he realized that personal gains could be achieved through lying and deception, he adopted a pattern of chronic lying. There were many times he would lie when the truth would have sufficed.

In his school career, he found that lying could produce benefits such as escaping responsibility for his actions or helping him feel clever when deceiving others. Frederick seemed oblivious to the personal and social costs of his lying. He was regarded as untrustworthy by peers and not desirable as a friend. He was usually the last to be chosen as a participant or partner in peer-controlled activities. Frederick continued this behavior pattern through middle and high school, where its consequences were more serious.

At age 18, he decided to join the military and immediately chafed against the requirement for compliance with its strict disciplinary code. He began associating with other soldiers who held similar views to his and got into serious trouble when he was identified as a material witness in a serious criminal act committed by one of them. When Frederick was questioned by an investigator about his knowledge of the incident and surrounding circumstances, he lied and said he had no knowledge of them. However, he had previously told several soldiers about his knowledge of details about the incident. When this fact was discovered, he was charged with lying to a federal investigator and referred for court martial. His trial resulted in a guilty verdict and after serving his sentence of 8 months in a military jail he was dishonorably discharged.

This case study illustrates one of the many reasons children and youth should be encouraged not to lie. In Frederick's case, his chronic lying had a severe and permanent impact on his life and future prospects.

Cheating

Cheating is a dishonest act that prevents an objective assessment of a student's actual performance. It should be defined early on in the school year and described as unacceptable. Students should know that being caught cheating will result in zero credit for the work on which the cheating occurred. Further, students should learn that supporting academic dishonesty by classmates results in a loss for everyone and is a violation of both personal and classroom acceptable standards of behavior. The following are some specific strategies for managing cheating (Shore, 2007):

- Debrief privately with the student about the cheating and the possible reasons for it. Communicate that you value the student but cheating is unfair to classmates, is the wrong thing to do, and cannot be allowed in your classroom.
- Describe consequences for cheating that are costly, such as receiving zero credit for the work on which cheating occurs and the potential loss of respect from classmates.
- Try to help the student deal with the reasons for the cheating and refer him or her for counseling if appropriate.

- Carefully monitor the performance of students who chronically cheat in order to prevent it.
- If the problem cannot be resolved, consider involving the student's parents in solving it.

Reducing Cheating Opportunities

Electronic devices that can be used to acquire or distribute answers and notes from and to other students should be strictly controlled by the teacher—especially during tests but also when independent work is expected of all students. Students who use phones to photograph and distribute answers to other students should be sanctioned, and text messaging or sending emails for the same purpose should be carefully controlled and restricted as appropriate and feasible. The following case study shows how undue pressure from parents can cause their children to cheat in order to meet their expectations.

CASE STUDY: SAMANTHA'S CHRONIC CHEATING

Samantha was a fifth-grade student in Ms. Tyler's classroom who sometimes struggled with her schoolwork. She came from a family of high achievers who were worried about her schooling and very concerned about her grades. They felt she should be achieving higher grades than she was and had expressed this view to teachers in the past. Samantha's older siblings had all done well academically in school and they were constantly held up to her as models to emulate. Samantha seemed depressed, guilty, and unhappy that she was not able to meet her parents' academic expectations.

One of Samantha's classmates reported to Ms. Tyler that she had asked her for answers for items on a test. The peer said this was not the first time it had happened and that she had asked other classmates for answers on previous tests. Ms. Tyler scheduled a private meeting with Samantha to review the situation. At first she denied the cheating but eventually admitted to it. Ms. Tyler explained to Samantha that any schoolwork on which cheating occurs results in zero credit for it, and that in addition to it being unacceptable to all teachers and most classmates, cheating reflects badly on the kind of person you are and is unfair to others.

Ms. Tyler told Samantha how much she had going for her, how supportive she was of her, and how much she wanted her to be successful in school. She asked why Samantha resorted to cheating in school. Samantha said her parents were very concerned about her getting good grades, she felt pressure to excel, and she did not want to disappoint them. Ms. Tyler asked Samantha if it would be OK to discuss the situation with her parents to see if they could come up with a solution. Samantha agreed and said she felt good about Ms. Tyler doing that.

Ms. Tyler scheduled a parent–teacher conference with Samantha's parents, who were surprised that their concerns about Samantha's schooling had contributed to her cheating. They and Ms. Tyler discussed ways of supporting Samantha and relieving the pressure on her to get good grades. The parents volunteered to hire a tutor to work with Samantha on her assignments and to tone down their interactions with her about grades. Ms. Tyler promised to call the parents weekly to provide a status report and to discuss Samantha's progress. Over the next six months, these supports had a positive effect: There were no more cheating incidents and Samantha seemed to be happier and less stressed about her academic performance.

Stealing

Stealing at school is a rare, serious, and disrespectful act that results in a loss of the victim's property or valued possession and is highly objectionable to teachers. It is important to note that accusing a student of stealing is a very serious matter, and teachers should exercise caution in doing so. Usually stealing comes to the teacher's attention through a student complaint that a valued possession is missing accompanied by a suspicion that it was stolen. The incident should be reported by the teacher to the principal's office. If a student is accused, he or she should be identified in the referral as the suspected thief according to the victim's report or that of classmates who may have knowledge of it.

While teachers should participate in the investigative and resolution processes, they should not try to investigate or resolve a case of stealing on their own. This should be the responsibility of the school's leadership, as it may require involvement of the accused student's parents and/or the legal system if the theft is substantial. At a minimum, the stolen item should be returned to the victim in the same condition as before, accompanied by an apology and a commitment to avoid such behavior in the future. It is the responsibility of the school and the student's parents to work out a satisfactory resolution to the theft. The following case study illustrates stealing in a schooling context and how it was resolved.

CASE STUDY: SKYLAR'S STEALING AND DEVIANT PEER GROUP

Skylar was enrolled in sixth grade in a middle school that served a number of neighborhoods with high crime and poverty rates. Skylar's family background was problematic, with high levels of dysfunction and drug use, and poor monitoring of Skylar's activities. While healthy and intellectually talented, Skylar chose friends growing up who displayed a number of antisocial traits resulting in destructive behavior. As they matured, their shared values supported vandalism, stealing, and other destructive acts. Skylar and his peers formed what is known as a deviant peer group, whose members are at high risk for juvenile delinquency and eventual arrest (Patterson et al., 1992).

Skylar and his friends posed a severe management challenge for their teachers from the beginning of their school careers. As a group, they had a very high frequency of ODRs to the school administration for a range of offenses, including insubordination, teacher defiance, and severe disruptions requiring room clears. Skylar and his group showed little interest in school or in structured activities involving peers during free-play periods, preferring to hang out with each other instead. In a very real sense, Skylar and his peers functioned as a small gang within and outside of school. When two or more members of this closely bonded group of peers were enrolled in the same classroom, it posed a nightmare scenario for the teacher. The principal's office made ample use of suspensions and exclusions in coping with the challenges of this group, which did very little to abate their problem behavior.

Skylar was a natural leader and, combined with his intellectual gifts, he was influential among his chosen friends. He played a powerful role in determining their covert activities as a group, and they decided to steal concealable merchandise (e.g., cell phones, small items of clothing) or possessions of value from fellow students that could be used or sold to peers. Partly to cement his status with his peers, Skylar informed them that he would steal a cell phone from a fellow student that could be sold for several hundred dollars. He waited until recess when he could search the student's desk with no one looking and found the phone that the student had left. However, another student happened to witness the theft and reported it to the teacher.

When the teacher confronted Skylar about it, he denied taking the phone and threatened the student who reported it. The teacher referred the matter to the principal, who contacted Skylar's parents about the theft. Skylar's father accused the school of falsely accusing his son, who assured him he had not taken the phone. The principal decided to involve the police, who conducted an investigation that determined Skylar had in fact taken the phone. The victim's parents insisted on Skylar being held responsible for his actions. Skylar was accused of a misdemeanor theft, required to return the phone, and registered as a juvenile offender. He also received disciplinary consequences at school resulting from the theft. These actions had a sobering effect on Skylar and his peer group going forward. The remaining classmates in Skylar's class showed satisfaction with how the case was handled and turned out.

IMPLEMENTING CHARACTER EDUCATION
TO PREVENT LYING, CHEATING, AND STEALING

Implementing character education on a schoolwide basis is a viable option in attempts to prevent dishonesty and promote student acceptance of behavioral standards. Character education teaches life skills in the social–emotional realm, such as learning to (1) communicate effectively, (2) make informed decisions, (3) set and achieve realistic goals, (4) resolve conflicts, (5) solve problems, and (6) respect others. A variety of materials, instructional activities, and student assignments are used in its implementation.

Character Counts! (Peterson, O'Connor, & Fluke, 2014; *www.charactercounts.org*) is an ethics- and character-building program designed for school-age students . It is the most widely used curricular framework for character education (Gruener, n.d.). The program was developed by respected researchers and is intended to teach and develop a consensus on ethical values that transcend race, politics, gender, and socioeconomic status. Character Counts! provides a framework for teaching the six pillars and core values of character education: trustworthiness, respect, responsibility, fairness, caring, and citizenship. It also provides lessons and activities that address the CASEL core competencies: self-management, self-awareness, social awareness, relationship skills, and responsible decision making.

Character Counts! is a universal program designed as a school-, district-, and/or communitywide program. Thus, individual teachers should not attempt to implement this program by themselves. Ideally, an entire school staff should participate in the adoption decision and receive training in the program's implementation, assisted by related services staff such as school psychologists, counselors, and behavioral specialists. Some parents may object if a character education program's adoption and implementation are initiated by an individual teacher rather than the school's leadership and staff. In any event, parents should always be accorded the opt-out choice for their children.

There is no guarantee that teaching character education values and principles will prevent lying, cheating, and stealing. However, character education can have numerous positive effects on school climate and student/staff interactions. If students are receptive to the schoolwide teaching of programs such as this, they may also be positively impacted.

Note: Extensive information regarding the Character Counts! program is available at *www.charactercounts.org,* including materials and staff training resources. Also, the Character Counts!: Program Brief of the Student Engagement Project, jointly produced by the University of Nebraska and the Nebraska Department of Education, can be accessed at *http://K12engagement.Unl.Edu/Character-Counts.*

CHAPTER 6 TAKEAWAYS

- Lying, cheating, and stealing are highly objectionable forms of stealth behavior.
- Lying has become pervasive in school and instances of it are rarely detected by teachers.

- As they develop, young children gradually learn that lying is frowned upon and being honest should be encouraged.

- Cheating is something that teachers can cope with effectively by seeking the reasons for its occurrence and developing a plan to correct and prevent it.

- Stealing is a serious instance of violating a person's space and victimizing them through theft of possessions or property.

- Addressing stealing is the responsibility of the school's leadership, and teachers should not attempt to deal with it by themselves.

- Consider referring the student to mental health services if stealing is sufficiently serious or habitual and cannot be controlled by the school's intervention(s).

PART III

Strategies for Increasing Desirable Behavior,
Decreasing Undesirable Behavior,
and Sustaining Achieved
Behavior Change over Time

How to Increase Desirable Student Behavior

The material in this part of the book focuses on a behavioral approach to classroom management and is for professionals who may be unfamiliar with this behavioral technology. Knowledge of these principles and techniques will make implementing the solutions described in Parts I and II more understandable and easier to apply. Portions of the material in this part of the book are adapted from Walker (1995).

There are two major tasks in achieving successful behavioral improvements. These are procedures for changing behavior and procedures for sustaining it. Procedures differ for achieving each of these objectives. Once positive behavior change is achieved, the remaining task is to ensure that it becomes a permanent feature. Behavior change is not regarded as effective unless it can be sustained over time and across settings. A main goal of this part of the book is to provide enabling information that can be used for achieving both these outcomes. The behavioral improvement techniques described in this chapter are accompanied by discussion of correct application guidelines and critical issues to consider in their use.

TEACHER PRAISE

One of the easiest and most powerful tools available for teachers in managing student behavior is praise and approval. Further, the cost in time and effort for using it is miniscule. Students vary in how responsive they are to adult praise but most students will respond positively at some level to it.

Definition and Examples of Teacher Praise

Approval from the teacher can be an effective strategy for enhancing student behavior and performance. This is especially true of very young students who are dependent upon frequent teacher direction and feedback. Praise is defined as delivery of a positive verbal, physical, or gestural action that communicates teacher approval of student performance. It can be dispensed in multiple ways, such as with a thumbs-up, a wink or nod of approval, a smile, or via a verbal statement or compliment. Some examples of teacher praise are listed below.

- Ms. Sanchez gives Joey a thumbs-up and smile for assisting another student with his assignment.
- "Billy, you and Jason are doing the flash card drills the right way—nice work!"
- "Andy, your math problems are 100% correct. Nice work!"
- "Suzy, you read that passage perfectly!"

Praise statements can also be directed to the entire class, as in "Class, I like the way you're all getting organized for our next in-class exercise."

Guidelines for Correct Application of Teacher Praise

There are a number of rules that should be followed to maximize the efficacy of praise.

- Praise is considered most effective when it is "behavior descriptive"—when the teacher communicates exactly what the approval is for, as in "John, I really liked how you worked through those problems without assistance. Good job!"

- Praise should always be applied to effort that is deserving of it.

- Praise should be delivered immediately after the target behavior occurs. This allows the student to learn to differentiate appropriate from inappropriate behavior or correct from incorrect performance so that some nonpreferred intervening response is not reinforced instead. An exception to this rule would be when praising continuous stream behaviors such as attending to task and certain types of ongoing peer-to-peer interactions (i.e., peer tutoring).

- The quality of praise is extremely important. It should always be positive, natural, and sincere in tone, and never superficial.

- Teacher praise statements should be varied so that praising does not become monotonous.

• As a general rule, one should try to deliver three to four praises for each criticism or disapproval of a child's behavior, although sustaining this ratio can be a problem for busy teachers. In the early stages of learning, one should strive to praise approximately once every 10 minutes with the frequency of praise gradually reduced as the target behavior or skill is developed.

Issues to Consider When Implementing Praise

It is important to note that while adult praise is reinforcing and is sought by most children, for reasons that are not completely understood adult approval has a limited impact on many children with very challenging behavior patterns. This is especially so for extremely aggressive children, who seem to actively reject the adult attention. I have found this to be the case repeatedly with young aggressive children, particularly within free-play settings (Walker et al., 1995). Thus, using praise alone to cope with the behavior of such students may not be a good idea in many instances.

REINFORCEMENT PROCEDURES

Reinforcement procedures have been used extensively in applied contexts to improve the human condition: Incentives occur at organizational, group, and individual levels and even in relations among nations. The following section provides information on how to use reinforcement effectively and for constructive purposes with students.

Definition and Examples of Reinforcement Procedures

Reinforcement refers to providing a rewarding event for the purpose of increasing a target behavior or response. An event is said to be rewarding when its occurrence increases the frequency or magnitude of the behavior to which it is applied.

There are differing types of reinforcement as well as different methods of delivery. There are also different schedules for the delivery of reinforcing events that have differential effects on the behavior to which they are applied.

Types of Rewarding Events

As to the types of reinforcement, there are both social and nonsocial forms. Teacher praise (discussed above) is a primary form of social reinforcement. In addition to verbal praise, social rewards include smiles, nods of approval, winks, a thumbs-up, and so on. Nonsocial rewards include preferred activities, free time, extra TV time at home, extra recess, being a teacher's helper, and so forth. There are a wide variety of rewards available at both home and school that can be used to motivate children and assist in the teaching of skills, concepts, and appropriate behavior patterns. The classroom teacher is in a unique position to take advantage of these rewards in teaching and managing the classroom.

Delivery of Rewarding Events

The two primary methods of delivering rewarding events are *token versus non-token reinforcement* and *group versus individual reinforcement*. Tokens earned in the form of points, check marks, punches on a card, or stars, exchangeable for backup rewards, can be a very effective means of reinforcement delivery. They are easy to use in classroom and playground settings and a variety of backup rewards can be provided that may appeal to a broader range of individual student preferences. Backup rewards can also be arranged according to their perceived value, with more mileage gained from higher value rewards.

Non-token reinforcement is used by many teachers and parents on an informal and sometimes unsystematic basis. With this approach, there is usually a one-to-one relationship between the reward and the behavior that earns it. For example, parents often set up if–then contingency arrangements, such as "After you clean up your room, you can watch TV." Similarly, teachers frequently set up contingencies where students can talk quietly with each other or have free time after completing their assigned work.

A form of non-token reinforcement that has been successfully adapted for classroom use is *activity-based contingency management*. This procedure was originally developed by Homme, DeBaca, Devine, Steinhorst, and Rickert (1963), and is similar to parents' use of contingency arrangements. It relies on the *Premack principle,* whose basic premise is that what an individual likes to do (i.e., a high frequency, preferred activity) can be used as a reward to enhance what they don't like to do (i.e., a low-frequency, non-preferred activity). It has also been described as "Grandma's law": "You get to do what you want after you do what I want." The Premack principle can be used with individual students, small groups, and the entire class. In most classroom applications free time (a preferred activity) has been used to reward academic work (not a preferred activity), or in the case of the whole class, as a positive consequence for classwide academic engagement. As a rule, small amounts of time spent in free-time activities can be used to reward larger amounts of time spent on academics. This technique seems to work best with younger children but has been used effectively with many students and groups in the K–12 grade range.

A second method of delivering reinforcement concerns group versus individual procedures. Individual reinforcement is a private, individualized arrangement between the teacher and student or between a teacher, parent, and student. The teacher defines focus behaviors or tasks for the student and then rewards the student for displaying them on some sort of schedule. At the other extreme, the entire class may be treated as a single group: The teacher verbally reinforces class members for following rules and the whole class is treated as if it were an individual student. There are many possible variations and possible combinations of group and individual reinforcement. However, experts have cautioned that group reinforcement procedures should be monitored carefully because of (1) the possibility that one or more members of the target group is unable to perform the focus behavior, (2) the resulting pressure on an individual who is responsible for the group's failure to meet the reward criterion, and (3) the possibility that one or more individuals may find it rewarding to subvert the system (O'Leary & Drabman, 1971). Both individual and group reinforcement procedures have been demonstrated as efficacious in literally thousands of studies reported in the professional literature. With classwide group reinforcement, a wall chart should be used to display the number of points earned toward some classroom-preferred group activity or goal. A thermometer-type chart generally works well for this purpose.

Some teachers object to providing individual rewards for students at school, but do not necessarily oppose using them on an individual basis to help students succeed in school. This arrangement can work quite satisfactorily for all parties. For example, the student's parents can provide appropriate rewards at home when the student brings home a note or Good Day Card indicating that the reward criterion was met at school.

Figure 13.1 shows an example of a Good Day Card (similar to the version of this card in Chapter 1) that can be used to reinforce good school behavior and good schoolwork for an individual student, with backup rewards delivered at home. An X is placed on the card on the student's desk each time the teacher awards a point for good student behavior or good schoolwork. Behavior-specific praise is then written next to the X to indicate what the point was earned for. It is a good idea to divide the number of points evenly between good student behavior and good schoolwork.

You can divide the school day into class periods on the point card with a certain number of points available in each class period or subject area. There are many possible variations of point cards either for school use only or as Good Day Cards. The card should remain on the student's desk throughout the school day so the student can see what points are awarded for. At the end of the day, the teacher should use the card to review the school day before sending it home.

| Student Name _____ |
| Date _____ |
| Teacher's Initials _____ |

Good Student Behavior	Good Schoolwork
Great job!	Excellent work on your math.
You were very helpful to Sarah.	Nice job on your reading.
Good listening	You got all of them right!

Total Points Today: 6

Teacher Comments: Jamie had a really good day! Keep up the good work.

FIGURE 13.1. Good Day Point Card for student behavior and schoolwork.

Schedules of Delivering Reinforcement

There are three basic scheduling options for delivering reinforcers: continuous, ratio, and interval. Ratio and interval schedules can be fixed or variable, and continuous schedules mean a response is reinforced each time it occurs. Continuous schedules build new behavior rapidly and are typically used in the early stages of learning when a new skill or behavior is being acquired.

After it has been acquired, a ratio schedule is used to sustain a behavior or skill and means that a certain ratio of responses to reinforcers is used in delivery. A ratio schedule of 1:5 means that one reinforcer will be delivered for every 5 responses; similarly, a 1:10 ratio schedule delivers one reinforcer for every 10 responses. Ratio schedules are typically used by teachers to reinforce academic responses for things such as number of math problems completed or number of pages read. An interval schedule, in contrast, refers to an arrangement where a reinforcer is delivered after a certain period of time has passed. Interval schedules are often used to reinforce continuous stream behavior such as social interaction or time spent academically engaged. Reinforcement schedules can be either fixed or variable. A fixed schedule means that one reinforcer is delivered after every so many responses have occurred, whereas a variable schedule means that one reinforcer is delivered after every so many responses *on average*. That is, the individual cannot tell exactly when the reinforcement will occur, in contrast to fixed schedules.

Table 13.1 includes the four types of fixed and variable schedules and their effects on behavior. Interval schedules are used much less often in the classroom than ratio schedules. Fixed interval schedules are used when students are rewarded for spending certain amounts of time in a particular activity. An example would be two students each receiving one minute of free time for every five minutes spent in a joint activity of some type, such as flash card drills or a more skilled student tutoring a less skilled classmate. Fixed ratio schedules are used much more frequently by teachers. A common practice is for teachers to assign X number of math problems that must be completed correctly before a reward is available.

Use of both variable ratio and variable interval schedules is much more typical in classrooms. In fact, due to limited time, most teachers are only able to reinforce student behavior intermittently. This has the effect of maintaining higher levels of student performance. It is usually not necessary to reinforce student behavior or performance on a strict variable schedule: reinforcement of an arbitrarily determined percentage of student responses will suffice.

As noted, continuous schedules are recommended in the early stages of learning or skill mastery. While strict adherence to this type of schedule is nearly impossible for busy teachers, when teaching a new skill or behavior every effort should be made to reinforce as often as possible when acceptable forms of the target behavior occur.

TABLE 13.1. Effects of Reinforcement Schedules on Behavior

Fixed ratio (FR)	Reinforcer is given after each X responses	High response rates	Irregular bursts of responding
Variable ratio (VR)	Reinforcer given after X responses on average	High response rates	Very resistant to extinction
Fixed interval (FI)	Reinforcer is given for first response occurring after each X minutes	Stops working after reinforcement; works hard just prior to time of next reinforcement	Slow gradual decrease in responding
Variable interval (VI)	Reinforcer is given for first response occurring after each X minutes on average	Steady rates of responding	Very resistant to extinction

Guidelines for Correct Application of Reinforcement Procedures

There are a number of best-practice guidelines for maximizing the effectiveness of reinforcement procedures. Fox example, it is of paramount importance that the reinforcement system used have incentive value for the student(s) to whom it is applied. If not, the system will not be effective no matter how well-designed. The more diversity there is in the backup activities and items that can be earned, the more effective reinforcement will be. Thus, both home and school reward options should be considered whenever possible depending on parental agreement. It is recommended that activity rewards be primarily earned at school, with special privileges or tangible items made available as a home option. In this option, the student earns points on a Good Day Card that is taken home and exchanged for a prearranged backup item or special privilege.

Backup rewards should be arranged according to the value they have for the student, with the most valued requiring the most effort to earn. In this way, students can learn to delay gratification by waiting to accumulate sufficient points or credits for more preferred items/activities. In a similar vein, the criterion for reinforcement can be gradually raised to stimulate higher quality performance or longer periods of appropriate behavior. Essentially, you redefine over time what a reinforceable response is and withhold reinforcement until the new criterion is met by the student.

The following are some additional rules for individual reinforcement:

- Students should have frequent opportunities to exchange their earned points for a backup item—on a daily basis when a skill or behavior is just being learned.
- Do not allow students to hoard earned points excessively, as it dilutes their value.
- As a general rule, students should be able to exchange earned points once per day for the least expensive item or activity of value on the backup reward list.
- A good reinforcement criterion for student behavior is that if it has been at 80% or better, it should qualify for reinforcement. Similar standards for academic productivity and correctness are also a good way to clearly communicate teacher expectations.
- When delivering reinforcement to ongoing behavior or performance, it is a good idea if the delivery is as subtle as possible to not disrupt the student's performance.
- Some form of teacher praise should always accompany the awarding of points in order to enhance the reinforcing value of teacher approval.

Issues to Consider When Using Reinforcement Procedures

Moral and ethical objections to the use of reinforcement to motivate students inevitably arise in connection with their use in school settings. Nevertheless, there are numerous unmotivated and behaviorally challenged students who are unable to achieve school success in their absence. A common objection to reinforcement's use is that it restricts a student's choices as well as limiting behavioral diversity by teaching the student to engage in a very limited behavior pattern so as to achieve reinforcement. Other objections are that it teaches the student to respond appropriately only in the presence of reinforcement and not at other times, and that it undermines a student's creativity and natural interest in activities. Logical arguments can be developed for and against each of the above-cited positions. Advocates on either side of them have passionately argued their respective merits endlessly with little resolution.

However, there is no question that reinforcement works and that it is effective in teaching students to achieve more and behave better. It should be viewed as a short-term remedial tool for teaching new skills and behaviors. After they are acquired, the formal reinforcement system can be gradually withdrawn or phased out. The challenge is to remove the reinforcement system in a way that preserves as much of the achieved gains as possible with appropriate maintenance procedures. The hope is that eventually the student's improvement(s) will be sustained by natural rewards in the environment, such as feelings of mastery and achievement; expressions of approval from teachers, peers, and parents; or access to new social opportunities such as inclusion in peer activities.

Self-control and self-management are the ultimate goals following interventions based on external reinforcement. However, it is not an easy task to get students with behavioral challenges to the point where they will accept responsibility for maintaining changes produced by an externally controlled intervention. A three-stage strategy is recommended for this purpose. First, an intervention is implemented with integrity to produce behavior changes. Second, control and management of the intervention is gradually transferred to the student. Third, when the student is able to manage it sufficiently well, the system is phased out with support from naturally occurring social rewards. My colleagues and I have accomplished this multiple times in phasing out recess and classroom interventions. However, regular follow-up monitoring is always recommended to determine how well the target behavior is being sustained and whether supplements to the intervention are warranted. Later on in this chapter, more-detailed procedures are described for teaching students self-control and self-management strategies.

SHAPING

Shaping is used to build totally new responses that have not previously been a part of a child's behavioral repertoire, with a combination of positive reinforcement (encouraging the response) and ignoring (discouraging an incorrect response). Its use is appropriate when a child does not perform a target behavior but is capable of doing so.

Definition and Examples of Shaping

In using shaping, the adult begins by reinforcing a form of the target behavior that may be only a rough approximation of the desired form of the behavior being taught. This is called reinforcing an approximation of the desired performance. Shaping is a process of reinforcing closer and closer approximations and ignoring ones that are less close to the desired final form. Ignoring puts the less close approximation on extinction while waiting until a closer one occurs. In this way, the child learns to discriminate correct from incorrect responses and is able to demonstrate the desired form of the behavior being taught.

Shaping is frequently used by speech therapists in early language training. As a child matures, the diversity and size of the sounds they make increases. Parents pay close attention to these sounds that approximate spoken language, model the correct sound or word, and then reinforce the child for imitating them. As a result, the child learns to listen to the spoken language of parents and siblings, then seeks to imitate it and is socially reinforced when successful. Complex language is acquired through this basic process.

As an applied example of shaping, child care workers and related services personnel working in school settings often use shaping procedures to gradually teach children with internalizing behavior problems (e.g., social avoidance, anxiety, phobias, social behavior deficits) new patterns of more adaptive social behavior. Many withdrawn children are quite limited and suppressed in their verbal and nonverbal interactions with peers due to social phobias, weak social skills, or having been punished in their peer initiations. Participating in ongoing peer interaction opportunities is essential for social growth and development. Following instruction on how to both approach others and respond to peer initiations, a socially withdrawn child could initially be reinforced for simply being in closer proximity to peers. Next, they might be prompted to engage in parallel play that requires no verbal interaction. Joining a peer-controlled activity might be the next step. Responding to a peer initiation could be followed by making an initiation to a peer with the goal of greater social engagement. The recruitment of special peer helpers to provide support and guidance in this overall process is a very effective technique often used in this context.

Guidelines for Correct Application of Shaping

To reiterate, shaping is used to develop skills or responses of a child who currently does not have them in their behavioral repertoire but who is capable of producing an approximation of what is being taught. Basically, shaping is the alternating application of reinforcement and extinction procedures in conjunction with gradually increasing criteria for what is a reinforceable attempt of the target behavior being developed. The child learns that a closer approximation of the target behavior is reinforced and other, more distant approximations are not reinforced (i.e., placed on extinction by ignoring). Through this gradual process, the child learns to produce closer and closer approximations to the new target behavior that is being developed.

The following are some specific guidelines for the process of shaping:

- When raising the reinforcement criterion for a new approximation, one should ensure that the required response is sufficiently different from prior approximations to be discriminated by the child.
- When a prior form of the target behavior has been placed on extinction, it should never again be reinforced.
- Each occurrence of the required approximation to the target behavior that meets criterion should be reinforced so that mastery can be rapidly built.

Issues to Consider When Implementing Shaping

One should know that while shaping can be highly effective, it is a complex procedure. It is demanding of the implementer and requires very careful monitoring and management of the target child's behavior. There is no limit on the age an individual needs to be in order to benefit from it, but shaping is especially useful for teaching young students needed skills. Because of the intensity of effort required by shaping, one should ensure that it is actually required. As a general rule, shaping should be used as a last resort in teaching new skills and behaviors after it has been determined that other methods would be inappropriate or ineffective. Otherwise a less labor-intensive procedure should be considered first.

MODELING PLUS REINFORCEMENT

If it has been determined that shaping is called for but the child is not capable of producing a rough approximation of the target behavior, a procedure such as modeling plus reinforcement should be tried as an alternative.

Showing the child the target behavior and requiring an imitation of it, followed by reinforcement of same could be effective in this instance. Often
clinicians and teachers use a combination of modeling plus reinforcement
in developing competencies among their clients or students. For example,
young children with autism or severe learning disabilities often need to
have the desired form of the focus skill or behavior demonstrated for them
so they can be reinforced for matching responses or approximations. The
latest successful approximation is then placed on extinction via ignoring
and the next closest approximation is prompted and reinforced. This process is repeated until criterion performance is reached.

Definition and Examples of Modeling Plus Reinforcement

Modeling plus reinforcement of matching responses refers to a teaching
procedure in which a behavior or skill is demonstrated by a model (usually
a teacher or parent) and attempts to imitate the model are then reinforced.
This procedure is extremely powerful and combines the instructional precision of modeling and imitation along with the motivational properties of
reinforcement. It is most often used when the instructor is uncertain if the
child can produce the desired skill or response on demand.

Modeling plus reinforcement is especially useful for speech therapists
in teaching children with articulation disorders how to enunciate sounds
and words correctly. The following is the step-by-step process used in this
task.

1. Sounds and words the child has difficulty pronouncing correctly
   are identified.
2. The therapist then models the sound or word and asks the child to
   imitate it.
3. Corrective feedback is given after each attempt.
4. Responses that closely approximate those of the therapist are positively reinforced.
5. This process is repeated until mastery is achieved.

This technique is also very useful in teaching social skills and social
interaction strategies. Many children are socially rejected by peers because
they either do not know how to make or respond to peer initiations or
they are negative and aggressive in their social interactions. I have used
a technique called "special helpers" for enlisting peers in the teaching of
social skills within free-play settings. A socially skilled peer is selected to
be a special helper who models how to forge positive peer interactions and
provides praise and approval for correct imitation. Four or five other peers
are identified who will support the focus child's efforts. The lead special

helper usually prompts the focus child with something like, "Now, you watch what I do!" and demonstrates initiating and responding with the peer confederates who respond positively to the lead peer helper. The focus child is then invited to try it with a similar response from peer confederates.

The following actual example provides a case study of how effective this tool can be.

CASE STUDY: TEACHING SIGN LANGUAGE USING MODELING PLUS REINFORCEMENT

I was doing behavioral consulting at the California School for the Deaf and observed this successful sign language teaching procedure using modeling plus reinforcement. The child in question was a male adolescent with very limited communication skills and equally deficient social skills. His teachers had been only minimally successful in teaching him sign language. The school's psychologist designed and supervised this procedure.

Three individuals were involved in the teaching procedure. They were the hearing impaired student, one of his peers, and the resident dorm counselor. The teaching procedure was carried out daily in a private area and went as follows. The counselor asked the peer a simple question using sign language, such as "What is your name please?" The peer responded in sign language with "My name is _____." The peer was rewarded with praise and an M&M each time she responded correctly using sign language. After observing this sequence, the counselor would then ask the boy the same question in sign language. If he responded correctly, he was also rewarded with praise and an M&M, and if not he received no reward and another question was asked of the peer and the routine repeated. This proved to be a highly effective teaching procedure. However, a number of learning trials were necessary before the boy would respond appropriately to the counselor's queries. Though fully capable of learning sign language he seemed not especially interested in doing so.

There are many situations in school where this technique can be used effectively to teach skill mastery and desired forms of behavior. Some guidelines for its use are discussed in the next section.

Guidelines for Correct Application of Modeling Plus Reinforcement

Modeling plus reinforcement is perhaps most appropriate in direct instructional situations where the teacher is not sure whether the target skill or behavior is within the student's behavioral repertoire. Because of its power and precision, it can be highly effective for teaching complex social, language, and academic skills and is less labor-intensive than shaping. The following is a list of guidelines for correctly applying this technique.

1. The target skill or response must be modeled correctly for the student. It is literally true that a child will learn what is demonstrated and selectively reinforced by the model.
2. The target skill must be modeled consistently for the student.
3. The model should ensure that the student is paying close attention to what is being demonstrated. Obviously, skill acquisition and mastery will be disrupted by poor attention on the child's part.
4. Precise, descriptive feedback as to correctness should be provided following each learning trial.
5. Correct matching responses should be selectively rewarded with praise and/or points exchangeable for backups.
6. Finally, cues and prompts should be used as needed to help the student discriminate and produce the correct form of the desired skill/response.

Issues to Consider in Using Modeling Plus Reinforcement

This process must be carefully designed and implemented in a private or semi-private area where direct observation, communication, modeling demonstrations, and positive feedback are feasible. In certain situations and with some students (i.e., younger, less skilled), it may be possible to enlist an older, more sophisticated student as a model and instructor. In other situations, a same-aged peer already skilled in the target behavior could play this role. However, close supervision by the teacher is necessary in either case. Whenever possible, it is desirable to involve a peer as a model and facilitator in the teaching process similar to the teaching routine used in the sign language example described above. This is an ideal teaching situation, particularly for teaching complex social skills. Involving a peer or peers (i.e., special helpers) can also facilitate the transfer of learned behavior from the private teaching situation to other school settings.

Often such transfer is assumed rather than documented as having occurred. As a general rule, skills and behaviors taught in this manner within a private setting require follow-up monitoring, support, and prompting to ensure that they occur in natural settings.

VERBAL FEEDBACK

Providing children and youth with verbal feedback regarding their actions is a time-honored tradition of both teaching and parenting. Aside from being a useful reminder of behavioral appropriateness or inappropriateness, it helps children learn to become more aware of their behavior and its effects on others. Thus, it provides the means for changing course if needed.

Definition and Examples of Verbal Feedback

Verbal feedback refers to the process of giving students direct information about the appropriateness or inappropriateness of their classroom behavior or academic performance. Teachers rely heavily on verbal feedback in teaching academic concepts, managing the classroom, and providing necessary corrections. Precorrections, cueing, prompting, coaching, providing second chances to get the right answer, and debriefing are all examples of feedback that helps learning. Computer-assisted instruction makes use of instantaneous feedback to facilitate the acquisition of new concepts and skills.

Verbal feedback is used constantly by teachers in managing student behavior. Feedback can be positive, negative, or neutral. Unfortunately, many teachers are more likely to reprimand inappropriate behavior than praise or give neutral feedback regarding inappropriate behavior. Many studies have shown that such reprimands and negative attention can increase rates of the problem behavior to which they are applied due to the teacher attention and engagement that they provide (Walker & Buckley, 1973; Morgan & Jenson, 1988).

Feedback to a student that communicates essential information but does not involve criticism might look like the following: "Sarah, you attempted all the problems in the assignment. Excellent! Can you help me find the mistakes in just the three problems you missed?" or "Freddie and Andy, I'd like you to focus on the assignment now. You can finish your discussion in between class periods or at recess or lunch." The latter is a form of redirecting student behavior that is not negative or critical but is quite clear. Being neutral or even positive in this process is extremely important.

Guidelines for Correct Application of Verbal Feedback

The now classic research of Brophy and Good (1986) and their associates casts a revealing light on the role that teacher expectations of students can play in their interactions with students when they provide verbal feedback on academic performance. This research was reviewed in the preface to this volume and shows that high-expectation students tend to receive more praise, cues, prompts, and second chances than the class average, and low-expectation students in the same classroom receive fewer instances of the latter on average. The behavioral expression of such different expectations communicates low esteem, deprives students who need assistance the most, and can limit their academic performance. It should be noted that this practice does not characterize all teachers by any means. Many teachers make it a point to be aware of and control the formation and expression of such different expectations in their student interactions.

The following are some general guidelines for providing verbal feedback.

1. Corrective feedback should be given immediately, or as soon as possible following a student's completion of assigned academic tasks.
2. The feedback should be as positive as possible and focus on what the student needs to do.
3. Feedback should be delivered so the student learns something and the chances are increased that a correct response will be given in a similar subsequent situation.
4. Correct responses should be confirmed with behavior-specific praise.
5. For incorrect responses, the teacher should communicate in a nonpunitive way that the answer is incorrect and the student should be given another chance to supply the answer with prompts provided as appropriate.

Issues to Consider When Using Verbal Feedback

If used correctly, verbal feedback can be a valuable tool in helping students acquire complex academic skills and concepts. However, verbal feedback can be a trap for the teacher when used in managing student behavior; over the long term this can potentially do more harm than good, especially with disruptive, oppositional students.

Reprimands that accompany terminating commands of a public nature are the usual method in trying to manage the inappropriate behavior of these students. However, reprimands rarely work effectively and can open the door to hostile student–teacher confrontations. Minor behaviors that are not disruptive but are irritating should be ignored whenever possible. More serious problem behavior should be dealt with via redirection, where the teacher communicates what they want the student to do. Attempted redirection can also prompt a hostile response with an agitated student but is more effective than reprimands, which have likely been heard so often by these students from parents and teachers that they have little beneficial effect. Further, the negative attention they provide can actually strengthen and reinforce the behavior they are designed to stop or reduce.

The timing and delivery of redirection attempts using verbal feedback are critical. For academic performance, the feedback to individual students should be private and as immediate as possible as to correctness.

For redirection of maladaptive behavior, the feedback should not be public; other students should not be able to hear what is being said. Also, the redirection should focus on what the teacher wants the student to do rather than what they should stop doing.

SELF-MONITORING AND SELF-CONTROL

The ultimate goal of an externally managed behavioral intervention is to transfer its control and management to a self-monitoring and self-control regimen managed by the individual student. This process makes it more likely that the target student will have a greater investment in sustaining the gains achieved.

Definition and Examples of Self-Monitoring and Self-Control

Self-monitoring requires that aspects of one's behavior or performance be systematically counted and recorded by the target individual. Three student examples that are typically addressed by self-monitoring are as follows: process measures (e.g., paying attention, being socially engaged with others), counts of discrete events (e.g., number of social bids made to others, number of times a newly taught social skill is used at recess), or by-products of one's performance (e.g., percentage of math problems completed correctly, number of pages read). Lloyd, Landrum, and Hallahan (1991) reported a procedure in which a student was prompted regularly during academic periods to stop, reflect, and record at the sound of a tape-recorded beep. At the sound of the beep, the student asked himself, "Was I paying attention?" He then marked *yes* or *no* on a form placed on his desk. Cueing systems such as this are especially helpful for younger students in learning to self-record.

Elementary-school-age students can learn how to count the number of occurrences of target behaviors as they occur, to rate the quality of their performance after it occurs, and to graph the products or results of their performance so they can gauge their progress. Simple golf wrist counters have been a popular way for children to record forms of their behavior that involve counts (e.g., number of turns taken, number of social bids initiated/received). The student simply counts and records each occurrence of the target behavior as it occurs throughout a time period. For this recording to work, the target behavior must be discrete in nature and have a start and end point.

As part of self-monitoring and evaluation, students can be asked to judge their overall performance following its occurrence. For example, at the end of a period the target student can make a judgment on a Likert 1–5 or 1–7 rating scale regarding the quality or effectiveness of their just completed performance. A rating of 1 would be very poor and well below average, and a rating of 5 would be very good and well above average. As a way to teach accuracy in making judgments, the teacher can also rate the student's performance for the period and compare ratings. Bonus points could be awarded for accuracy. This procedure can help the student learn to make realistic judgments.

In an ingenious use of self-recording and self-evaluation, Rhode, Morgan, and Jensen (1983) successfully promoted the transfer of behavior gains, achieved in a resource room, for the same students when they were subsequently assigned to a general education classroom. Prior to their new placement, the students were taught to judge their own behavior and to use self-evaluation and self-recording tools to do so. They rated their own performance daily, as did their general education teacher, and compared their ratings with the teacher's. They received bonus points for matching the teacher's rating. This matching procedure was gradually phased out until they were judging their own behavior and awarding themselves points accordingly. This was a very successful demonstration of self-evaluation and self-management of student behavior in a challenging task—preserving gains within a new classroom placement.

There are numerous examples that can be cited of this effective and valuable tool. It is highly recommended as a way of sensitizing students to their own behavior, teaching them to make accurate and realistic self-evaluations, and managing their behavior more effectively.

Guidelines for Correct Application of Self-Monitoring and Self-Control

Self-monitoring/self-control is a very useful strategy in making students more sensitive to their own behavior in relation to standards of behavior for others, in producing changes in relatively mild forms of problem behavior (e.g., low academic engagement, noncompliance with teacher commands, minor disruptions), and for facilitating the transfer and durability of achieved intervention effects within and across settings.

The following general guidelines should be considered in using this approach.

- The self-monitoring and self-control process and its purpose should be thoroughly explained to the target student.
- The student's active cooperation in making it work should be sought. Presenting it as a fun partnership between student and teacher can be helpful.
- After explaining the intervention, have the student practice observing, recording, and evaluating their behavior and/or performance. Ask the student if they would like to self-award their earned points.

- Ensure that the target student thoroughly understands the process and how it works.
- Consider arranging home rewards for earned points and provide regular communication with parents regarding the intervention's effects.
- Hold a daily debriefing session with the student about their behavior, and fine-tune the system as needed.
- Use the student–teacher "matching" feature to teach the student how to make accurate performance appraisals.
- Once the student has mastered the process, begin phasing out some of its external features (i.e., cues, prompts, reminders) and transfer as much control to the student as possible while still maintaining behavioral gains.

Issues to Consider in Using Self-Monitoring and Self-Control

Children with challenging behavior patterns have well-developed habits of resisting adult influence and are often inured to the social impact of their behavior on others. Self-monitoring and self-control interventions can reduce these problems by providing opportunities for students to work proactively with adults in shaping their behavior toward desirable outcomes. However, this approach should not be used to address severely disruptive and aggressive forms of behavior. As a general rule, adult-controlled and -managed interventions are necessary to successfully address such problems.

Students should also be held accountable for making accurate and honest self-judgments when using this approach. Teaching them realistic self-appraisal through teacher monitoring of the same behavior they themselves are monitoring is very important.

CONTINGENCY CONTRACTS

A contingency contract is a useful procedure for teaching responsibility and accountability for schoolwork. It is easy to implement and widely used.

Definition and Examples of Contingency Contracts

A contingency contract is typically a two-party agreement between a teacher and student that sometimes includes parents. It specifies the role each participant will play in achieving a certain goal—usually of an academic nature. It may also specify positive consequences for one or both parties for meeting the contract's terms. Its goal is to individualize rules and expectations as well as consequences for meeting them.

In this procedure, the teacher evaluates the student's behavior or academic performance at regular intervals during the school day, provides feedback as appropriate, and makes an overall judgment regarding whether the terms of the contract have been met. If so, the teacher praises the student and signs a Good Day Card for them to take home. Figure 13.2 is an example of a contingency contract.

A contingency contract can specify a series of behaviors, tasks, or terms that a student must meet or it can be built around a single behavior or task. The contract in Figure 13.2 deals only with a series of behaviors that facilitate the student's academic performance and clearly specifies the teacher's expectations.

Guidelines for Correct Application of Contingency Contracts

The terms of the contract should be negotiated with the student and should be fair and reasonable. The outcome of following the contract should be specified within it and the student's ability to meet the contract's requirements should be carefully monitored. If the terms are not met for 2 or 3 days in a row, the requirements may be too difficult and need to be readjusted. Backup outcomes for meeting the contract's requirements should also be evaluated regularly and varied as necessary.

Issues to Consider in Using Contingency Contracts

There appear to be no deleterious risks associated with the use of contingency contracts to motivate students to achieve and behave better. A primary caution would be that they are not complex and are agreeable to the student and/or parents, who can be an important resource in their effectiveness.

SOCIAL SKILLS TRAINING

The quality of one's social relationships has a great deal to do with school success and with general quality of life. In school, students are required to negotiate two critically important social relationships: one with teachers (*teacher-related*) and one with peers (*peer-related*). Failure in one of these relationships carries personal risk but failure in both puts one's school success at risk. Long-term studies show that students who fail to make these adjustments early in their school careers experience a host of problems and a lower quality of life in their development (Parker & Asher, 1987). While systematic social skills training (SST) can be successful within any grade level, it is most effective when it occurs early on in a student's schooling (Walker, 1995). Over the past several decades, substantial interest has

_____ **agrees to do the following:**
    (Student Name)

1. Listen to instructions from the teacher   _____
2. Complete schoolwork accurately and on time   _____
3. Follow teacher directions   _____
4. Take part in class discussions   _____
5. Raise hand when asking a question or needing help   _____
6. Cooperate with peers in group activities   _____
7. Comply with teacher corrections   _____

                                       (total)   _____

The teacher agrees to:

1. Check _____'s behavior/performance at regular intervals during the school day and give feedback.
2. Award a check mark if _____ has shown good student behavior and work during the school day.
3. Sign a Good Day Card if five of seven check marks are earned at the end of the day.

Consequence
At the end of the school day, the teacher reviews _____'s performance during the school day and awards a check mark for each behavior that was satisfactory.

If _____ earns five or more check marks for the school day, the teacher signs a Good Day Card to take home that can be exchanged for a special privilege.

FIGURE 13.2. Example of a contingency contract. From _Solutions to Critical Behavioral Issues in the Classroom_ by Hill M. Walker. Copyright © 2023 The Guilford Press. Permission to photocopy this material is granted to purchasers of this book for personal use or use with students (see copyright page for details). Purchasers can download enlarged versions of this material (see the box at the end of the table of contents).

developed among educators in addressing the social effectiveness of K–12 students. Many see SST as a viable means to improve schooling outcomes by addressing students' social skills deficits.

Definition and Examples of SST

Systematic SST refers to the teaching of social skills that contribute to school success and improve social effectiveness. In a widely referenced reformulation of the social skills concept, McFall (1982) clarified the relationship between social skills and social effectiveness. In his definition, social competence refers to an overall judgment or perception by others about someone's social effectiveness. Social skills, in turn, are the basis that others use for making this judgment. Thus, one who has good social skills is likely to be perceived as socially effective and vice versa.

The following social skills are most commonly prioritized by teachers and support teacher-related adjustment.

- Complies promptly with teacher directives and commands
- Makes assistance needs known appropriately
- Cooperates with others
- Works independently
- Focuses and sustains attention on academic tasks
- Responds to teacher corrections
- Displays self-control
- Participates in small- and large-group instructional arrangements

In a similar vein, the social skills that are essential for successful peer-related adjustment and peer acceptance as indicated by peers are:

- Positively initiates with others
- Knows how to make friends
- Displays high rates of positive behavior toward peers
- Uses low-risk tactics in joining ongoing peer activities (does not interrupt activity, hovers and waits for invite)
- Achieves athletically and academically
- Has a sense of humor
- Avoids getting in trouble with teacher
- Is helpful to peers

These skills were identified in a national survey of K–12 students and are reported in Walker (1986) as well as reviewed in the preface to this book. There are a wide range of social skills curricula and instructional programs available for teaching these important skills, and a number of reviews of the curricula and approaches have been reported in professional literature (Cook et al., 2008; Gresham, Mai, & Cook, 2006; Park, 2017).

Systematic SST is part of a cohesive evidence base on social–emotional learning that has developed over the past four decades (Durlak, Domitrovich, Weissberg, & Gullotta, 2015). A large number of studies have been conducted on its effectiveness in improving teacher and peer relationships in schooling. Reviews of this research show that SST produces moderate treatment outcomes for general education students and at-risk subgroups (Gresham et al., 2006). However, research also shows that treatment effects vanish in follow-up studies unless steps are taken to monitor and support their transfer to natural settings and to sustain them within the intervention setting (DuPaul & Eckert, 1994).

My colleagues and I developed an example of a social skills curriculum for K–6 students. This SST program is called *ACCEPTS: A Curriculum for Children's Effective Peer and Teacher Skills* and is based on principles of direct instruction (Walker et al., 1983). It has 28 skills distributed across five areas as follows: (1) classroom skills, (2) getting along skills, (3) basic interaction skills, (4) making friends skills, and (5) coping skills. These skill areas are designed to address the two most important relationships students have in school: with teachers and with peers. This program can be taught in individual, small-group, and large-group formats, with small-group instruction being the most feasible and easiest to implement. ACCEPTS is suitable for use within regular and specialized school contexts.

A basic rule is taught for each skill in the ACCEPTS program. For example, for the skill of joining others, the rule is "Say your name and ask to play." Using provided teaching scripts and guidelines, students are taught how to do this using the following nine steps.

1. Define and discuss the basic skill rule.
2. Provide a positive skill example (video).
3. Provide a negative or non-example of the skill.
4. Review and restate the skill's definition.
5. Provide a second positive example.
6. Conduct teaching activities.
7. Provide a third positive example.
8. Conduct criterion role plays.
9. Implement an informal contracting procedure.

This teaching routine is repeated for each of the 28 ACCEPTS skills.

Guidelines for Correct Applications of SST

The most effective application of SST is when it is combined with behavioral contingencies that support the integration of newly acquired skills into a student's ongoing behavior pattern. Walker, Schwarz, Nippold, Irvin, and Noell (1994) developed a list of cardinal rules and guidelines for conducting SST from which the following skills list is adapted.

- Social skills should be taught as academic subject matter using instructional procedures identical to those for teaching basic academic content (e.g., math, reading, and language).
- When possible, social skills should be *directly* taught along with possible variations in their appropriate application.
- The critical test of SST is their functional integration into a student's behavioral repertoire and their demonstration within natural settings like the playground.

- Both the social context and situational factors influence the use of social skills and must be taken into account systematically.
- SST procedures are not an effective intervention for complex or severe behavior problems and disorders. They should not be used alone to remediate aggressive or severe disruptive behavior patterns.
- SST can complement the use of behavioral reduction techniques, as it teaches adaptive alternatives to maladaptive behavior.
- To be effective, SST must be accompanied by provision of response opportunities, feedback, and incentives within natural settings.
- There are two types of deficits in social–emotional behavior: skill deficits (can't do) and performance deficits (won't do). They should be treated differently, as skill deficits require instruction and performance deficits require behavioral incentives since the individual can already demonstrate the skill.

Adherence to the above guidelines in conducting SST will do a great deal to enhance its success. However, additional considerations are necessary: These include investing adequate time in the initial training process; ensuring that the SST teaching process is of sufficient duration; and using coaching and other strategies to help ensure that initial skills mastery is incorporated into students' ongoing behavior patterns, persists over time, and transfers to natural settings (e.g., the playground and other peer-controlled settings).

Gresham, Mai, and Cook (2006) reported that on average SST sessions last approximately 2.5 to 3 hours per week over a 10- to 12-week period. They suggest this time investment is insufficient for remediating long-term deficits and recommend doubling it in order to achieve satisfactory effects. Further, their study demonstrated superior treatment outcomes of SST by selecting students for their small-group training who shared similar social skills deficits, which allows greater streamlining of instructional procedures. A similar SST approach has been recommended by LaGreca and Mesibov (1979) and is considered a best practice. Helping enhance the durability of SST gains and facilitating their transfer to natural settings are very important issues and are discussed in the next section. In addition, a more complete description of such strategies for sustaining generic treatment outcomes are described in Chapter 15.

Issues to Consider in Conducting SST

As noted, the "gold standard" of effectiveness for applied interventions is whether their effects are sustainable and transfer to natural school settings. Addressing this issue, DuPaul and Eckert (1994) conducted an important study of the generalization of social skills effects from curricular programs implemented in the classroom to natural school settings. The investigators evaluated seven SST programs in relation to these outcomes and found that the least effective strategy was the "train and hope" strategy that often occurs, where systematic SST training is implemented with the effects expected to persist automatically over time and spontaneously transfer to other settings.

The combination of SST and the alteration of consequences (i.e., providing incentives to use the skills) led to the most significant maintenance of results. The most effective programs were those that used the greatest diversity of techniques during SST, including role playing, monitoring, providing incentives to use the skills, coaching, and prompting. These techniques facilitated the integration and demonstration of the skills being taught. This study provides an important lesson on what we can expect regarding the sustainability of social skills taught in school settings.

The foregoing material on enhancing students' desirable behavior can be very useful if the described techniques are implemented according to best-practice guidelines for teaching and sustaining target behaviors and skills. Increasing a student's adaptive classroom and playground behavior should always be a first option in dealing with students who have challenging behavior. However, for severely challenging behavior it may be necessary to also implement behavioral reduction techniques at the same time. These techniques are discussed in Chapter 14.

CHAPTER 13 TAKEAWAYS

- As a rule, students respond better to positive behavior-change strategies that encourage them to behave appropriately as opposed to negative strategies that discourage their inappropriate behavior.

- Praise and positive reinforcement can be highly effective behavior-change strategies if used correctly.

- The ultimate goal of behavior management is to have students learn to regulate and control their own behavior.

- The use of positive behavior-improvement strategies takes longer to work than do negative strategies but they produce fewer side effects in the teacher–student relationship over the long term.

- Teaching primary grade level, and above, students to self-monitor and manage their behavior can yield many benefits for the student, such as making them more aware of their behavior and its effects on others and helping generalize their improved behavior to non-intervention settings.

- For severe forms of challenging behavior that prove resistant to ordinary behavior management procedures, it may be necessary to involve parents and to develop a joint, school–home behavior-improvement plan.

CHAPTER 14

How to Decrease Undesirable Student Behavior

This chapter describes techniques for reducing undesirable or challenging forms of student behavior in school. With rare exceptions, these techniques should not be applied in isolation. Whenever feasible, they should be implemented in concert with positive strategies for increasing desirable, appropriate behavior so the focus is not just on a student's negative behavior. The exception to this rule would involve a student whose normal behavior pattern is positive and appropriate but is involved in something that requires a brief time-out or suspension.

Some behavioral reduction strategies, such as time-out, response cost (i.e., fines), or loss of privileges are commonly referred to as mild punishment procedures because they are designed to discourage the behavior to which they are applied. They focus on challenging behavior that cannot be dealt with effectively by nonpunitive techniques such as ignoring, debriefing, or stimulus change. Behavioral reduction strategies should be reserved for moderate to severe forms of challenging behavior that prove unresponsive to positive intervention techniques such as those described in Chapter 13. The behavioral reduction techniques described in this chapter are accompanied by discussion of correct application guidelines and critical issues to consider in their use.

DEBRIEFING BEHAVIORAL ALTERNATIVES

Debriefing is a positive strategy for helping students understand why they behave as they do in the face of clear information about what they should do differently, and for clarifying how they can do better going forward. It is especially important for use with antisocial and aggressive students who often resort to coercive strategies as a way of navigating their social environments and dealing with conflicts—particularly with peers (Patterson et al., 1992; Walker, Sprague, & Severson, 2016). These students suffer from a limited ability to consider different ways to deal with situations when their preferred strategies (coercion or escalation) fail. Being able to do so is a critically important social skill.

Definition and Examples of Debriefing

Debriefing is a strategy that addresses both intervention and prevention goals. It is typically used in school contexts following incidents of challenging behavior that involve classroom disruptions and/or peer conflicts in settings not controlled by adults, such as hallways, playgrounds, and so forth. However, a recognized good parenting practice is to debrief with children about the school day, discussing what was good as well as how they handled any difficult situations. This is an excellent method for teaching children how to develop alternatives when a preferred strategy or a natural reactive response does not work. Appendix 3 contains a short tutorial on how to conduct debriefings of this type.

Debriefing following an incident of challenging behavior allows the teacher to reconnect with the student in private and to problem-solve alternative ways of behaving. Doing so can help repair any relationship damage that may have occurred. This strategy allows a reboot of sorts that can be very useful in reestablishing peer relationships (e.g., after a bullying incident).

Guidelines for Correct Application of Debriefing

In school settings, a debriefing session can take the form of a teacher–student interaction or discussion and can include behavioral rehearsal and role-playing of possible alternatives. It may include homework assignments depending on the grade level of the student. The following are critical steps in the debriefing process (PENT, n.d.):

1. Reviewing and understanding the incident that prompted the debriefing
2. Repairing the relationship damage that occurred
3. Identifying and/or role-playing an agreed-on behavioral alternative
4. Developing a plan for how to handle the problem situation better next time

The following case study illustrates how the debriefing of a playground bullying situation was conducted by a school psychologist (Ms. Gonzales).

It involved a problem-solving dialogue between the bully (Billy), the victimized student (Darrin), and two peers (Carl and Owen) who witnessed the incident.

CASE STUDY: DEBRIEFING A BULLYING SITUATION

Darrin was a sixth-grade student in Mr. Knox's classroom. He was a socially unskilled student who often had clumsy interactions with peers. He ranked in the bottom third of his class in popularity and suffered from a slight but noticeable articulation disorder for which he was seeing a speech and language therapist. Billy was an aggressive student with a short temper. He was the source of numerous angry exchanges with peers over the rules of recess activities. His best friends were other students with challenging behavior. Carl and Owen were good students who were liked and respected by peers.

Debriefing Dialogue

Ms. Gonzales convenes the group in her office and opens the discussion as follows:

Ms. GONZALES: Hi, everyone. Thank you for participating in this session today to review yesterday's playground incident between Billy and Darrin. Our goal today is to understand what happened, repair any damage that occurred, and to develop a plan going forward that avoids a repeat of this situation. Now, Darrin, would you tell us how it started and what happened?

DARRIN: A group of us were playing kickball at recess. Billy was not playing in the game but he came up, grabbed the ball, and tried to throw it so the ball would hit me in the head when my back was turned.

Ms. GONZALES: Thank you, Darrin. Is there anything you want to add?

DARRIN: Yes, I asked him why he did it and called him a name. Then he shoved me and asked if I wanted to do anything about it. He's bigger than I am so I said no but asked him not to do it again.

Ms. GONZALES: Owen and Carl. Is that right? Do you want to add anything else? (*Both Carl and Owen say that Darrin was accurate in his account of what happened.*) We want to know what happened but also why it happened. Billy, can you tell us why you threw the ball at Darrin the way you did?

BILLY: I didn't get asked to play kickball and I think Darrin had something to do with it.

Ms. GONZALES: Is that true, Darrin?

DARRIN: No, I had nothing to do with whether he was asked to play or not. But I'm not surprised he wasn't invited since he always argues about the rules and insists that his way is right.

(*Carl and Owen agree with Darrin's explanation but say Darrin shouldn't have called Billy a name.*)

Ms. GONZALES: Thanks to each of you for your honesty. Billy, you should know that displaying your anger as you did against Darrin when you had no proof that he was involved was not right. You made the situation worse by asking him if he wanted to do anything about it. And Darrin, it was wrong of you to call Billy a name. Asking him why he threw the ball at you and telling him not to do it again, as you did, was a better way to handle things.

(*Carl and Owen both say that they told Billy he was wrong to act as he did but that Darrin shouldn't have called him a name.*)

Ms. GONZALES: So how do we move forward from here? Any suggestions?

CARL: I think Billy should apologize to Darrin for falsely accusing him and acting as he did.

Ms. GONZALES: Billy, what do you think about that? Would you expect an apology if you were Darrin?

BILLY: I guess so, but I still don't know if he wanted me to play kickball or not. (*Apologizes.*)

Ms. GONZALES: Good, Billy. This is a first step toward making things better between you. So, what can we learn from this situation? First, Billy got angry and he expressed his anger the wrong way by trying to hurt Darrin with the ball. Second, physical retaliation is never the right way to act when one feels wronged. Third, it's best to confront someone when you feel you've been wronged and get their side of things. Often, it's a matter of poor communication and misinterpretation of someone's intentions.

So how do we make sure this doesn't happen again? What do you think, Billy?

BILLY: I guess I need to learn how to handle my anger better.

OWEN: It would help too if you didn't assume the worst in others when you think you've been wronged.

Ms. GONZALES: Very good, Billy and Owen. You're both right! Billy, in the future, if you need help with any situation that concerns you, feel free to talk with me or the school counselor about it before taking action. OK? Thank you all for your participation. I think we made some good progress today.

In debriefing, it is important to have students be held accountable for their actions, to minimize blame in the process, and to develop a prevention plan in going forward. This case study covers the four critical steps mentioned above for conducting a debriefing session.

Issues to Consider in Using Debriefing

Debriefing is a valuable tool for getting at why a challenging behavior incident occurred and for teaching students to consider alternatives before acting on their initial impulses. It is a nonpunitive technique but requires restraint in assigning blame within situations such as bullying, harassment, aggression, and teacher defiance where students need to be held accountable for their actions. Students should come away from debriefing with a clear idea of how they could have handled things better or differently.

REDIRECTING STUDENT BEHAVIOR OR PERFORMANCE

Guided redirection of a child's behavior is a form of discipline intended to redirect behavior from inappropriate to appropriate. It is a time-honored strategy that parents use to protect children and prevent them from getting into trouble, and sometimes must be physically guided with very young children. As a usual practice, it is preferable to the use of loud reprimands such as "No!" or "Stop It!" unless the child is in imminent danger of injury. In schooling, redirection is preferred as a tool in dealing with inappropriate behavior whenever possible. It is a step up from ignoring in its likely effects in encouraging behavior change.

Definition and Examples of Redirecting Student Behavior

In schooling, redirection is a proactive management strategy used to address challenging behavior that interferes with learning and productive teacher or peer interactions. Redirection maximizes academic engagement for individual students as well as the class as a whole. Redirection lets the student know what they're doing wrong in a few words and quickly points the way toward correcting the situation. It changes a negative situation into a positive one through the appropriate use of teacher language. The following are some examples of redirection.

- "Sarah, I see you are not working on the assignment. How can I help you with your work?"
- "Frank, I'd like you and Jason to focus on your joint task assignment now."
- "Peter, please put your smartphone away and work on your math problems now."
- "Brian, I want you to stop pestering Jon so he can concentrate."
- "Willie, it's time for you to get to work."

Guidelines for Correct Application of Redirecting Student Behavior

Respectful, positive redirection asks a student to stop what they are doing and to do what's called for in the situation. The language used should be neutral to positive and clearly point the student in the correct direction.

Redirection strategies are incorporated into the PBIS program (PBIS, 2021). Some PBIS guidelines for using this strategy are:

1. Provide students with a quick reminder of what they should be doing and the rule(s) governing the focus activity.
2. Limit the redirection to one student at a time.
3. Give the redirection and continue on with your teaching. Don't wait for a student comment or response to your directive.
4. Be clear and concise with your redirection statement.
5. Make your redirection to the point.
6. Consider also using nonverbal redirection such as eye contact, physical gestures, and proximity control.
7. Deliver the redirection privately while standing in close proximity to the student. Avoid calling out redirections to individual students but consider using them for the entire classroom if needed.

Consider Using Reinforcing, Reminding, and Redirecting Teacher Language in Managing Student Behavior

A useful concept in verbally managing student behavior is for the teacher to pay careful attention to their language. The teacher's tone and messaging are very powerful influences for most students. The Responsive Classroom is an evidence-based program that incorporates three different types of teacher language for positively influencing student behavior: reinforcing language, reminding language, and redirecting language (Rimm-Kauffman et al., 2012). These three language types have considerable utility in managing teacher–student interactions effectively.

Reinforcing language refers to focusing on a student's strengths and what they do well, and avoiding criticism and negative feedback whenever possible. It involves having high expectations for all students while recognizing the individual differences that exist among them. It highlights not only a student's academic performance but also the student's effort and attitudes. The use of behavior-specific praise is very important in this regard.

Reminding language is used for problem student behavior for which ignoring is not feasible because it will likely not lead to cessation of the behavior (e.g., not engaging an assignment, disrupting a cooperative learning group). These student reminders function much like "precorrections" and are designed to prevent errors or problem behavior early in their trajectory. They are especially helpful for less skilled students for whom lower performance expectations are held. Calmly using positive, supportive language should be the norm in their use.

Redirecting language is called for when students engage in behavior that could be harmful to themselves or others or disrupts the classroom.

The language should be neutral in tone but direct and specific regarding the activity being targeted, and it requires follow-through to see that the student complies with the directive. If the student resists the redirection, they should be asked to reflect on why their behavior was redirected. However, it is important that this request be brief and not come across as a lecture.

These three types of teacher language apply respectively to student behavior that is reinforceable, neutral, and challenging. Thus, they provide tools for comprehensively managing teacher–student interactions productively. Their use is highly recommended.

Issues to Consider When Redirecting Student Behavior

Teacher redirection of a student's behavioral or academic performance is a proactive strategy with many benefits that can prevent the development of severe problems by catching them early in their trajectory. It is not a form of punishment, but there are risks to its use with agitated students having challenging behavior. Teacher redirection with such students can sometimes lead to teacher defiance and, in a worst-case scenario, necessitate a room clear—a last resort for use in managing an out-of-control student who poses a safety risk to their classmates and teacher.

The risk of the attempted redirection leading to teacher defiance should always be taken into account when using this strategy. Thus, the redirection's timing, tone, and form of delivery (i.e., private versus public) should be carefully considered. Reinforcing and reminding language should also be used with such students as feasible to help strengthen the teacher–student relationship and lower the risk of escalation.

STIMULUS CHANGE

One of the most efficient ways to effect behavior change is to alter the conditions or events that stimulate occurrence of a deficit or behavior of concern. Stimulus change is based on the premise that desirable behavior change can be achieved by altering the relationship between a stimulus and the resulting behavior or performance prompted by it. Stimulus change is a proactive, nonpunitive way of preventing problem behavior and resolving difficult situations.

Definition and Examples of Stimulus Change

Stimulus change requires that an assessment of the student's behavior or performance be conducted and analyzed to identify possible controlling stimuli. Once a likely controlling stimulus is identified, it can be altered to see if it changes the resulting target behavior of concern. Sometimes multiple stimuli prompt and control the same deficit or behavior. For example, a student who is frequently noncompliant with teacher directives may be doing so for a variety of reasons: They may not fully understand the directives because they are too vague, complex, unclear, or are accompanied by mini lectures that reflect the teacher's frustration. Another possibility is that the student has a comprehension problem due to a hearing impairment. A third possibility is that the student has been allowed to comply only haphazardly with parental directives at home and this behavior pattern generalizes to the teacher.

In these examples, stimulus change would involve determining the most likely causal factor and ruling out others. For instance, if an audiology exam revealed a hearing deficit in certain sound ranges, that could be the cause. If a hearing aid led to a marked reduction in noncompliance rates, then this stimulus change would be validated. In contrast, if there were no change in the rate of noncompliance, then other possibilities would need to be considered, such as using alpha rather than beta commands in directing the student's behavior.

Another example involves a young student experiencing severe reading problems, who will likely be referred to a reading specialist if the teacher is unable to identify the cause. If after a diagnostic/prescriptive evaluation of the child's reading the specialist discovers the student has no knowledge of phonics, that would be a likely cause of the reading difficulty. Provided that an intensive training program in phonics were developed and applied to the child's reading, and was associated with improved reading over time, it is likely that a lack of phonics knowledge would account for the reading problems.

Yet another example is of a teacher who gives vague, poorly organized instructions for assignments. As a result, many students are confused, request clarification, and end up doing assignments incorrectly. The teacher then streamlines instructions and directions for each assignment, dramatically reducing the rate of confusion about assignments; the frequency of follow-up clarification questions decreases and the number of students completing their assignments correctly increases. The changed stimulus conditions in this instance were the likely cause of the improvement in student outcomes.

It should be noted that the variables changed in each of the above examples were not absolutely established as the cause of the changes observed. However, it is very likely that they were, as demonstrated by the stimulus change results.

Guidelines for Correct Application of Stimulus Change

The successful use of stimulus change requires an analysis of potential causal factors and the selection of one that potentially prompts the behavior of concern, followed by a demonstration as to whether that is actually the case. This process is called the *functional analysis of behavior* and is the bedrock tool of applied behavior analysts who are expert at analyzing problem behavior and its causes. Understanding and being able to conduct such an analysis is an invaluable skill for the classroom teacher.

Functional Behavioral Analysis

In the past several decades, the scientific study of behavior has produced an approach that allows for the functional behavioral analysis (FBA) of deficits and problem behavior. FBA allows for understanding the nature and causes of problem behavior, and developing cost-effective interventions for changing or reducing that behavior. A classic treatment of this topic was contributed by O'Neill, Horner, Albin, Storey, and Sprague (1990). There are hundreds of studies in the professional literature that demonstrate the efficacy of this technique.

FBA has three main goals: (1) to describe the deficit performance or problem behavior, (2) to predict the occasions or times in which the behavior of interest is and is not likely to occur, and (3) to identify and define the functional purpose the problem behavior serves. The following strategies are used to achieve these goals. First, an interview of the student and a profile analysis are conducted of possible causal factors (i.e., interviews of peers and/or parents, review of school history, analysis of school records). Based on this information, the most likely causal factor(s) is identified and a process is initiated for its validation or confirmation. Figure 14.1 is a sample form that can be used for collecting information about the behavior of interest. This form provides useful information about critical features of the problem behavior and conditions surrounding its occurrence that can be used in an FBA.

Next, the target behavior is monitored and tracked to identify its situational variations and to find out what maintains it (i.e., what specific purpose does the behavior serve?). As a general rule, the problem behavior serves one of two purposes: to obtain something of value or produce a desired effect, or to escape or avoid something. Therefore we speak of attention-seeking and escape-motivated forms of behavior. Two questions should be asked in this regard: What does the behavior get or produce for the student, and what condition or event does it allow the student to avoid. These are powerful motivators and maintain large amounts of problem behavior. To successfully change problem behavior, its primary purpose or goal must be identified and changed.

Finally, an optional component of FBA is to systematically manipulate the conditions surrounding the problem behavior and certify that they are

Target behavior	Intensity of the behavior	Frequency	Duration	Where?	Context or cause
Shoving and hitting peers	High	2–3 times daily	5–10 seconds	Recess	Arguing about game rules

FIGURE 14.1. Sample form for describing a problem behavior in FBA.

the maintaining variable(s) or causal agents. If a student's defiant behavior during certain instructional periods is suspected to be due to academic material that is too difficult, the teacher could vary the student's assigned material to test this presumption. If the teacher defiance is reduced during the period of easier assignments and covaries with reassignment of more difficult material, then it is likely that the student is engaging in escape-motivated behavior.

FBA is a valuable tool that allows teachers to understand, predict, and intervene successfully with student behavior problems and performance deficits. However, given the demands on teachers' time, conducting a full FBA is often beyond the scope of a teacher's responsibilities. If possible, teacher support staff such as behavioral coaches, school psychologists, or school counselors should be enlisted to assist the teacher in conducting an FBA.

Issues to Consider in Using Stimulus Change

In the process of teaching and managing a classroom, a teacher makes thousands of social comparisons among students and acquires extensive information about students' behavioral characteristics, capabilities, and factors that motivate and prompt students' actions. In collaborating with school support staff on conducting an FBA, the teacher's knowledge and perspective should be given paramount importance. As the teacher will likely be the implementing agent for an FBA intervention, their involvement in planning an FBA intervention is essential for its success. However, the time required in conducting a full FBA may be beyond the time limits of many teachers. Thus, collaboration in planning and conducting them is highly recommended.

The following case study illustrates how careful behavioral analysis can lead to a function-based intervention for reducing social isolation, increasing social participation, and making friends.

CASE STUDY: FROM SOCIAL ISOLATION TO SOCIAL INVOLVEMENT

Lydia was 7 years old and the youngest of five children. Early on, she was shy and showed signs of isolate behavior, preferring to play alone rather than with neighborhood children. She liked her siblings and got along well with them.

Lydia was in second grade and had no problems with her schoolwork. However, she was socially awkward, not popular with classmates, and had few friends. At recess she was often neglected and rarely participated in peer-controlled activities. Her teacher, Ms. Sumi, noticed this and decided to initiate an FBA of Lydia's low participation and peer contact to see if she could identify the source of her isolation. When Ms. Sumi asked Lydia about her low peer contact, Lydia said she would like more peer contact and to have friends but didn't know how to go about making them. When asked about games at recess, she said she was not invited to play them and didn't know their rules anyway.

Over several days, Ms. Sumi observed Lydia in the morning, noon, and afternoon recess periods to see if she could better understand the nature of Lydia's social behavior and peer relationships. Lydia spent most of her recess time alone and when she did interact with peers, it was clear she did not know how to initiate, respond to, or continue interactions with them: She was socially awkward and hesitant, and did not participate in any games over the three recess periods.

Ms. Sumi consulted the school psychologist about her observations, who confirmed them along with several additional observations. Together, they designed a three-pronged intervention for Lydia that (1) taught her the rules of games played at recess; (2) provided her with training and role playing in how to initiate to peers, respond to their initiations, and then continue the interaction; and (3) recruited some socially skilled peers to serve as special helpers for Lydia at recess. First, the teacher and some peer volunteers agreed to help teach Lydia the rules of the most-played games at recess. Discussion, role playing, and coaching were used in this process. Next, the teacher and school psychologist taught Lydia how to start, respond to, and continue social interactions with peers. Role playing with peer volunteers was again used in this training: For example, initiating an interaction would be, "Hi. I'm Lydia. Want to play?" A response to a peer initiation or request could be, "Yes, thanks. I'd love to," and continuing an interaction might be, "Want to climb on the jungle gym?" or "Can we try the seesaw?" Finally, the special peer helpers were recruited to serve as peer mentors for Lydia on the playground, to help her gain access to games and to coach and support her during the game.

The special peer helpers proved to be especially adept at helping Lydia learn and follow the rules of games, in getting her more involved with her peers, and in reducing her social isolation. When Lydia was not involved in a game or a peer interaction, they made sure she was not alone and would play with her. They used coaching strategies very skillfully in teaching Lydia to improve her skills in playing games and in her social interactions with peers. They had many other creative ways of getting her socially involved that they brought to the situation. Due to Lydia's cooperation, greater social involvement, and the special helpers' advocacy, support, and coaching, some of her classmates began seeking her out as a playmate and casual friend.

This intervention addressed the three conditions that seemed to be holding back Lydia's social involvement with her peers: not knowing the rules of popular games at recess and how to play them well; not being skilled in forging interactions with peers; and an absence of special peer helpers to mentor, support, and coach her. The stimulus change procedures implemented during the intervention for remediating these conditions proved very helpful in improving Lydia's social involvement. FBA analysis, planning, and implementation procedures identical to those used in this case study should be implemented with stimulus change for challenging, undesirable student behavior.

TIME-OUT

Time-out is a form of mild punishment that, when combined with positive management procedures, can be effective in reducing severe, undesirable behavior such as aggression, teacher defiance, tantrums, and classroom disruption. Despite its efficacy, the fact that it is a form of mild punishment makes it controversial. Time-out, as well as response cost—another mild punishment discussed later in this chapter—should only be considered for very serious forms of behavior that cannot be reduced to within normal limits using positive-only techniques such as those described in Chapter 13. Use of these two techniques requires careful planning and preparation (including prior parental consent) along with considerable skill and monitoring in their implementation.

Definition and Examples of Time-Out

Time-out is defined as a form of mild punishment in which a child is temporarily removed from a reinforcing situation immediately following the occurrence of some type of undesirable or inappropriate behavior. Time-out is based on the premise that removal from a reinforcing situation is unpleasant for the child and will discourage future occurrences of the behavior to which it is applied. It differs from ignoring in that ignoring removes a rewarding stimulus (e.g., adult attention) from a previously reinforced behavior, while time-out removes the child from a reinforcing situation. Both time-out and ignoring deny access to reinforcement.

Time-out generally involves removal from a reinforcing situation for anywhere from 3–30 minutes depending on the child's age and the inappropriate behavior to which it is applied. Time-out appears to be used more frequently with students in lower rather than higher school grades. It is certainly easier to use logistically with younger students.

Time-out can be thought of as part of a set of techniques for discouraging out-of-control student behavior. These techniques range from planned ignoring (withdrawal of teacher attention), to nonexclusion (passive time-out in place), to exclusion (removal from classroom activity), to isolation (physical removal from classroom), and finally to a room clear as a last resort (removal of all students from classroom except teacher and out of control student).

Time-out has a storied history as a parental means of socializing children and shaping them toward appropriate developmental behavior. It has been recommended by the American Academy of Pediatrics, the American Academy of Child and Adolescent Psychiatry, and the Centers for Disease Control and Prevention for use by parents in raising children. The dual advantage of time-out is that it interrupts and stops the problem behavior, and also reduces the likelihood that it will occur in the future. Decades of research on time-out show it has proven effective in both home and school settings when implemented correctly (Ortiz, 2018; Wolf, McLaughlin, & Williams, 2006). However, implementation of time-out in school is much more complicated than in the home setting due to a range of logistical and delivery issues.

Guidelines for Correct Application of Time-Out

As noted above, time-out should be reserved for student behavior that is challenging, severe, and cannot be tolerated, and that has been unresponsive to attempts to discourage or reduce its occurrence. Appropriate targets for time-out, for example, would be tantrums, classroom disruptions, and teacher defiance.

The first rule to consider in the correct application of time-out is that the setting or activities from which the child is removed must be reinforcing. If not, time-out will have only limited or no effect in reducing the target behavior to which it is applied. Secondly, if a student is so chronically disruptive or defiant of teacher authority that time-out has to be considered, the parents should be contacted and informed of this decision. This will allow them to have input in resolving the problem and opens up consideration of other options to deal with the situation. The principal should always be informed when time-out is used.

The third rule is that the area or place to which the child is removed should be supervised by the teacher but also be relatively uninteresting. In other words, time-out should not be an escape from an unpleasant situation nor should it be something to look forward to. Some teachers designate a quiet area of the classroom for time-out that may or may not be screened off with a partition. Taking along reading materials, objects to play with, or work assignments should not be allowed. However, an exception would be a child who asks to go to a quiet area temporarily to collect themselves or seeks an area free of distractions in which to better concentrate. If a student has to be isolated for a brief period, a chair placed just outside the classroom would likely serve this purpose well. The principal's office should be notified in this case. A student should never be placed in a closed space such as an adjoining closet. Some schools establish detention class-rooms to accommodate chronically challenging students who have diffi-culty tolerating a general classroom.

Finally, one needs to determine how long time-out will last. For young children, experts suggest 1 minute per year in age. Most commonly, studies in the professional literature have reported time-out periods from 3 to 15 minutes. Studies by Wolf and colleagues report that longer periods of time-out are no more effective in discouraging challenging behavior than are shorter periods. For young children (preschooler, kindergarten), a time-out period longer than 5 minutes does not generally result in additional efficacy (Wolf et al., 2006).

Some general guidelines for using time-out are provided next, followed by a procedure for time-out administration. These guidelines apply to both home and school settings.

- Select a place.
- Prepare the place.
- Explain the time-out procedure.
- Label the behavior that results in time-out.
- Be consistent.
- Remain calm when applying time-out.
- Use a timer.
- Have a backup plan if there is a refusal to go to time-out.

Administering Time-Out

1. *Label the problem behavior.* A simple statement such as "You didn't stop arguing: That's a time-out." is sufficient.
2. *Wait 10 seconds.* If the student refuses to enter time-out, imple-ment a backup plan such as contacting the principal's office.
3. *Set a timer or check your watch for passage of the time-out inter-val.*
4. *Control your anger.* Be respectful of the student's emotions and feelings.
5. *Remove yourself from the situation during time-out.*

6. *Remain neutral.* Disapproval of the student's behavior can be communicated but do not personally blame the student.
7. *Carry on with regular activities after time-out.*

Adherence to these time-out rules, guidelines, and administration procedures should maximize the efficacy of time-out and help minimize problems in its use.

Issues to Consider in Using Time-Out

There are some important issues to consider in preserving time-out's efficacy and safeguarding against its potential abuse in schools. A key issue in this regard concerns how the student is treated following time-out. It has been my experience that students tend to be ignored by their teachers for relatively long periods of time after emerging from time-out. This is likely due to teachers carrying residual anger due to the student's challenging behavior, as well as to a generally held belief that students should not be socially reinforced closely in the time following punishment. Thus the student's appropriate behavior following time-out may be ignored for too long and could eventually be extinguished. The student might then learn that the most reliable and consistent way to gain teacher attention, albeit negative, is to behave inappropriately.

Over past decades, there have been occasional episodes of time-out abuse by educators that have been profiled in the media. They have involved young students being detained within locked confines such as closets and other confined spaces. There is absolutely no excuse for such abuses. Time-out simply removes a student from an ongoing, reinforcing activity for a brief period of time and can be effective simply by separating a small classroom area with a portable screen. If a student becomes disruptive while in time-out, they can be removed to another area for the time-out, such as the front office or health room.

Finally, as noted above, the length of time a student spends in time-out is a critical issue that has often not been handled well. Time-out is not more effective for longer durations. Overall, studies reported in the professional literature show that relatively brief time-out durations (i.e., 5–15 minutes) are generally effective in reducing inappropriate behavior (Ortiz, 2018); spending more than 5 minutes in time-out for younger children and more than 15 minutes for older children is actually counterproductive. Typically, a category of disruptive or inappropriate student behaviors is defined (e.g., teacher defiance, disturbing others, tantrums) and a standard time-out duration is applied to those behaviors unless special circumstances indicate otherwise. If a student is unresponsive to repeated 15-minute time-out durations, then other procedures should be considered for addressing the problem behavior.

RESPONSE COST

Like time-out, *response cost* (RC) can be used to directly reduce serious types of challenging behavior. It has been a relatively popular way to do so among educators and has been used by school staff in preschool through high school contexts. The accumulated research shows that RC is effective in reducing and preventing the challenging behavior to which it is applied (Kazdin, 1972; Walker, 1983; Walker et al., 1995; Tanol, Johnson, McComas, & Cote, 2010). My colleagues and I have investigated this technique extensively with elementary students having serious challenging behavior and have found it to be highly effective with students throughout the elementary grade range. Further, Reynolds and Kelley (1997) reported that an RC-based treatment package for managing aggressive behavior in preschoolers was highly effective and acceptable to teachers. RC is a useful adjunct to point-based token systems and can enhance their efficacy.

Definition and Examples of RC

RC, also known as *cost contingency,* is a technique applied to behavioral infractions to reduce and prevent their occurrence. Unlike time-out, it does not interrupt or stop the challenging behavior when delivered. Instead, RC operates much like fines do and refers to the removal of previously awarded or earned reinforcers for the purpose of reducing and eliminating forms of behavior that are considered inappropriate. A penalty or cost is incurred each time the student engages in the targeted inappropriate behavior. There are numerous examples of response cost in everyday life: Parking tickets and traffic violation fines are good examples, as are football, basketball, hockey, and soccer with their built-in penalties for rule infractions.

Two forms of delivery exist for RC (Weiner, 1962). In the first, points or tokens are awarded noncontingently (unearned) at the beginning of a period and the student can lose these points for engaging in inappropriate behavior. In the second form, points or tokens for appropriate behavior can be earned during the period and these already earned points can also be subtracted for instances of inappropriate behavior. An RC procedure can be applied either alone or in combination with positive reinforcement: There is little evidence that one method is more effective than the other (Tanol et al., 2010), however, RC alone is substantially easier to implement (Walker et al., 1983, 1995). Both the utility and efficacy of RC have been amply demonstrated in the professional literature over many decades. This technique has been applied successfully to a large number of behaviors within classroom, playground, and specialized settings.

In a series of single case studies, my colleagues and I (Walker, Hops, & Greenwood, 1981, 1984) used RC point systems combined with praise, group and individual reinforcement procedures, and school rewards to remediate aggressive and negative social behavior on the playground for K–5 students. A representative study from this series is described below.

During initial, preintervention behavioral observations, approximately 30–40% of the students' social interactions with peers were of an aggressive or negative nature—our research indicated that elementary-school-aged peers are typically positive with each other approximately 90–95% of the time during recess periods (Walker et al., 1981). This student intervention plan initially involved reviewing the definition of negative/aggressive social interactions and the rules governing playground behavior. The target student also role-played with the teacher and several volunteer peers. After this training, the student was awarded one point on a card for each minute of recess at the beginning of recess periods (e.g., 15 points for a 15-minute recess) maintained by the playground supervisor. The student's goal was to keep the points. Five points were subtracted for each instance of aggressive or negative social behavior and two points for rule violations. If all the student's points were lost, the remainder of that recess period was forfeited and the student had to sit it out. However, he could exchange the number of points remaining at the end of recess for prearranged special privileges at home. In addition, if no episodes of aggressive/negative social behavior occurred in any of the three recesses across the school day, he could also earn a special group activity for himself and classmates near the end of the school day.

This was an easy intervention to implement: Once trained in its implementation, the recess supervisor was able to monitor, award praise, and manage points for the student's positive behavior. The intervention was highly effective in almost totally eliminating the student's aggressive/negative behavior on the playground. Also, there appeared to be some evidence of spontaneous transfer or spillover of the student's improved behavior with peers to periods in which the program was not currently in effect. This was a highly unusual outcome but can occur occasionally when positive, peer-related behavior is established early on in the school day. Sometimes these positive social exchanges continue during subsequent recess periods (Walker, et al., 1981).

Guidelines for Correct Application of RC

Regardless of setting or context, there are some preconditions and implementation rules that should be observed and followed carefully in using RC.

Essential Preconditions

1. The RC system should be carefully explained to the student before it is implemented.
2. RC should be tied to a reinforcement system.
3. An appropriate delivery system should be in place.

Implementation Rules

1. RC should be implemented immediately after a target behavior occurs and for each occurrence.
2. The student should never be allowed to have negative points (where more points are lost than they have earned).
3. The ratio of points earned to those that can be lost should be carefully monitored.
4. The teacher should never be intimidated out of applying RC by a student.
5. The subtraction of points should never be punitive or personalized.
6. When using RC, the student's positive, appropriate behavior should be praised and reinforced as opportunities permit.

My experience in using RC with elementary-school-aged students having very serious disruptive and aggressive behavior leads me to recommend its use on playgrounds and also within specialized classroom settings (e.g., classrooms for disruptive students, resource classrooms) as well as general classroom settings. However, within general education classrooms, it should be implemented in a private arrangement between the student, teacher, and parents and should adhere to the following guidelines.

- The student should know exactly how points can be earned and subtracted.
- During the school day, the student should receive frequent feedback about the number of points that have been awarded and subtracted and what they have been awarded and subtracted for. A point-awarding/RC card should be maintained by the teacher and reviewed regularly with the student during the school day.
- The ratio of points awarded to those subtracted should be monitored carefully so that the student never ends up with a negative point total.
- At the end of the school day, the teacher should review the day's performance with the student and award the net number of points earned so the student can take them home and exchange them for prearranged backup rewards.

- Parents should be regularly debriefed regarding how the procedure is going. The logistics of managing a point system with RC are much more feasible within specialized classroom settings having substantially fewer students than general education classrooms.

For 9 years, my colleagues and I operated an experimental, demonstration classroom for students in grades 3–5 having very serious disruptive behavior problems (Walker, 1995). We established a point system with RC where each student could earn and lose points daily depending on their behavior. They also received an intensive academic program in the basic skills of reading, math, and language arts. Points and praise were delivered to each student for academic performance and for appropriate classroom behavior. RC was applied to instances of inappropriate behavior as they occurred. Observations, academic measures, and teacher reports all showed impressive results for this intervention program (Walker & Buckley, 1974; Walker, 1995).

It is essential that a delivery/feedback system be developed that tells the student when RC is applied, which behavior it has been applied to, and how many points are lost as a result. Unless this information is communicated effectively, RC will not impact the target inappropriate behavior. Figure 14.2 provides an example of an RC delivery/feedback form used to record inappropriate behaviors for individual students and the corresponding point-loss values. These delivery forms were taped to each student's desk for recording. A second point card was used to deliver points for appropriate academic and social–emotional behavior. However, opposite sides of the same card could be used for awarding and subtracting points accordingly.

A factor that greatly affects the impact of RC on inappropriate behavior is the ratio of points earned to points lost. This ratio affects the degree to which RC functions as an effective consequence (i.e., its relative strength). For example, if a student has a total of 3 points and loses 1, the impact of RC is substantial; however, if the student has 24 points and loses 1, the impact of RC is minimized by comparison. In our use of RC in a specialized classroom, point losses ranged from 1 to 5 points per infraction and 35 points could be earned each day. There is no standard rule for determining an appropriate ratio but the student should learn that challenging behavior will result in a fine or cost.

A related issue concerns the relationship of the magnitude of RC cost to the severity of the problem behavior. Figure 14.2 illustrates this relationship as well, where more severe problems result in a greater cost in points lost. This is an important factor in making RC effective.

Probably *the* most important rule to remember regarding RC is that a student's point total should never be allowed to go below zero and into

Behaviors	Point values	M	T	W	Th	F
Out of seat	2					
Talk outs	2					
Off task	1					
Noncompliance	3					
Disturbs others	2					
Aggression	5					

FIGURE 14.2. Example of an RC delivery/feedback form.

minus points. If the student is allowed to go into debt, the efficacy of RC is lost. If a student should lose all his/her accumulated points, some other consequence, such as a brief time-out, should be used to address further instances of inappropriate behavior until additional points are earned.

Consistency in the application of RC also helps determine its effectiveness. RC should be applied each time its use is called for. Otherwise the student may be inclined to risk engagement in the undesired behavior on the presumption that RC might not be applied.

Verbal interaction with the student in the delivery of RC can be counterproductive and is unnecessary since the delivery process tells the student what prompted its use and how many points were lost. Sometimes students are inclined to argue or protest the teacher's application of RC. The teacher should not argue with the student nor be intimidated out of using RC because of the student's emotional reaction. A calm, nonjudgmental delivery by the teacher is best.

Issues to Consider in Using RC

Like time-out, RC is a form of mild punishment for inappropriate behavior. Its use raises the question as to whether undesirable side effects associated with punishment (e.g., avoidance, escape, emotional effects) are also side effects of RC. Opinion among experts regarding this issue has been divided. It probably depends very much on circumstances surrounding its use. In using RC my colleague and I have never seen it prompt escape or avoidance from a therapeutic situation. Emotional reactions to its use have been very rare in our experience. Even when RC was used to reduce aggressive playground social behavior, it did not affect the frequency with which a target student interacted with peers. Claims that RC tends to suppress appropriate behavior in order to avoid losing points seem to have very little merit.

As noted earlier, if RC is to be implemented in general education classrooms with individual students, a private arrangement involving the teacher, student, and parents is recommended. In some circumstances, it may be logistically difficult for a teacher to monitor student behavior and simultaneously deliver points, praise, and RC in a classroom of 25–30 students. Thus, teachers may need support from an aide or the school's related services staff in such cases.

Because the techniques described in this chapter are designed to reduce, eliminate, and prevent undesired forms of classroom behavior, it is important that they be used judiciously and always implemented according to best-practice guidelines and with adequate administrative support. Generally, positive-only techniques that support and strengthen appropriate behavior are preferred and should be the first option in managing student behavior. Chapter 15 describes strategies for sustaining gains produced by these intervention approaches.

CHAPTER 14 TAKEAWAYS

- With very rare exceptions, negative techniques such as time-out or RC should never be used in isolation to discourage undesirable student behavior.

- In the case of students with severe challenging behavior, they should be given a clear choice of positive strategies for desirable behavior versus negative strategies for undesirable behavior—in other words only use negative strategies in combination with positive strategies.

- Parents should always be informed when negative strategies are necessary to reduce undesirable behavior at school.

- Debriefing following challenging behavior episodes is a very useful strategy for helping the student develop more adaptive responses to difficult situations.

- A time-out period longer than 15 minutes or so rarely increases the efficacy of the time-out.

- When using RC, a student should never be allowed to lose earned points so that the student goes into a minus situation with earned points.

CHAPTER 15

How to Sustain Behavioral Change(s) over Time and across Settings

As discussed in Chapters 13 and 14, improving student behavior is a two-stage process. There are strategies for changing existing behavior and strategies for sustaining the changes and ensuring their transfer to non-intervention settings and contexts. Unfortunately, changed behavior is typically less likely to reflect these maintenance and generalization outcomes. This chapter describes techniques, strategies, and tools that my colleagues and I have found to be cost-effective, focused on enhancing stage two of the behavioral improvement process.

In a major conceptual advance, Stokes and Baer (1977) contributed a new formulation of generalization and maintenance that laid the groundwork for development of a technology governing them. They described nine techniques or practices that should be included in such a behavioral technology, including the following:

- Train and hope
- Sequential modification
- Introduce to natural maintaining contingencies
- Train sufficient exemplars
- Train loosely
- Use indiscriminate contingencies
- Program common stimuli
- Mediate generalization
- Train to generalize

Unfortunately, applied interventions in schools for decades have continued to be dominated by "train and hope" practices (DuPaul & Eckert,

1994) rather than by active efforts to actually ensure the persistence and transfer of applied treatment effects. My colleagues and I have collectively investigated numerous techniques and strategies over the years to help facilitate positive maintenance and generalization outcomes for students with behavior problems. They can be grouped under the categories of *introduce to natural maintaining contingencies* and *train to generalize* where we have attempted to plan for and program these outcomes. The specific approaches used in these studies can be grouped under the following major categories: (1) strategies for sustaining treatment gains within the classroom and playground settings where the intervention occurs; (2) facilitating the transfer or generalization of treatment gains from intervention to non-intervention settings while the intervention is ongoing; and (3) designing and evaluating transition strategies to support teachers, and students with challenging behavior, in their reintegration from specialized intervention settings into general education classrooms.

STRATEGIES FOR SUSTAINING TREATMENT GAINS IN THE INTERVENTION SETTINGS

The strategies we have used to sustain behavioral changes are as follows: implementing a low-cost version of the intervention, repeated reintroductions of the intervention, phasing out program components, substituting teacher praise and approval for points, and special peer helpers.

Low-Cost Version of the Intervention

The goal of this strategy is to maintain approximately 80% of the treatment gain by implementing 10–15% of the intervention that produced it. This involves shifting to a strategy that requires much less effort and is sustainable long term. The following guidelines should be followed with this strategy.

1. Wait until the student's behavior has improved to acceptable levels and is in the normal range as defined by the class average for peers.
2. Discuss with the student your intention to reduce the intervention.
3. Reassure the student that a part of the intervention will remain in effect but you want to see how they do with a reduced version.
4. Monitor the student's behavior carefully and provide frequent feedback as to how it's going.
5. Readjust the maintenance strategy as necessary.

The following case study illustrates how this can work.

CASE STUDY: IMPLEMENTING A LOW-COST
FOLLOW-UP INTERVENTION FOR JODY

The target student of this intervention had a diverse array of challenging behaviors that gave him an unfortunate reputation with teachers and peers. Jody was variously referred to as incorrigible, mean, out of control, a bully, and unteachable. He experienced problems from the first day of school and had received the full gamut of school psychological services with very little effect. The schoolwide assistance team was tasked with coming up with a behavior intervention plan for him to prevent his exclusion from school.

It was decided Jody needed a powerful intervention plan with multiple components in order to impact his behavior problems. The plan that was developed had three major components: (1) specifying his appropriate and inappropriate behavior to which the intervention would apply; (2) specifying the consequences at school and home that would apply to his behavior; and (3) specifying the roles that he, his teacher, and his parents would play in the intervention. The program was explained in detail to all, prior to implementation.

The intervention consisted of teacher praise and points awarded for appropriate behavior and RC backed up by time-out for inappropriate behavior. A total of 24 points could be earned each day, and point loss values ranged from 5 for aggression toward others to 1 for persistent inattention. Points were exchanged for backup rewards prearranged at home. This intervention had a powerful impact on Jody's behavior, improving his overall level of appropriate behavior from an average of 30 to 40% to more than 80% on most days.

After the program had been in effect for a month, plans were made by the school psychologist and teacher to transition Jody to a lower cost version of the intervention. The goal was to try and maintain his improved behavior with only minimal teacher support compared to that required by the full intervention. The following steps were taken to design, explain, and implement the maintenance plan.

1. Jody's parents were informed of the decision and briefed on the importance of continuing to praise and support Jody's improved school behavior.

2. Jody was told that since he was doing so well, the intervention was moving into a new phase with some changes that would help him make his improved behavior permanent.

3. The point awarding and RC system were replaced with a simple rating system where the teacher would award Jody a + or − (on a form that he kept) for following classroom rules. One point could be earned for each 15 minutes of class time. If Jody earned a + rating for 80% of the 15-minute intervals, he could receive a special privilege at home as before. This daily form was sent home and shared with his parents. An example is shown in Figure 15.1.

Student	Teacher	Date

Time	Teacher Rating
9:00–9:15	+
9:15–9:30	+
9:30–9:45	+
9:45–10:00	–
10:00–10:15	+
10:15–10:30	+
10:30–10:45	+
10:45–11:00	+
11:00–11:15	–
11:15–11:30	+
11:30–11:45	+
11:45–12:00	+
	83% of Points Earned

Tried my best?　　　Yes ____　No ____　? ____

FIGURE 15.1. Sample rating form for student behavior.

4. At regular times during the school day, the teacher reviewed Jody's ratings with him.

5. The teacher and school psychologist agreed it was necessary to maintain a high level of praise for Jody's improved behavior.

The maintenance plan worked well after a few slip-ups by Jody in the first few days. Ultimately he maintained his improved behavior with much less implementation effort than before. The teacher appreciated the reduced effort and felt the program was sustainable going forward. The school psychologist continued to provide regular progress reports to Jody's parents on his progress and to debrief regularly about Jody with the teacher.

Repeated Reintroductions of the Intervention

This strategy involves introducing, withdrawing, and briefly reintroducing a treatment with the goal of getting its effects to maintain following a primary intervention period. It has been referred to as a repeated treatments procedure. Repeated treatments are feasible for relatively simple interventions such as increasing a student's social interaction rate using prompts and praise that are relatively simple to introduce, withdraw, and reintroduce. This procedure has shown some success in maintaining treatment gains in studies reported in the professional literature (Kolko & Lindhiem, 2014).

Paine et al. (1982) used repeated treatments to sustain prior treatment gains of five children having low interaction rates with peers: The five children had previously received treatment for social withdrawal. The goal of the study was to see whether maintenance effects would accumulate with repeated exposure to and withdrawal of treatment, which consisted of social skills tutoring and a recess point system. Four of the five children increased their peer interaction rates to within normative levels following three repeated treatments of the intervention. Ratings by parents, the teacher, and peers all showed positive improvements. It is possible that this study succeeded in behaviorally entrapping these students into supportive peer networks that served to maintain the target children's behavior via natural supports existing in the recess environment, for example social reciprocity, peer acceptance, greater social involvement, and so forth (Baer & Wolf, 1970).

Results of this study showed the promise of repeated treatments in the maintenance of previously achieved behavioral gains. Though the study focused on social withdrawal, this strategy may have applicability to a range of other mild problem behaviors in the school setting, provided the interventions involved are not too complex and can be easily introduced, withdrawn, and then reintroduced. Examples of such interventions include improving academic engagement through peer tutoring, increasing positive interactions on the playground via supervisor praise, and prompting social initiations to peers through behavioral coaching.

Phasing Out Program Components

School interventions that have multiple components tend to be more effective than single-component interventions (Reid, 1993). My colleagues and I have found this to be the case in our program development efforts for students with challenging behavior. However, implementing such multicomponent interventions within general education settings can be logistically challenging. We have found that a substantial amount of an achieved treatment effect can be sustained by gradually phasing out program components.

For example, in our work in developing and evaluating the CLASS (Contingencies for Academic and Social Skills) program for acting-out students (Walker & Hops, 1979), we were able to successfully phase out nearly all of its major components over the course of intervention and during a brief maintenance period. The CLASS program consists of three phases: consultant, teacher, and maintenance, spanning 30 program days for full implementation. It involves supportive participation roles by parents, teachers, and peers, and each participant signs a behavioral contract attesting to their role in the program's implementation. The CLASS program has the following major components:

- Support by a consultant or program specialist (school psychologist, resource teacher, counselor) during the intervention, who coordinates teacher, parent, and peer activities
- Teacher, parent, and peer praise
- A nonverbal feedback system that communicates to the student whether their behavior is inappropriate or appropriate using a red and green card
- A daily point system backed up by school activity rewards shared with peers, and individualized special privileges accessed at home
- A recycling procedure where a failed program day involves repeating a prior successful day
- The therapeutic use of time-out and suspension

Over the first 10 program days, the CLASS program is fully implemented and gradually extended to those parts of the school day where the target student is having problems. The consultant sets up and operates the CLASS program for brief periods during the school day. During this phase, the CLASS consultant transfers control of the program to the cooperating teacher. At the beginning of the teacher phase, the planned gradual removal of key program components is begun. By the end of the maintenance phase, all components except teacher praise have been removed. The program teaches the student to work for multiple days in succession to earn backup activity rewards for themselves and classmates.

From day one of the CLASS program, plans are in place to begin removing its intervention components in order to lighten the implementation load while sustaining the student's appropriate behavior. In phasing out, we find that while there is a slight loss of treatment gains, the student's behavior generally remains in the normal, acceptable range when CLASS program components are gradually reduced (Hops et al., 1978; Walker &

Hops, 1979; Walker, Fonseca-Retana, & Gersten, 1988). Following this, the maintenance phase of CLASS provides four options to help facilitate longer-term sustainability of achieved behavioral gains.

The following case study presents an example of how the CLASS program was successfully applied.

CASE STUDY: RESPONDING TO FELIX'S DISRUPTIVE BEHAVIOR

Felix was a disruptive, sometimes out-of-control third-grade student in Mr. Thompson's classroom. He came from a difficult family background and had experienced problems adjusting to school from the first day of kindergarten. He was highly coercive with peers and insisted on getting his way most of the time. Felix was consistently noncompliant with requests and directives from Mr. Thompson and was frequently sent to the principal's office for detention as a result. Felix also carried high levels of agitation and was prone to escalate disagreements into intense behavioral challenges with both staff and students. His parents were highly critical of how the school dealt with these behavioral challenges but Mr. Thompson was exasperated with Felix's continuation of them. He decided to ask the school psychologist, Ms. Turner, if there was anything different that could be tried.

Ms. Turner had attended a workshop at a conference on implementing CLASS and described the program to him. She explained it was a consultant-supervised intervention for use with disruptive students in general education. After learning about the program, Mr. Thompson agreed to participate in implementing it for Felix in his classroom. Ms. Turner contacted Felix's parents and explained the program to them, along with their role in praising, supporting, and rewarding Felix at home for doing well in the program at school. They agreed that Felix could participate in the program and that they would cooperate in its implementation. Next, Ms. Turner met with Felix and explained how she wanted him to help her with a game to be played with his classmates called the red/green card game. She explained that he could earn praise and points for following classroom rules and that his points could be traded for a special activity for himself and classmates as well as special privileges at home. Felix agreed to give it a try.

Ms. Turner explained to the class that Felix had volunteered to assist her with a new game that helps students learn better and faster:

"When Felix follows the classroom rules, I will show him the green side of the red/green card and he will earn points on the green side. But if he earns a point on the red side by not following the rules, it doesn't count toward earning a free-time activity. Green means keep doing what you're doing; red means stop what you're doing. So Felix needs to keep the card on green by following classroom rules. [Note: Points are awarded randomly on the green or red side of the card according to a randomized, predetermined schedule. If the card is on the green side at a point delivery occasion, the point counts toward the reward; if on red, it does not.]

"If he earns most of his points [80%] on the green side of the card, he can exchange them for a brief, free-time activity for everyone after the game. He will have a chance to play the game in the morning and in the afternoon."

Ms. Turner asked how classmates could help Felix earn points and received a number of helpful suggestions. Immediately after this explanation, Ms. Turner ran the morning 20-minute session of the game. There were 40 points available in the 20-minute session (i.e., one point awarded every 30 seconds). Felix needed to earn 30 points, or 80% of the available points on the green side of the card. He earned 35 points and exchanged them for a game activity for the whole class. Felix liked the game and asked when the next session was.

Over the 10-day consultant phase, the following happened:

- The program reduced the number of points available per session from 40 to 5, making it much easier to implement.
- Ms. Turner turned operation of the red/green card game over to Mr. Thompson.
- Ms. Turner assumed a supervisory role in the program.
- Preparations were made to extend the CLASS program to the entire school day.

Beginning on day 10, Felix began working to earn points in blocks of 2-, 3-, and 5-day periods. The magnitude of school and home rewards were increased to compensate for these longer periods.

During the first 10 days of the program, Felix adjusted quite well, needing to recycle to an earlier successful program day in only two instances. However, he struggled with having to work for multiple days to meet the reward criterion. Ultimately, he learned to tolerate these longer periods and completed the program in a reasonable time frame. After CLASS was terminated, Felix needed frequent praise from Mr. Thompson, occasional program booster shots, and covert monitoring/recording of his behavior to sustain his improved performance. Over the long term, all parties in the intervention expressed general satisfaction with the results.

This is an example of how a highly structured program can have a large impact on the behavior of a student with an emotional or behavioral disorder (EBD). Often these students need such structure for a period of time to assist them in meeting the ordinary demands of schooling.

Substituting Teacher Praise and Approval for Points

Whenever using a point system to motivate student behavior, it is always recommended to deliver behavior-specific praise in conjunction with awarding a point. Though teacher attention is generally reinforcing when used alone, pairing it with points backed up by rewards at school or home makes it even more important. A recommended way to withdraw a point system is to gradually reduce the number of points that are paired with praise. Some options for doing so are presented here.

Sample Schedule for Phasing Out Points

A schedule for phasing out points can be fixed or variable, such as moving from one point accompanying each praise, to one point for every two praises, then one point for every three and so on, until a majority of praises are no longer accompanied by a point. An alternative is to use a variable phasing out schedule so the student cannot predict exactly which praises will be accompanied by a point. Which one is selected depends on teacher preference and ease of delivery.

Reducing Available Points and Raising the Criterion for Reinforcement

In researching the CLASS program (Hops & Walker, 1988) we found that the number of points awarded daily could be substantially reduced while simultaneously raising the criterion for reinforcement in order to earn X number of points per day. At the same time, the value or magnitude of backup school and home rewards were substantially increased in value as the student learned to work for longer periods and with fewer reinforcements. Table 15.1 shows how this scheduling process can gradually work to reduce the implementation burden and simultaneously sustain the student's appropriate behavior with fewer reinforcements.

The Role of Special Peer Helpers

There is a strong tradition of best practice in using peers as therapeutic agents in the behavioral change process (Strain, 1981; Walker, Hops, & Greenwood, 1981). My colleagues and I have found that the peers and classmates of at-risk students who are targets of intervention are very supportive and capable therapeutic agents. Often, they will participate in supporting interventions voluntarily without needing to be reinforced for their role. We and others have conducted studies of maintenance effects where the target student is monitored by selected peers (peer monitoring) and, in

TABLE 15.1. CLASS Program Schedule for Phasing Out Points

Program phase	Session length	Length of point award interval	Program day	Show red/ green card	Total points available
Consultant	20 minutes	30 seconds	1	1:1	40
Consultant	20 minutes	1 minute	2	1:1	20
Consultant	20 minutes	2 minutes	3	1:1	10
Consultant	20 minutes	4 minutes	4	1:1	5
Consultant	30 minutes	6 minutes	5	1:1	5

contrast, where they themselves monitor the social behavior of peers. In both instances, we have seen positive outcomes with young (K–3) aggressive children. Two studies are described below that illustrate these important outcomes.

The RECESS (Reprogramming Environmental Contingencies for Effective Social Skills) program has been used as a vehicle to investigate peer- and self-monitoring procedures among socially aggressive elementary-school-age students (Dougherty, Fowler, & Paine, 1985; Fowler, Dougherty, Kirby, & Kohler, 1986). My colleagues and I have found that young students, as well as those with disabilities, can be effective wherein they monitor, coach, reinforce, and support the social behavior of an aggressive student following that student's exposure to the RECESS program (Walker, Hops, & Greenwood, 1988). They are also effective as peer monitors where the target student monitors the social behavior of other selected aggressive peers. In both roles, clear therapeutic-maintenance effects were achieved.

Dougherty et al. (1985) studied effects of the RECESS program with a student having a mild disability. There were substantial reductions in negative-aggressive interactions with peers, and following adult-monitored phases the effects were maintained when peer-monitoring and self-monitoring strategies were implemented in subsequent study phases. Similarly, Fowler et al. (1986) successfully replicated these effects and found that peer monitoring of the target student, implemented in the morning recess, showed evidence of transfer or generalization to the noon and afternoon recess periods. This was an unanticipated positive finding from this study.

These two studies illustrate how special peer helpers can be utilized effectively as therapeutic agents following their involvement in a powerful intervention. The economic impact of this finding is potentially huge for overburdened related services personnel and teachers charged with intervening in schools to effect positive behavioral change. It appears that special peer helpers could be enlisted profitably in a range of such contexts.

TRANSFERRING TREATMENT GAINS
FROM INTERVENTION TO NON-INTERVENTION SETTINGS

In developing the CLASS program and the RECESS program, my colleagues and I investigated both the extent to which treatment effects would spontaneously transfer from intervention to non-intervention settings, and how to facilitate this process efficiently and economically in terms of required effort. Regarding the first point, only very rarely did such transfer occur, and when it did it was sporadic and we were unable to attribute the transfer to the intervention. However, we found that such transfer could be reliably achieved if steps were taken to directly facilitate its occurrence. Examples of these strategies are described in the next sections.

Teacher Monitoring and Rating of Student Behavior
in Non-Intervention Settings

The positive effects of the CLASS program can be extended to non-intervention classrooms and the playground, with the following simple procedure:

- The coach or primary teacher extends the red/green point card from the intervention classroom to other classrooms where the teacher is enlisted to monitor, rate, and praise the student's behavior during that period.
- The student carries the card throughout the day and gives it to each new teacher at the beginning of the class period.
- The card has spaces for each new teacher to provide a 1–5 rating of the student's behavior according to how well the class rules are followed.
- At the end of the day, the cooperating CLASS program teacher reviews the ratings and discusses the student's behavior with the student. The numerical rating for each teacher's student rating is converted into an equivalent number of points earned for that period.

The student Good Behavior Card and teacher ratings system, as shown in Figure 15.2, was developed to extend behavioral improvements from intervention settings and has a number of potential school applications.

A further example of the efficacy and economy of this basic strategy is provided in the next section and shows the positive effects of covert monitoring and recording of student behavior.

Student _____ Teacher _____ Date _____

Classroom Rules:
- Talk quietly.
- Follow your teacher's instructions.
- Focus on your assigned task.
- Do your best work.
- Ask for help in the right way.

Teacher Rating (1 to 5): **1** = *not good*, **3** = *good*, **5** = *very good*

Class Period	Teacher Rating	Teacher Initials
1	_____	_____
2	_____	_____
3	_____	_____
4	_____	_____
5	_____	_____

Total Points Earned: _____

FIGURE 15.2. Sample student Good Behavior Card. From *Solutions to Critical Behavioral Issues in the Classroom* by Hill M. Walker. Copyright © 2023 The Guilford Press. Permission to photocopy this material is granted to purchasers of this book for personal use or use with students (see copyright page for details). Purchasers can download enlarged versions of this material (see the box at the end of the table of contents).

Transferring Treatment Gains from One Recess Period to Another

My colleagues and I used a simple version of this maintenance strategy in a study of negative social interactions by an aggressive boy in the primary grades (Walker et al., 1995). The full intervention was implemented in the morning recess, consisting of social skills tutoring, prompts, praise, and an RC point system backed up by group and individual rewards. Only a covert stopwatch recording of the boy's negative interactions with peers was implemented in the noon and afternoon recesses. The recording process was not visible to the student but he was aware that it was happening. If he met the reward criterion for four of the five days of the week, he earned a group activity reward for himself and classmates. No intervention components were implemented in these recess periods. This procedure was highly effective in extending the treatment outcome from the first to second and third recesses of the day.

Covert recordings of this type, following a full intervention in a primary setting, are highly recommended to address both maintenance goals within the intervention setting and generalization goals in non-intervention settings. However, the target student should be aware of the recording procedure and debriefed daily about how they performed for it to work as intended.

Strategies for Reintegrating Students into General Education Classrooms

In fall 2018, an average of 36% of the individuals served across the 13 disability categories of IDEA (Individuals with Disabilities Education Act) were assigned to nongeneral education settings for 20% or less of the school day (separate schools, self-contained settings, residential schools); this figure was 50.4% for individuals with EBD (National Center for Education Statistics, 2018). This doubtless results from a host of factors that work against these students being able to access less-restrictive school settings (e.g., resources, cultural attitudes, accommodation challenges). However, with EBD students, it has a great deal to do with the challenging forms of behavior they present to general educators and the resistance it engenders (Simpson, 2004). There is a continuing need for models and systems that make general education classrooms more accessible to EBD students, and for supporting successful adjustment and academic achievement within them (Bradley, Doolittle, & Bartolotta, 2008).

My colleagues and I conducted 15 years of research on the reintegration of grade 3–5 students with very serious disruptive behavior problems and disorders (Hersh & Walker, 1983; Walker & Rankin, 1983; Walker, 1984, 1986). The stimulus for this research was an experimental demonstration classroom we established for elementary-school-age EBD students as part of a larger research project. We designed an intensive program of instruction in basic academic and social skills, combined with a well-designed and implemented behavior management program (Walker & Buckley, 1972, 1974), to which all students responded quite well. Two groups of six students spent approximately 4 months each in the classroom and were then returned to their referral schools and classrooms. At the beginning of the next school year, we were asked to take six of the 12 students back who we thought had been cured. Our subsequent follow-up inquiry along with the experiences of others taught us the following:

- At-risk students who respond well in a self-contained classroom will not necessarily perform well in a general education classroom.
- The reintegrated students were not sufficiently prepared for or supported in the reintegration process.
- Post-placement interviews revealed that the students' general

education teachers did not believe any meaningful behavioral or academic changes could be produced by assignment to a different, 4-month alternative placement.
• We needed to develop a radically different approach if our efforts were to be successful.

In response to these challenges, we designed a comprehensive reintegration process based on a behavioral–ecological frame of reference whose central principle is "person–environment fit or match" (Romer & Heller, 1983). The central challenge EBD students have is that their characteristic behavioral profiles do not match the behavioral ecology or expectations of general education classrooms. Thus they are a classic example of a lack of fit or match with teacher expectations. Research shows that general education teachers prefer the behavioral profile of high-expectation students, initially identified by Brophy and Good (1970), and replicated by Hersh and Walker (1983), which involves following classroom rules, complying promptly, cooperating, working independently, expressing anger appropriately, and producing work of acceptable quality given one's skill level. Unacceptable behavior for most teachers involves teacher defiance, tantrums, ignoring teacher feedback and directives, aggression toward peers, damaging others' possessions, and dishonesty. These challenging behaviors depend on salience and intensity rather than frequency of occurrence for their psychological impact; they function much like behavioral earthquakes, are considered by teachers to be very serious infractions, and are highly destructive of the teacher–student relationship. Teachers tend to initiate referrals out of the general education classroom of students who display them (Gerber & Semmel, 1984).

Wong, Kauffman, and Lloyd (1991) have noted that too often in reintegration efforts the match between the receiving teacher and the target student is left to chance and is guided by intuition rather than by a systematic, rational decision-making process. Achieving the best possible fit or match between the demands of the receiving setting and the characteristics of the target student is of paramount importance in reintegration. This can be accomplished by a combination of carefully selecting general classroom settings as target sites for reintegration and thorough preparation of the student to meet receiving teacher behavioral expectations.

Preparing for Reintegration

We relied on a generic strategy, called *transenvironmental programming,* as a vehicle for planning and supporting the reintegration of EBD students into mainstream, general education settings. Transenvironmental programming is a set of procedures and guiding principles for preparing individuals to succeed in similar but different settings (Anderson-Inman, 1981; Anderson-Inman, Walker, & Purcell, 1984), and is an especially effective strategy for reintegration. Its four major components are:

1. Assessment of target general classroom environments to identify their critically important social–behavioral and academic expectations and use of this information as an aid in selecting a placement setting
2. Instruction and intervention in the more restrictive setting (i.e., separate school program, self-contained or resource room) to teach the identified skills and behavioral competencies required in the selected general education classroom
3. Selection and use of transition techniques and support strategies (e.g., student-focused coaching, reinforcement, and briefing of receiving teachers) for ensuring the transfer of newly acquired skills and competencies between the sending and receiving settings
4. Monitoring and follow-up assistance provided to the teacher and student in the new placement setting to ensure maintenance and durability of effects over time

The AIMS Assessment System for Reintegrating At-Risk Students

In 1986 I developed an ecological assessment process called AIMS (Assessments for Integration into Mainstream Settings) that enabled achievement of the above steps. AIMS has three primary purposes: to help select potential placement settings in the educational mainstream, to determine the minimum behavioral demands necessary for entry into and satisfactory adjustment within these settings, and to assess the receiving teacher's technical assistance needs in accommodating challenging students who are reintegrated into a less restrictive setting.

The primary AIMS instrument used for these purposes is the SBS (Social Behavioral Survival) Inventory (Walker & Rankin, 1983). The original version of this inventory contains 56 items describing adaptive behavior and 51 items describing maladaptive behavior. A copy of the short form of the SBS Inventory ($N = 40$ items) is included in this book as Appendix 1. It is used in the reintegration process as a classroom selection vehicle, as a means of negotiating the terms of reintegration with the receiving teacher, and as a planning tool in preparing the student for reintegration.

The SBS Inventory has three sections. In Section 1 teachers rate descriptions of adaptive student behavior in terms of whether they are critical, desirable, or unimportant to a successful adjustment in the teacher's classroom. In Section 2, descriptions of maladaptive student behavior are rated along an acceptability dimension of unacceptable, tolerated, or acceptable.

Definitions are provided in the instructions for each section. Section 3 asks the teacher to re-rate items they marked as critical and unacceptable in Sections 1 and 2 along a technical assistance dimension according to one of the following options: (1) a student who is deficient on a critical item or is outside the normal range on an unacceptable rated item would have to be at average competency or within the normal range prior to being socially integrated into the receiving teacher's classroom, (2) the student can be integrated with the deficit or behavioral excess but technical assistance must be provided following integration to address them, or (3) the student can be integrated with the deficit and/or behavioral excess and no technical assistance is required.

Teacher Profiles on the SBS Inventory

Extensive research has been conducted on the SBS Inventory's psychometric characteristics (Hersh & Walker, 1983; Walker & Rankin, 1983; Walker, 1986). The SBS Inventory has high internal consistency and demonstrated acceptable test–retest stability. Teachers who receive higher scores on the instrument (i.e., they rate a larger number of items as critical and unacceptable) tend to fit the profile of the effective teacher. Typically, general education teachers on average rate 22% of the Section 1 items as critical and 71% as desirable, and 55% of the Section 2 items as unacceptable and 44% as tolerated (Walker, 1986). Special education teachers had very similar profiles as general education teachers on the two sets of items.

However, there are some teachers who have extreme profiles on the SBS Inventory. Table 15.2 shows the scoring profiles of six individual teachers from a sample of 50 general education teachers who scored radically differently from each other. These atypical scoring profiles generally show up in any group of 25–30 teachers or more. The profiles for teachers 3 and 6 in Table 15.2 are very typical of teachers in general; fortunately, the profiles for the other teachers in the table occur relatively infrequently. In my view, general education teachers who receive such extreme scores should be avoided as potential mainstream placement settings for at-risk students generally and especially EBD students.

Using the SBS Inventory to Select a General Education Classroom Setting for Reintegration

The following steps should be completed in this process.

- *Step 1:* Teachers in potential placement classrooms should be asked if they would consider accepting an at-risk student. If yes, they should be asked to complete the short form of the SBS Inventory. The number of items rated as critical and unacceptable should be noted and tabulated for each

TABLE 15.2. Normative and Extreme SBS Profiles of General Education Teachers

Section 1	Critical	Desirable	Unimportant
Teacher 1	0	36	20
Teacher 2	47	9	0
Teacher 3	15	40	1

Section 2	Unacceptable	Tolerated	Acceptable
Teacher 4	51	0	0
Teacher 5	8	42	1
Teacher 6	28	22	1

teacher who completes the inventory. All teachers should be assured of the confidentiality of their ratings.

• *Step 2:* When considering reintegration of a student into a general education classroom, one should look for a teacher profile on the short form of the SBS Inventory that shows reasonable behavioral expectations. That would be 22% of Section 1 items rated critical (5 items), 71% of items rated desirable (14 items), and around 7% of items rated unimportant (1–2 items). Similarly, on Section 2 about 55% of items should be rated unacceptable (10 items), 44% of items rated tolerated (8 items), and 1% unacceptable (0 items).

• *Step 3:* An interview should be scheduled with any teacher who has a favorable SBS Inventory profile. The behavioral expectations and technical assistance needs of the receiving teacher should be reviewed thoroughly and negotiated as appropriate in this interview.

• *Step 4:* A transition plan should be developed that lists the student's behaviors that will be addressed prior to and following reintegration as negotiated between the sending and receiving teachers.

• *Step 5:* The critical and unacceptable items that need to be addressed prior to integration should be the focus of the sending teacher's priorities prior to scheduling its occurrence.

• *Step 6:* The reintegration process should be scheduled when the student is judged ready to enter a general education classroom and the terms of reintegration have been satisfactorily negotiated.

The student's parents should be consulted about the potential change in placement and give their approval. They will be most directly affected by the reintegration process other than the student. For reintegration to be successful, it must have the support of all parties.

Implementing a Transition Plan Governing Reintegration

A transition plan to enable reintegration should have four key elements: (1) procedures to prepare the receiving setting for the student's reintegration, (2) procedures to prepare the target student to meet the minimum behavioral demands of the receiving setting, (3) procedures to manage and coordinate the transition process as the student moves from the sending to receiving setting, and (4) monitoring of the student's progress following reintegration.

Preparing the Receiving Setting for Reintegration. An interview should be scheduled with the receiving teacher to discuss and plan for the student's reintegration. The goals of this interview are to inform the receiving teacher of the student's behavioral characteristics and what to expect, review the SBS items rated as critical and unacceptable by the receiving teacher, and determine the receiving teacher's technical assistance needs in accommodating the student and negotiate this assistance.

The following areas of the student's behavioral profile should be reviewed as part of this discussion: social skills, impulse control, ability to handle anger and avoid emotional outbursts, attention span, peer acceptance, and ability to cooperate with others and work in groups. Though not necessary, one could assign the target student a rating of 1–5 in each of these areas in which 1 is unacceptable, 3 is acceptable, and 5 is outstanding. This rating could be best made by the sending teacher and/or the consultant coordinating the transition/reintegration process. These ratings could be useful in helping the receiving teacher know what to expect from the student, as would information on background factors that could negatively influence the student's response to the ordinary demands of schooling.

The student's behavioral status on the receiving teacher's critical and unacceptable items should be reviewed with the receiving teacher and a joint plan should be developed to address each one. For critical-rated, adaptive behaviors, they could be coded as 1 = displays the behavior consistently, 2 = the behavior is improving, or 3 = the student lacks the appropriate behavior. Similarly, unacceptable-rated, maladaptive behaviors could be coded as: 1 = does not display the behavior, 2 = displays the behavior but is improving, or 3 = frequently exhibits the behavior. This is a very useful way to communicate the student's current behavioral status to the receiving teacher. Next, the type of technical assistance required by the receiving teacher for each critical and unacceptable item should be determined. Options A and B in Section 3 of the SBS Inventory are most frequently chosen by receiving teachers; however, option C (does not need assistance) is selected by a surprisingly large number of receiving teachers. Technical assistance and support provided in this way is very positively viewed by most receiving teachers.

Finally, it is a good idea to interview the receiving teacher about his or her classroom rules, which typically reflect teacher expectations. Knowledge of them can be valuable to the sending teacher in the reintegration process. Pre-teaching them in the sending setting can greatly facilitate reintegration.

Preparing the Student to Meet the Behavioral Demands of the Receiving Setting. There are four areas that should be addressed in preparing students to enter and be successful in general education settings: (1) adherence to the general classroom rules of the receiving setting, (2) achieving acceptable mastery of specific critical and unacceptable behaviors that the receiving teacher says must be addressed prior to reintegration, (3) displaying cooperation with the receiving teacher and peers, and (4) displaying friendship-making skills that support positive peer relations.

As a first step in preparation, the target student, sending teacher, and/ or reintegration coordinator should review the classroom rules of the receiving teacher and rehearse them as needed. The student should understand their meaning and be able to recognize examples and nonexamples of each rule. He or she should know that all students in the receiving classroom are expected to follow the rules.

The critical-rated behaviors that must be dealt with prior to placement should be reviewed next. Each behavior should be defined, role-played as necessary, and incorporated into the student's behavior management plan. This procedure should also be repeated for the unacceptable-rated behaviors and the student should be corrected to avoid the unacceptable behaviors in the receiving setting.

It should be emphasized to the student that it is very important for them to display cooperative behaviors with classmates and the receiving teacher. The student should be taught what it means to be cooperative with others and should be behaviorally coached in demonstrations of it.

Finally, positive peer relations are critical to a student's mental health, quality of life, social adjustment, and acceptance by classmates. Numerous social skills curricula are available for teaching the friendship-making skills that support this goal. Hollinger (1987) compiled a list of social competencies and skills that are required for successful peer relations:

- Dispensing and receiving positive reinforcements (praise, compliments) to/from others
- Use of low-risk tactics for entering ongoing peer group activities, such as "hovering, waiting for invitations and avoid talking about self, asking questions, or making requests"
- Use of appropriate social initiations likely to be accepted by peers (helping others, volunteering, inviting others)

- Displaying positive social behavior toward peers
- Knowing how to make friends
- Communicating effectively
- Being academically skilled
- Having a sense of humor
- Displaying low levels of inappropriate behavior

Coordinating and Managing the Transition Process. The guiding rule for managing the transition process well is to provide the student, parents, and receiving teacher with the right amount of assistance and support, which should be provided as confidentially as possible. The reintegration process should follow a daily schedule for the first week and then be adjusted as circumstances require. At least weekly contact should be maintained with the receiving teacher after the first week, with regularly scheduled debriefings and planning sessions thereafter. Daily contact with the student is likely necessary for the first week and regularly thereafter. Weekly communication with the parents is recommended until it is clear the student is adjusting well.

Monitoring Student Progress Following Reintegration. Careful monitoring of the student's behavior in the receiving classroom is extremely important in order to problem-solve challenges and provide needed support. It is a good idea to develop a transition "How Did I Do?" Card to provide feedback on the reintegrated student's performance in the receiving setting to all parties as appropriate.

Figure 15.3 shows a sample of this type of card. Versions for both the student and the receiving teacher can be developed so that the student's self-rating and the teacher's rating can be compared, reviewed, and discussed with the student. This card should be used by the reintegration coordinator to conduct daily debriefings with the student early in the transition process. It can also be used as a parent communication device and serve as a means of delivering home privileges for good performance at school.

For at-risk students who experience substantial behavioral adjustment problems upon reintegration, one option is to implement the CLASS program (see earlier description) or a similar program that uses direct intervention procedures. This will provide a vehicle for building peer support and substantially assist in teaching the student to better meet the teacher's expectations. It is an excellent way to introduce a reintegrated student to a new general education classroom context. However, CLASS should only be used in a reintegration context if the student's behavior problems in the new classroom are relatively severe. A number of professionals have anecdotally reported their successful use of CLASS as a post-intervention, transition–reintegration vehicle.

Student Name _____	Date _____	Grade _____	
1. Followed general classroom rules?	Yes ____	No ____	?____
2. Cooperated with others?	Yes ____	No ____	? ____
3. Did my work well and on time?	Yes ____	No ____	? ____

FIGURE 15.3. Sample student "How Did I Do?" Card. From *Solutions to Critical Behavioral Issues in the Classroom* by Hill M. Walker. Copyright © 2023 The Guilford Press. Permission to photocopy this material is granted to purchasers of this book for personal use or use with students (see copyright page for details). Purchasers can download enlarged versions of this material (see the box at the end of the table of contents).

This concludes Part III of this book. I hope this material will prove valuable in providing tools for implementing the strategies in Parts I and II and enabling the sustainability and transfer of improved student behavior resulting from their application.

CHAPTER 15 TAKEAWAYS

■ There are two major tasks in achieving successful behavioral improvements; that is, procedures for changing behavior and procedures for sustaining it.

■ There is no guarantee that behavior changes achieved in one setting will automatically transfer to other settings.

■ Regarding behavioral improvement, the general rule seems to be "Where you teach it is where you get it!"

■ There are a number of effective techniques for prompting and supporting students to display their improved behavior in non-intervention settings (i.e., boosters, verbal instructions, priming, adult and peer self-monitoring, adult praise, and verbal encouragement).

■ Positive behavior changes are more likely to be sustained in the setting in which they were produced over the long term if a low-cost variation of the behavior improvement strategy is implemented from time to time.

Short Form of the SBS Inventory

Hill M. Walker, PhD, and Richard Rankin, PhD

GENERAL INSTRUCTIONS

This inventory, reprinted with author permission and freely reproducible, consists of two sets of items descriptive of student behavior in the classroom. The first set of items (Section 1) describes student social behavior competencies and skills that are considered appropriate to the classroom. The second set (Section 2) describes student behavior that is considered maladaptive, challenging, and disruptive to the classroom. Section 3 of the inventory asks you to review the Section 1 and 2 items you rated as either *critically important* or *unacceptable* and indicate the ones for which you would want assistance in working with a student displaying that behavior. Please make *one* of three rating judgments about *each* item in Sections 1 and 2 and then complete Section 3. Thank you for your willingness to complete this inventory and planning tool.

SECTION 1: DESCRIPTIONS OF ADAPTIVE, APPROPRIATE STUDENT BEHAVIOR

Instructions

For the items in this section, please indicate whether the behavior described is **critical, desirable,** or **unimportant** to a successful adjustment in your classroom.

Critical means that possession of the behavior is absolutely essential to a successful or satisfactory adjustment in your classroom.

Desirable means that possession of the behavior is not essential or critical to a satisfactory classroom adjustment but is encouraged.

Unimportant means that you perceive the behavior as not being necessary or required for a satisfactory adjustment in your classroom.

Please circle the appropriate choice to the right of the item: C for **critical**, D for **desirable,** and U for **unimportant**. The line to the left of each item will be used later.

_____ 1. Student seeks teacher attention at appropriate times. [C] [D] [U]

_____ 2. Student makes his or her assistance needs known in an appropriate manner (raises hand, asks for help, etc.) [C] [D] [U]

_____ 3. Student listens carefully to teacher instructions and directions for assignments. [C] [D] [U]

_____ 4. Student complies with teacher commands. [C] [D] [U]

_____ 5. Student improves academic or social behavior in response to teacher feedback. [C] [D] [U]

_____ 6. Student produces work of acceptable quality given his or her skill level. [C] [D] [U]

_____ 7. Student cooperates with peers in group activities or situations. [C] [D] [U]

_____ 8. Student compliments peers regarding some attribute(s) or behavior. [C] [D] [U]

_____ 9. Student has independent study skills, that is, works adequately with minimal teacher support, attempts to solve problem(s) before asking for help. [C] [D] [U]

_____ 10. Student copes with failure in an appropriate manner, that is, doesn't give up on tasks or assignments. [C] [D] [U]

_____ 11. Student behaves appropriately in nonclassroom settings (restrooms, hallway, lunchroom, playground), that is, walks quietly, follows playground rules, etc. [C] [D] [U]

_____ 12. Student resolves peer conflicts or problems adequately on her or his own without requesting teacher assistance. [C] [D] [U]

_____ 13. Student can accept not getting his or her own way. [C] [D] [U]

_____ 14. Student ignores the distractions or interruptions of other students during academic activities. [C] [D] [U]

_____ 15. Student can participate in and contribute to group instructional situations or activities. [C] [D] [U]

_____ 16. Student has good work habits, that is, makes efficient use of class time, is organized, and stays on task. [C] [D] [U]

_____ 17. Student makes productive use of time while waiting for teacher assistance, that is, continues to work on problems that do not prove difficult. [C] [D] [U]

_____ 18. Student completes tasks within prescribed time limits. [C] [D] [U]

_____ 19. Student expresses anger appropriately, that is, reacts to [C] [D] [U]
situations without being violent or destructive.

_____ 20. Student does seatwork assignments as directed. [C] [D] [U]

SECTION 2: DESCRIPTIONS OF MALADAPTIVE, INAPPROPRIATE STUDENT BEHAVIOR

Instructions

For the items in this section, please indicate whether the behavior described is
unacceptable, tolerated, or **acceptable** in your classroom.

Unacceptable means that you would not tolerate the behavior occurring in
your classroom. Should an instance of the behavior occur, you would initiate active
methods to (1) suppress or eliminate it and (2) prevent its future occurrence.

Tolerated means that while you will put up with the behavior in question (at
least temporarily), you would prefer to see it reduced in frequency or replaced by
an appropriate, incompatible behavior.

Acceptable means the behavior presents no problems for you and you would
not initiate procedures to reduce or eliminate it.

Please circle the appropriate choice to the right of the item: **U** for **unacceptable**, **T** for **tolerated**, and **A** for **acceptable**. The line to the left of each item will be
used later.

_____ 1. Student is easily distracted from the task or activity at [U] [T] [A]
hand.

_____ 2. Student has tantrums. [U] [T] [A]

_____ 3. Student lies. [U] [T] [A]

_____ 4. Student ignores teacher warnings or reprimands. [U] [T] [A]

_____ 5. Student cheats, that is, copies work from others. [U] [T] [A]

_____ 6. Student becomes visibly upset or angry when things do [U] [T] [A]
not go his or her way.

_____ 7. Student damages others' property, that is, academic [U] [T] [A]
materials, personal possessions, etc.

_____ 8. Student asks irrelevant questions, that is, questions [U] [T] [A]
serve no functional purpose and are not task-related.

_____ 9. Student reacts with defiance to instructions or [U] [T] [A]
commands.

_____ 10. Student steals. [U] [T] [A]

_____ 11. Student does not follow specified rules of games or [U] [T] [A]
class activities.

_____ 12. Student obeys only when threatened with punishment. [U] [T] [A]

_____ 13. Student argues and must have the last word in verbal [U] [T] [A]
exchanges with peers or teacher.

_____ 14. Student appears to be unmotivated, that is, not [U] [T] [A]
interested in schoolwork.

_____ 15. Student displays high levels of dependence, that is, [U] [T] [A]
needs excessive amounts of assistance, feedback, or
supervision to complete tasks.

_____ 16. Student does not respond when called on. [U] [T] [A]

_____ 17. Student creates a disturbance during class activities, [U] [T] [A]
that is, is excessively noisy, is out of seat, bothers other
students, etc.

_____ 18. Student interrupts the teacher when the teacher is [U] [T] [A]
engaged in a presentation or activity.

_____ 19. Student engages in inappropriate sexual behavior, that [U] [T] [A]
is, masturbates, exposes self.

_____ 20. Student does not follow or give in to necessary rules of [U] [T] [A]
games and class activities.

SECTION 3: TECHNICAL ASSISTANCE NEEDS

Instructions

The purpose of this section of the SBS Inventory is to identify your technical assistance needs in teaching and managing at-risk students who, at some future point, could be integrated into your classroom. These students are likely to be deficient in some of the skills and competencies listed in Section 1 and outside the normal range on some of the maladaptive behaviors described in Section 2.

Please make one of three judgments for each item in Section 1 that you rated as **critical** and also for each item in Section 2 you rated as **unacceptable**. On the line to the left of each of your critical and unacceptable rated items, enter an **A**, **B**, or **C** to indicate the following.

(A) You would insist that the student have mastered the skill or competency **prior to entry into your classroom.**

(B) Following entry, you would accept responsibility for developing the skill or competency, but you would expect technical assistance in the process of doing so.

(C) Following entry, you would accept responsibility for developing the skill or competency and would **not** require technical assistance.

Similarly, for each item you marked as unacceptable (**U**) in Section 2, enter **A, B,** or **C** to indicate the following.

(A) The student must be within normal limits on the social behavior in question **prior to entry into your classroom.**

(B) Following entry, you would take responsibility for moving the student to within normal limits on the social behavior in question, but only with technical assistance provided.

(C) Following entry, you would take responsibility for moving the student to within normal limits on the social behavior and would **not** require technical assistance.

APPENDIX 2

Recommended Additional Resources for Use by Teachers

This appendix contains recommended best-practice resources, including assessment procedures, intervention programs, books on critically important topics, and systemwide frameworks for dealing with problems that are schoolwide or that extend beyond the classroom and require collaborations among teachers, related services personnel, school administrators, and sometimes families. Problems and needs addressed by these resources include bullying and harassment, behavioral assessment, identifying students early who may experience reading failure at the end of the primary grades, teaching violence prevention skills, behavioral screening to detect students with social–emotional and behavioral challenges, creating a positive school climate, severe tantrumming, and so forth. These resources are described herein with a brief notation as to the problems or issues each addresses, an overview of the resource, access information, and evidence for its effectiveness. A listing of these resources is provided below, followed by an annotated bibliography for them.

- Steps to Respect—Addresses schoolwide bullying and harassment.
- Positive Behavioral Interventions and Supports (PBIS)—Provides a structure for intervention strategies to create a positive school climate.
- Second Step Violence Prevention Curriculum—Instructional program that teaches social–emotional skills and lessons on how to avoid and prevent violence.
- Family Check-Up (FCU)—Proven process for assisting parents and teachers in improving the school success of elementary and middle school students with challenging behavior.
- Classroom Check-Up (CCU)—Collaborative teacher support system for enhancing positive behavior management outcomes in the classroom.
- First Step Next (FSN)—Early intervention for preschool to second-grade students who need assistance in getting off to the best start possible in their schooling.

- Dynamic Indicators of Basic Early Literacy Skills (DIBELS)—Early assessment of literacy skills to preidentify reading failure prior to third grade.
- Systematic Screening for Behavior Disorders (SSBD)—Procedure to identify students with challenging behavior.
- Comprehensive, integrated, three-tiered (Ci3T) model (Lane, Menzies, Oakes, & Kalberg, 2020)—Organizational structure for integrating/coordinating social–emotional, behavioral, and academic intervention strategies for all students.
- *The Explosive Child* (Green, 2014)—Classic text for parents and teachers on how to deal with the defiant, out-of-control child.
- *School-Based Behavioral Assessment* (Chafouleas, Johnson, Riley-Tillman, & Iovino, 2021)—Classic book on behavioral assessment of social, behavioral, and emotional problems in schooling.

STEPS TO RESPECT (STR)

STR is a universal, anti-bullying curricular program for reducing bullying and supportive bystander behavior among general education students in grades K–5. The program increases prosocial beliefs regarding peer relations and teaches social–emotional skills via use of appropriate educational materials. STR has been endorsed as effective by the following organizations: Blueprints for Healthy Youth Development, CrimeSolutions, and OJJDP Model Programs. It is an established evidence-based program.

Program Contact Information

Sally Vilardi, Director of Marketing and Outreach
Committee for Children
2815 2nd Ave., Suite 400
Seattle, WA 98121
800-634-4449
Email: Svilardi@cfchildren.org
Website: *www.cfchildren.org*

Program Overview

STR is designed to reduce bullying through the following means: (1) increasing staff awareness and responsiveness, (2) fostering socially responsible beliefs, and (3) teaching social–emotional skills to counter bullying and promote healthy relationships. The program also aims to promote skills (e.g., group joining, conflict resolution) associated with general social competence. STR is comprised of a program guide, staff training, and classroom lessons for students in grades K–5. All school staff receive an overview of the program's goals and key features of the program content. Teachers, counselors, and administrators receive additional training in how to coach students who have been involved in bullying. The student curriculum consists of skills and literature-based lessons presented by third- through sixth-grade teachers over a 12- to 14-week implementation period. Ten semi-scripted lessons focus on social–emotional skills for positive peer relations, emotion management, and recognizing, refusing, and reporting bullying behavior. A 45-minute skill lesson and 15-minute follow-up booster sessions are taught weekly to provide review. Parents are provided information about the program throughout the implementation period.

Program Outcomes

STR has been established as an evidenced-based intervention in the prevention of bullying. Elementary schools using this program reported a drop in teacher reports of physical bullying and fighting (McElroy, 2011). These schools also saw gains in school climate and protective factors. A study by Brown, Low, Smith, and Haggerty (2011) provided partial validation of the STR program as a means of achieving this outcome. This study reported outcomes of a randomized controlled trial of STR conducted in 33 elementary schools. Schools were matched on demographics and then randomly assigned to intervention or wait-list control conditions. Study participants were selected teachers and their classrooms in grades 3–5 of participating schools. Outcomes showed statistically significant gains of the STR program over participants in the control condition on the following variables: (1) improved student climate, (2) reductions in physical bullying, and (3) fewer bullying related problems. Staff in these schools were also informed about the STR intervention and their support doubtless contributed to the positive outcomes of the study.

References

Brown, E., Low, S., Smith, B., & Haggerty, K. (2011). Outcomes from a school-randomized controlled trial of Steps to Respect: A bullying prevention program. *School Psychology Review, 40*(3), 423–443.

McElroy, M. (2011, September 21). Thirty-three percent drop in physical bullying using Steps to Respect. University of Washington blog post. Retrieved December 3, 2021, from *www.washington.edu/news/2011/09/21/33-percent-drop-in-physical-bullying-in-schools-using-steps-to-respect.*

POSITIVE BEHAVIORAL INTERVENTIONS AND SUPPORTS (PBIS)

PBIS is a framework for selecting and implementing the use of evidence-based prevention and intervention practices along a multi-tiered continuum that support improved academic, social–emotional, and behavioral competence. This positive approach is a powerful alternative to zero tolerance policies that have held sway among educators for so long in dealing with challenging behavior in schools. When implemented effectively, PBIS supports students in their academic success; schools experience less need for the use of suspension and exclusion; and teachers and school staff perceive themselves as more effective.

Program Contact Information

National Technical Assistance Center on Positive Behavioral Interventions and Supports
U.S. Department of Education
Office of Special Education Programs and Office of Elementary and Secondary Education Center on PBIS (2021)
Website: *www.pbis.org*
State-level PBIS coordinators can be contacted for additional information and how to initiate PBIS.

Program Overview

PBIS is a schoolwide, three-tiered framework for coordinating interventions that address the needs of all, some, or a few of a school's students. PBIS implements three levels of interventions and supports as follows: (1) Tier 1—all students, (2) Tier 2—some students, and (3) Tier 3—a few students. The program teaches three core values as follows: (1) be safe, (2) be respectful, and (3) be responsible. Students and the teacher together determine how these core values translate into specific behavioral expectations.

As noted, PBIS provides a scaffold or platform for delivery of evidence-based interventions that achieve goals at each tier of the continuum. Tier 1 is universal in that all students receive the intervention. Those students who do not respond to Tier 1 receive additional intervention and support in Tier 2. Tier 3 students, who don't respond to either Tier 1 or Tier 2, are the focus of intensive additional services and supports in addition to those already received in Tiers 1 and 2. PBIS has been broadly accepted by K–12 schools in the United States (Bradshaw, Waasdorp, & Leaf, 2012). PBIS maximizes the cost-effective allocation of school resources and addresses the needs of all students in general education classrooms. It is especially useful for addressing the needs of students having disabilities within mainstream, least restrictive environment settings.

Program Outcomes

There have been numerous studies of the impact of PBIS. Horner and Sugai (2015) provided an overview of the areas in which PBIS implementation has produced important outcomes over two decades resulting from 21,000 program adoptions. They include (1) reductions in office discipline referrals (ODRs), (2) improved social–emotional competence, (3) reductions in out-of-school suspensions and expulsions, (4) improved organizational efficiency, (5) improved academic outcomes, and (6) reductions in bullying. It is extremely rare to see a single program with this degree of impact across decades and diverse settings.

One of the most impactful scientific studies of PBIS is by Bradshaw and colleagues (2012), who conducted a randomized controlled trial of the PBIS program involving 37 elementary schools and over 12,000 students in grades K–2. The study spanned 5 years. Primary study measures included ODRs and the Teacher Observation of Classroom Adaptation (TOCA-C) Checklist. The student sample was 52% male and 45% African American. Students in PBIS schools had lower levels of aggressive and disruptive behaviors compared to students in control schools. There was also a reduction in concentration problems, prosocial behavior, and emotional regulation, favoring PBIS school students over control school students. PBIS students also had a 33% lower likelihood of receiving an ODR than students in control schools. This longitudinal intervention study provided powerful multidimensional impact of PBIS when implemented fully and correctly with young children. As such, it has many implications for long-term prevention of challenging behavior in schools.

References

Bradshaw, C., Waasdorp, T., & Leaf, P. (2012). Effects of school-wide interventions and supports on child behavior. *Pediatrics, 130*(5), 1136–1145.

Horner, R., & Sugai, G. (2015). School-wide PBIS: An example of applied behavior analysis implemented at a scale of social importance. *Behavior Analysis Practices, 8*(1), 80–85.

SECOND STEP PROGRAM

Second Step is a universal curriculum for teaching all students the social–emotional skills that are critical in preventing conflicts that can escalate into interpersonal violence. Second Step was developed by the Committee for Children and is used in approximately 20,000 U.S. schools. The Committee for Children dates its existence from 1979. There are versions of the program for use in preschool through middle school. Second Step is considered a social–emotional learning program and teaches skills such as self-regulation, empathy, getting along with others, friendship making, and problem solving. Second Step ranks as an evidence-based program that is highly respected.

Program Contact Information

Committee for Children
2815 2nd Ave., Suite 400
Seattle, WA 98121
800-634-4449
Email: *Support@secondstep.org*

Program Overview

]Second Step is a holistic approach for transforming a school into a positive learning environment where all students have the opportunity to be successful. There are separate program versions for preschool, elementary, and middle school. Spanish-language versions are also an option, as is an online option for remote learning. The developers of Second Step recommend staff training to foster quality implementation. This training can be delivered online.

For maximum impact, the following guidelines should be observed in Second Step implementation: (1) embed Second Step into the school schedule, (2) set aside time for Second Step lessons at the beginning of each day, and (3) implement the program so everyone is learning and practicing the same skills at the same time. Second Step also has a unit on managing disruptive behavior as well as video-based training modules to introduce Second Step and how to use it successfully. The cost of Second Step will vary by size of school. Prices range from a one-time cost of $2,200 to $3,100 for a single school's materials. Multisite prices for materials provide an economy of scale in cost savings.

Program Outcomes

A strength of Second Step is that it has been found effective by researchers other than the program developers. Some studies have evaluated the preschool, elementary, and middle school versions of Second Step. A randomized controlled trial investigation by Upshur, Heyman, and Wenz-Gross (2017) of the early learning version of Second Step showed that at the end of preschool, children in the treatment group had better executive function skills than students in the control group. A 2018 study by Wenz-Gross, Yoo, Upshur, and Gambino (2018) replicated these findings and showed that Second Step preschoolers significantly increased their executive function upon entering kindergarten. Growth in their executive function predicted corresponding gains in students' pre-academic skills and on-task behavior, which was associated with improved kindergarten readiness. Low, Cook, Smolkowski, and Buntain-Ricklefs (2015) conducted a study of the elementary version of Second Step that involved a randomized controlled trial of 7,300 K–2 students, 321 teachers, 61 schools within six participating school districts. The study found improvements in prosocial skills, empathy, and conduct benefiting students in the Second Step treatment group. Finally, Second Step has been found to reduce aggression among middle school students, and a longitudinal follow-up study showed that it improved students' sense of middle school belonging, which was related to reduced negative outcomes in high school (e.g., sexual harassment and victimization, bullying, and cyberbullying; see Espelage, Low, Polanin, & Brown, 2013). Second Step has been rated as effective in multiple studies cited in the National Institute of Justice CrimeSolutions compilation.

References

Espelage, D., Low, S., Polanin, J., & Brown, E. (2013). The impact of a middle school program to reduce aggression, victimization and sexual violence. *Journal of Adolescent Health, 53,* 180–186.

Low, S., Cook, C., Smolkowski, K., & Buntain-Ricklefs, J. (2015). Promoting social–emotional competence: An evaluation of the elementary version of Second Step. *Journal of School Psychology, 53,* 463–477.

Upshur, C., Heyman, M., & Wenz-Gross, M. (2017). Efficacy trial of the Second Step Early Learning Curriculum: Preliminary outcomes. *Journal of Applied Developmental Psychology, 50,* 15–25.

Wenz-Gross, M., Yoo, Y., Upshur, C., & Gambino, A. (2018). Pathways to kindergarten readiness: The roles of Second Step Early Learning Curriculum and social emotional, executive functioning, preschool academic, and task behavior skills. *Frontiers in Psychology, 9,* 1886.

FAMILY CHECK-UP (FCU)

The FCU is a strengths-based intervention approach for children ages 2–17 and their parents. It promotes positive child outcomes by improving parenting and family management practices. The FCU is an evidence-based and highly respected intervention with more than three decades of adoption and implementation with strong outcomes. Stormshak, Fosco, and Dishion (2010) have developed a highly successful school implementation of this program for use with parents of middle school students, which is described here.

Program Contact Information

Family Check-Up
Arizona State University REACH Institute
ASU Psychology North Building
900 S. McAllister Ave., Room 205
P.O. Box 876005
Tempe, AZ 85287-6005
480-965-7420

Program Overview

The FCU was designed as a family-centered intervention that is implementable in school contexts and other settings such as mental health clinics, health care settings, and other venues that serve the needs of families. The FCU teaches parents important family management practices and skills such as child monitoring and parent encouragement and involvement. Parents also become involved in their child's school participation, such as ensuring that homework is completed. The FCU motivates and engages parents to improve their parenting skills and to access needed services for which they qualify.

The FCU involves three meetings with a youth's caregivers. The first meeting is to identify the parents' goals and to assess their motivation for changing their parenting practices. The second meeting is focused on securing completion of a packet of assessments from the child, teacher, and parents. Parents also participate in an observational assessment of their interactions with their child. The third meeting reviews results of the assessments and a menu of intervention options for improving family management practices. Most parents choose to continue their FCU involvement over the long term. Related services staff in schools (counselors, behavioral specialists, service coordinators, and administrators) can be trained to implement the FCU model.

Program Outcomes

Stormshak et al. (2010) examined outcomes associated with FCU's impact on families and children in three middle schools. Goals of the intervention were to enhance the positive adjustment of middle schoolers and prevent problem behavior. The study sample involved 377 families who were assigned randomly to either FCU intervention or school as usual. Exposure to the intervention improved self-regulation over the 3 years of the study. Results also showed reductions in depression and increased school engagement. The FCU has been shown to reduce the growth of problem behavior, family conflict, and substance use among middle school youth (Dishion & Stormshak, 2007). The support that FCU parents provide children leads to important outcomes in self-regulation (Stormshak et al., 2010). These FCU results have important implications for the delivery of effective mental health services and healthy family management practices within school contexts.

References

Dishion, T., & Stormshak, E. (2007). *Intervening in children's lives: An ecological, family-centered approach to mental health care*. Washington, DC: American Psychological Association.

Stormshak, E., Fosco, G., & Dishion, T. (2010). Implementing interventions with families in schools to increase youth engagement: The Family Check-Up Model. *School Mental Health, 2*(2), 82–92.

CLASSROOM CHECK-UP (CCU)

The CCU is a valuable resource and implementation system for supporting teachers by school-based consultants (behavioral coaches) who serve in roles designed to improve classroom behavior management. The CCU was developed by Reinke, Lewis-Palmer, & Merrell (2008) as a way of reducing disruptive classroom behavior through increasing teacher praise rates for appropriate student behavior. It is focused on changing the ecology of the entire classroom via improved behavior management processes. Since its initial development, the CCU has been elaborated into a comprehensive system of teacher support having four modules through a large grant from the Institute of Education Sciences to Wendy Reinke and Keith Herman of the University of Missouri.

Program Contact Information

Classroom Check-Up
National Center for Rural School Mental Health
University of Missouri
16 Hill Hall
Columbia, MO 65211
888-473-5623
Email: *Support@3cisd.com*

Program Overview

The CCU contains Web-based tools and access to training via the following intervention modules: (1) classroom structure, (2) management of instruction, (3) classroom behavior management, and (4) classroom climate. Each module has a variety of training tools such as videos, assessment instruments, intervention options, and action planning strategies. The CCU provides participant roles for teachers, consulting coaches, and administrators. There are five essential steps involved in the implementation of the CCU.

1. *Assess the classroom.* The first step of the CCU is to assess the classroom environment through direct observation, conducting a teacher interview, and evaluating the classroom ecology. A key purpose of this interview is to establish rapport between the coach and teacher and to identify strengths and areas of teacher need and support.
2. *Discuss feedback from assessments.* The coach provides feedback on results of the Step 1 assessments and identifies strengths as well as teacher needs.
3. *Develop list of menu options.* Teacher and coach collaboratively develop a menu of options for intervening to create positive classroom outcomes.

4. *Select intervention.* Teacher chooses which intervention to implement and consultant provides support for the implementation.
5. *Self-monitor intervention.* The participating teacher is trained to self-monitor implementation of the selected intervention.

After implementation, maintenance and follow-up consultation is provided by the coach to troubleshoot the classroom situation and respond to the teacher's ongoing need for support and assistance.

Technical support for implementing the CCU is available via the following email address: *Support@3cisd.com.*

Program Outcomes

The CCU is a well-researched, evidence-based intervention. A study by Reinke, Lewis-Palmer, and Merrell (2008), its developers, provides an example of the kinds of outcomes it produces when implemented according to best-practice guidelines. The CCU provides training in the effective use of teacher praise through observation and feedback on the teacher's performance. The investigators found that the CCU had a significant impact on both teacher and student behavior as well as social validity outcomes indicating acceptance and perceived importance of the intervention by participants. Specifically, they found (1) an increase in overall teacher praise rates, including use of behavior-specific praise, (2) a corresponding reduction in classroom disruptions by students, (3) reduced use of reprimands, and (4) partial retention of intervention gains in outcomes despite declining trends in maintenance and follow-up periods.

Reference

Reinke, W., Lewis-Palmer, T., & Merrell, K. (2008). The Classroom Checkup: A classwide teacher consultant model for increasing praise and decreasing disruptive behavior. *School Psychology Review, 37*(3), 315–332.

FIRST STEP NEXT (FSN) PROGRAM

The FSN program is a Tier 2, selected early intervention designed to assist behaviorally at-risk students in getting off to the best start possible in their school careers. The program, originally called First Step to Success, was developed by the author and his colleagues (Walker et al., 1997; Walker, Severson, et al., 1998; Walker, Kavanagh, et al., 1998) through a 4-year model development grant from the U.S. Office of Special Education Programs. Since its original publication, First Step has been the focus of a large number of randomized controlled trials and single-case experimental designs. First Step was revised and updated in 2015 and renamed First Step Next (Walker et al., 2015).

Program Contact Information

First Step Next
Ancora Publishing, Inc.
21 W. 6th Ave.
Eugene, OR 97401
Website: *https://ancorapublishing.com*
866-542-1490

Program Overview

FSN is a social–ecological intervention for preschool through grade-2 students who present behavioral challenges in schooling that result in a poor fit between a student's behavioral characteristics and the routines and demands of school environments (Romer & Heller, 1983). Students who qualify for FSN often come from homes with dysfunctional family ecologies characterized by negative exchanges among family members (Patterson, 1982). Children bring coercive behavior patterns to school with them, which often get them into conflicts with teachers and peers.

FSN is designed to intervene early in this process and to assist the child in getting off to a good start in their schooling. It involves parents in supporting and participating in the intervention, which typically lasts 2–3 months from start to finish. FSN has three interconnected parts: (1) a screening-identification process, (2) school intervention, and (3) parent support. The school intervention has three phases as follows: (1) a coach phase lasting 10 days, (2) a teacher phase lasting 10 days, and (3) a maintenance phase lasting 10 days. Both school and home rewards are used to motivate the FSN focus student and peers to cooperate with the intervention. The FSN coach sets the program up initially and operates it for the first 5 days and then trains the cooperating teacher to assume control of the program in days 5–10. By program day 10, FSN is extended to all periods in which the focus student may be experiencing problems. During the maintenance phase, a number of strategies are used to help sustain achieved behavioral gains, including booster shots, peer and teacher praise, and brief reintroduction of the FSN intervention.

Program Outcomes

Since its initial development, a robust evidence base has been developed on the FSN program's efficacy and effectiveness. Most of this work has been produced by the FSN author and colleagues (Walker et al., 2009; Frey et al., in press) but some excellent work has also been conducted on the program and its outcomes by other investigators (see Nelson et al., 2009). To date there have been five efficacy and three effectiveness studies of the First Step program and its outcomes. These studies show positive outcomes, averaging a moderate level of impact, across a broad range of diverse measures, student participants, and school districts.

The First Step program has been endorsed by the What Works Clearinghouse of the Institute of Education Sciences as a promising program. It is also listed in the Model Programs Guide by the U.S. Office of Juvenile Justice and Delinquency Prevention.

References

Frey, A., Small, J., Walker, H., Mitchell, B., Seeley, J., Feil, . . . Forness, S. (in press). First Step Next: A synthesis of replication studies from 2009–2021. *Remedial and Special Education.*

Nelson, R., Duppong, K., Synhorst, L., Epstein, M., Stage, S., & Buckley, J. (2009). The child outcomes of a behavior model. *Exceptional Children, 76*(1), 7–30.

Patterson, G. (1982). *Coercive family process.* Eugene, OR: Castalia.

Romer, D., & Heller, T. (1983). Social adaptation of mentally retarded adults: A social-ecological approach. *Applied Research in Mental Retardation, 4,* 303–314.

Walker, H., Kavanagh, K., Stiller, B., Golly, A., Feil, E., & Severson, H. (1997). *First Step to Success: Helping young children overcome antisocial behavior.* Longmont, CO: Sopris West.

Walker, H., Kavanagh, K., Stiller, B., Golly, A., Severson, H., & Feil, E. (1998). First Step: An early intervention approach for preventing school antisocial behavior. *Journal of Emotional and Behavioral Disorders, 6*(2), 66–80.

Walker, H., Seeley, J., Small, J., Severson, H., Graham, B., Feil, E., . . . Forness, S. (2009). A randomized controlled trial of the First Step to Success early intervention: Demonstration of program efficacy in a diverse, urban district. *Journal of Emotional and Behavioral Disorders, 17*(4), 197–212.

Walker, H., Severson, H., Feil, E., Stiller, B., & Golly, A. (1998). First Steps to Success: Intervening at the point of school entry to prevent antisocial behavior patterns. *Psychology in the Schools, 35*(3), 259–269.

Walker, H., Stiller, B., Coughlin, C., Golly, A., Sprick, M., & Feil, E. (2015). *First Step Next* (rev. 2nd ed.). Eugene, OR: Ancora.

DYNAMIC INDICATORS OF BASIC EARLY LITERACY SKILLS (DIBELS)

DIBELS is a set of assessment procedures for measuring the acquisition of literacy skills of young students who are early in their schooling. DIBELS is based on the work of Deno and associates (Deno, 1985) on curriculum-based assessment. DIBELS was developed originally by Good and Kaminsky (1996) and has been further developed and extensively researched by researchers of the Center on Teaching and Learning at the University of Oregon. It is now in its eighth edition.

This widely adopted assessment procedure has proven effective in predicting those students who are likely to have reading problems at the end of grade 3, when students are required to begin using reading as a tool for learning other subject matter.

Program Contact Information

DIBELS
Center on Teaching and Learning (CTL)
5292 University of Oregon
Eugene, OR 97403
Website: *www.dibels.uoregon.edu*
541-346-4349

Program Overview

DIBELS was developed to be an economical, early indicator of a student's progress in reading and other subject areas. DIBELS consists of a series of 1-minute fluency subtests that can be used to regularly monitor development of early literacy and reading skills in kindergarten through eighth grade. DIBELS measures skills related to general reading outcomes. Each subtest is a valid and reliable indicator of early literacy development. These subtests contribute to a composite score that is the single best predictor of later reading achievement, which is an invaluable asset in preventing reading failure.

CTL offers a scoring and interpretation service for DIBELS. The center provides an administrative guide, student materials, scoring booklets, and testing resources for free. Extensive information about all aspects of DIBELS can be accessed through its website.

Program Outcomes

For the past two decades a large number of researchers have been involved in conducting DIBELS research and development activities that have (1) established its psychometric characteristics and (2) developed, trial tested, and expanded the features and options it now offers. CTL has compiled a list of technical reports on DIBELS as well as a large number of published articles on its outcomes and efficacy. All this information can be accessed on the DIBELS website. DIBELS is a thoroughly researched and highly effective assessment procedure.

References

Deno, 1985. Curriculum based measurement: The emerging alternative. *Exceptional Children, 52*(3), 219–232.
Deno, S., & Fuchs, L. (1987). Developing curriculum-based measurement systems for data-based special education problem solving. *Focus on Exceptional Children, 19,* 1–16.

Good, R., & Kaminsky, R. (1996). Assessment for instructional decisions: Toward a proactive/prevention model of decision-making for early literacy skills. *School Psychology Quarterly, 11*(4), 326–336.

SYSTEMATIC SCREENING FOR BEHAVIOR DISORDERS (SSBD)

The SSBD is a universal PreK through grade 9 screener designed to identify students having challenging behavior of two main types: internalizing versus externalizing. Internalizing refers to problems with self (internal); externalizing refers to problems with others (external). The vast majority of the behavior problems children and youth experience can be classified as either internalizing or externalizing. The SSBD uses a combination of teacher rankings, ratings, and behavioral observations to accurately screen and identify preschool through grade 9 students experiencing these problems so they can access appropriate services and supports. The SSBD comes in two versions: paper and pencil, and online. Scoring is by hand for the paper and pencil version and is automatic for the online option.

In addition to its role in screening and identification, the SSBD can be used as: (1) an added information source in a comprehensive evaluation process, (2) a program evaluation and research tool, and (3) an information source for determining staff training needs and technical assistance. The SSBD is a complete screening, identification, and monitoring system that allows school professionals to accurately identify behaviorally at-risk students as early as possible in their school careers.

Program Contact Information

SSBD
Ancora Publishing, Inc.
21 W. 6th Ave.
Eugene, OR 97401
Website: *https://ancorapublishing.com*
866-542-1490
Contact Sara Ferris of Ancora with information requests regarding the SSBD and its uses.

Program Overview

The SSBD (Walker & Severson, 1990) was developed and initially validated in the late 1980s (see Walker et al., 1988; Walker et al., 1990). This screening system is referred to as a multiple-gating assessment in that it utilizes multiple gates or sequential screening stages to screen and identify behaviorally at-risk students efficiently and accurately. The SSBD was revised and updated in 2013 and the second edition was published in 2014 (Walker, Severson, & Feil, 2014). The SSBD was extended to grades 7–9 as part of the revision process. The SSBD also offers screening for 3- to 5-year-olds. SSBD Stages 1 and 2 screening forms for PreK–K are specially designed screeners for use in identifying at-risk children early in pre-school and kindergarten. Originally published as the Early Screening Project (ESP; Walker, Severson, & Feil, 1995), this screener was designed as a downward extension of the first edition of SSBD (grades 1–5).

Gate 1 of the SSBD requires the teacher to nominate and rank-order a subset of five students from the classroom whose characteristic behavior most closely matches a behavioral description of internalizing. This identical procedure is then repeated for another group of five externalizing students. In screening Gate 2, the three highest-ranked students are evaluated on rating scales and a critical events checklist. Those students on each dimension (internalizing and externalizing) who exceed Stage 2 normative criteria on the rating scales and checklist are then either (1) observed in their classroom settings using optional behavioral coding systems for classroom engagement and peer interactions or (2) referred for additional evaluation for possible intervention or additional services. In grades 7–9 screening, the optional behavior observations codes are not used. Students who meet at-risk criteria at screening Gates 2 and 3 and/or all three gates have serious behavioral challenges. Following screening, scores are derived for each student who completes Stage 2 screening and compared to risk criteria to determine behavioral status on the SSBD measures and the need for further assessment and/or services. For students in grades 1–9, guidelines are provided for an optional Archival School Records Search (SARS), which can be administered as well to gain a picture of the student's behavioral and academic history in school and assist in the decision-making process.

The SSBD comes with a CD that contains the technical manual, providing information on the validation and technical adequacy of the SSBD procedure. The CD also contains forms that can be used in scoring and interpreting the SSBD results, including scoring charts to determine Stage 2 and 3 risk status as well as individual student summary forms for reporting more detailed results for identified students.

Program Outcomes

Since it was first published in the early 1990s, the SSBD has been referred to by some professionals as the "gold standard" of universal behavioral screening for students with challenging behavior. The second edition of the SSBD is one of a small number of tools that screen for both externalizing and internalizing behavior problems and disorders. The SSBD has been used by researchers as a validation criterion for establishing the validity of other screeners (Lane, Menzies, Oakes, & Kalberg, 2012). A large number of studies have been reported in the professional literature on the SSBD's psychometric characteristics and technical adequacy. The SSBD has adequate to good internal consistency, test–retest stability, and interrater agreement. There is strong empirical evidence for the SSBD's concurrent, discriminant, criterion-related, and predictive validity. See the SSBD Technical Manual on the CD for details of this evidence.

References

Lane, K., Menzies, W., Oakes, W., & Kalberg, J. (2012). *Systematic screenings of behavior to support instruction: From preschool to high school.* New York: Guilford Press.

Walker, H., & Severson, H. (1990). *Systematic Screening for Behavior Disorders (SSBD).* Longmont, CO: Sopris West.

Walker, H., Severson, H., & Feil, E. (2014). *Systematic Screening for Behavior Disorders (SSBD)* (2nd ed.). Eugene, OR: Ancora.

Walker, H., Severson, H., & Feil, E. (1995). *The Early Screening Project: A proven child-find process.* Eugene, OR: Applied Research Press.

Walker, H., Severson, H., Stiller, B., Williams, G., Haring, N., Shinn, M., & Todis, B. (1988). Systematic screening of pupils in the elementary age range at risk for behavior disorders: Development and trial testing of a multiple gating model. *Remedial and Special Education, 9*(3), 8–14.

Walker, H., Severson, H., Todis, B., Block-Pedgo, A., Williams, G., Haring, N., & Barckley, M. (1990). Systematic screening for behavior disorders (SSBD): Further validation, replication and normative data. *Remedial and Special Education, 11,* 32–46.

DEVELOPING A SCHOOLWIDE FRAMEWORK TO PREVENT AND MANAGE LEARNING AND BEHAVIOR PROBLEMS

This resource by Kathleen Lynne Lane, Holly Mariah Menzies, Wendy Peia Oakes, and Jemma Kalberg (2020) is a "must read" for the professional who wishes to establish, implement, and evaluate a comprehensive and integrated three-tiered (Ci3T) model of prevention for targeting academic, behavioral, and social–emotional problems. These authors demonstrate how to bring the best knowledge and research to bear on such problems. Each of the authors is firmly grounded and highly experienced in responding to the needs of teachers and students in both general and specialized school settings.

The second edition contains the following new features:

- Step-by-step descriptions of the continuing development of the Ci3T model
- Chapter on evidence for the effectiveness of tiered models of intervention
- Chapter on low-intensity, teacher-delivered strategies
- Chapter on sustaining effective implementation and professional development

- A lessons-learned feature containing reflections from educators in a range of settings

One of the greatest strengths of the book is the authors' promotion of low-intensity intervention techniques that are easy for teachers to implement and thus more likely for them to use. If ever there were a roadmap for creating an effective school, this is the template for doing so.

Contact Information

Guilford Publications (publisher)
370 Seventh Ave., Suite 1200
New York, NY 10001
800-365-7006, Ext. 1
Website: *www.guilford.com*

Reference

Lane, K., Menzies, H., Oakes, W., & Kalberg, J. (2020). *Developing a schoolwide framework to prevent and manage learning and behavior problems* (2nd ed.). New York: Guilford Press.

THE EXPLOSIVE CHILD

This highly recommended resource by Ross Green is suitable for use in school and family settings. This groundbreaking work, now a classic text, first published in 1998 and currently in its sixth edition, provides an insightful analysis of the explosive child for parents and teachers. *The Explosive Child* is essential reading for parents and professionals who have to cope with children and youth with poor self-regulation and self-control that causes them to have extreme reactions (tantrums, screaming) to routine problems. This book explains how children develop challenging behavior and describes a collaborative problem-solving approach for addressing it.

The author argues that the explosive child lacks some crucial skills in frustration tolerance, problem solving, and flexibility as well as adaptability. He presents a collaborative problem-solving model that engages explosive children to resolve the problems and skill deficits that contribute to this destructive behavior pattern. The success of his model has resulted in 750,000 copies sold to date.

Contact Information

HarperCollins (publisher; also available through Amazon)

Sixth edition, 2021
855-877-9820
Website: *www.harpercollins.com/page*

Reference

Green, R. (2014). *The explosive child: A new approach for understanding and parenting easily frustrated, chronically inflexible children.* New York: Harper.

SCHOOL-BASED BEHAVIORAL ASSESSMENT: INFORMING PREVENTION AND INTERVENTION

This second edition of a now classic text on behavioral assessment by Sandra M. Chafouleas, Austin H. Johnson, T. Chris Riley-Tillman, and Emily A. Iovino (2021) is a highly recommend resource for school staff who wish to profile and identify the social, emotional, and behavioral challenges that today's students face. As the authors note, the demand for tools and strategies in this realm has accelerated dramatically in the past decade, driven by (1) increasing school responsibility for addressing this priority and (2) the education field's move from diagnosis and detection to prevention and intervention. The material in this book provides an effective means to accomplish this goal and provides critical information on the following issues: (1) posing the right questions to drive the assessment process, (2) how to take advantage of existing data in assessment and decision making, and (3) best practices in conducting behavioral observations, behavior ratings, and direct behavior ratings that blend rating and observation approaches. Most importantly, the authors show how these different forms of behavioral assessment work when applied to realistic case examples. Having this book in one's professional toolkit will greatly expedite effective management of social, emotional, and behavioral challenges in schooling.

Contact Information

Guilford Publications (publisher)
370 Seventh Ave., Suite 1200
New York, NY 10001
800-365-7006, Ext. 1
Website: *www.guilford.com*

Reference

Chafouleas, S., Johnson, A., Riley-Tillman, T., & Iovino, E. (2021). *School-based behavioral assessment: Informing prevention and intervention* (2nd ed.). New York: Guilford Press.

Handout for Parents on How to Debrief Daily with Their Children about School

Debriefing is a process for talking with your children about what their school day was like. It has many advantages for the child and parents:

- Debriefing shows your interest in your child's schooling and how it's going.
- It's an opportunity to teach your child communication skills.
- Debriefing tells children you care for them and are concerned about what happens in their lives.
- It is an excellent form of screening to detect problems you might not find out about otherwise.
- Through debriefing, children can learn how to develop alternatives to problem situations and ways of responding to them effectively.
- Debriefing makes children more aware of their behavior and its impact on others.

WHEN TO DEBRIEF

Children should have some downtime after the stresses of the school day before being asked to engage in a debriefing session. Dinner time or after dinner may be a relaxed occasion for having a conversation about school and how it went. If a dinner time debriefing involves more than one child, each child should be asked different questions rather than the same question.

WHAT QUESTIONS TO ASK DURING DEBRIEFING

Debriefing about school will be easier if it has been an established practice prior to the beginning of schooling by asking questions like "Tell me what you did today that was fun", "Who did you play with today?", and "What did you like best about your day?"

Family psychologist Soroya Lakhani has written on the importance of debriefing about school and the kinds of questions that should be asked in family debriefing sessions (retrieved from September 2021 blog post, December, 2021). She suggests that open-ended questions like "How was your day?" should be avoided in favor of questions that require a specific answer. Too often children respond to open-ended questions with statements like "It was OK" or "Fine." She suggests using questions like the following.

- "What did you do during recess?"
- "What was the best thing that happened today?"
- "What was the worst thing that happened today?" "How did you handle it?"
- "Did you help anyone out today or did anyone help you?" (If so) "What for?"
- "Did anyone compliment you today?" (If so) "What for?"
- "Was anyone mean to you today?" (If yes) "Why so?
- "Did you play any game(s) today?" (If so) "What were they?
- "Was there a situation you didn't like at school today?"
- "Were there any problems that you needed your teacher's or classmates' help on?"
- "Did you have any problems today with schoolwork?" (If yes) "How did you solve them?"
- "Did you spend time with your friends today?" (If yes) "What did you all do?"

Debriefing in this way will yield many long-term benefits in your child's development.

Coping with the Impact of Psychiatric Disorders in School

There is voluminous evidence that the strategies and tools described in this volume are effective in improving the behavioral adjustment of most students who are exposed to them. But not all students respond well or respond at a level that educators expect. This outcome could well be due to the presence of an unrecognized or undiagnosed psychiatric disorder that may impact how a child responds to behavioral interventions (Konopasek & Forness, 2014). The presence of a psychiatric disorder such as attention-deficit/hyperactivity disorder (ADHD), depression, or an anxiety disorder might not always be recognized by parents or school professionals but could explain why a student is not responsive to a well-implemented behavioral intervention in school. Referral of the student to a community mental health practitioner such as a clinical psychologist, pediatrician, or child psychiatrist might well be warranted to rule in or rule out the role of a possible disorder and determine if treatment is needed. By law parents, not school professionals, have to initiate such a referral. Thus, it is important to explain in some detail to parents why such a referral is needed for their child.

Dr. Steven R. Forness of UCLA has been a long-term proponent of educators' understanding of how psychiatric disorders can negatively impact a student's academic and social–behavioral performance as well as reduce their responsiveness to school interventions. Dr. Forness has contributed some critical information on psychiatric disorders and their treatment that every educator should access. For many years he was the principal of the inpatient school for the UCLA Neuropsychiatric Hospital and was also chief of outpatient educational psychology. He has extensive knowledge of and experience with this issue.

Dr. Forness has contributed the following material for this appendix, including a valuable fact sheet of common psychiatric disorders, their symptoms, and their treatment. The goal of this material is to better enable school professionals to connect students and families to effective mental health interventions and services.

PSYCHIATRIC DISORDERS AND THEIR TREATMENT:
A FACT SHEET FOR SCHOOL PROFESSIONALS

by Steven R. Forness, UCLA

Children who have emotional or behavioral difficulties in school may have these problems for a variety of reasons. Family conflicts or other psychological stressors may leave many children with frustration, anger, and demoralizing or anxious feelings, as well as difficulties in concentration or learning. Their social or emotional problems require understanding and support from teachers and family members, and they may occasionally require counseling to help them deal with their feelings and explore ways of coping.

Psychiatric disorders, on the other hand, are generally more disabling, more difficult to diagnose correctly, and more likely to require very specific therapeutic interventions, such as cognitive-behavioral therapy or even psychopharmacology, that is, medications that are used to help the child control his or her emotional or behavioral symptoms. Child psychopharmacology, however, is a controversial field and has received a great deal of attention in the popular media, much of it over sensationalized. The media often suggest that large numbers of children are being prescribed medication for only minor problems. In actual fact, careful studies suggest that only a small fraction of children with serious psychiatric disorders are actually receiving such medication (Konopasek & Forness, 2014). In the hands of a competent pediatrician or child psychiatrist, moreover, these medications may be not only effective but also essential to an overall treatment program for many children with serious psychiatric disorders. Careful treatment with these medications has been shown not only to effect dramatic improvement in behavioral or emotional responses of these children but also to improve their social and even academic functioning. Specific behavioral and related therapies, however, may also be critical. These may be used alone, prior to, or concurrent with psychopharmacologic treatment. Combined behavioral and psychopharmacologic treatments are often found to be significantly better than either one used alone (Konopasek & Forness, 2014).

Psychiatric disorders are classified in the *Diagnostic and Statistical Manual of Mental Disorders* (5th ed., text rev.) of the American Psychiatric Association (DSM-5-TR, American Psychiatric Association, 2022). DSM-5-TR is used primarily by psychiatrists and psychologists to diagnose mental health problems in children and adolescents. It is sometimes the case that the behavioral interventions described in this teachers' desk reference may not work as expected because an undetected psychiatric disorder may be present, requiring much more intensive treatment. For this reason, a very brief "fact sheet" is provided below that is designed to acquaint teachers and other school professionals with the diagnosis and treatment of psychiatric disorders so that they can more readily detect children who

This section and the fact sheet are reprinted with permission from Steven R. Forness.

need to be referred to mental health professionals, when indicated, and also collaborate with these professionals in ongoing treatment when warranted. These disorders are presented briefly in terms of (1) primary symptoms and (2) psychosocial or psychopharmacologic treatments for each disorder.

Note that the attached fact sheet is neither an exhaustive nor a comprehensive description of childhood psychiatric disorders. It is intended merely as a brief introduction for teachers or other school professionals to some of the more common diagnoses that can impair school learning or classroom behavior. In addition, several other aids exist that may help school professionals recognize these disorders, such as:

- A behavioral checklist for teachers and parents has been developed by Gadow and Sprafkin (2015), which is based on DSM-5-TR and provides critical cutoff points that suggest the presence or absence of common psychiatric disorders.
- Introductory materials to educate teachers and parents about psychopharmacology have been developed for those interested in psychiatric medications (Konopasek, 2017; Wilens & Hammerness, 2016).
- Several clinical guidelines for specific evidence-based practices in both psychosocial and psychopharmacologic treatment have been developed by the American Academy of Child and Adolescent Psychiatry (AACAP) to assist families or other frontline professionals in making sure that mental health referrals are effective for diagnosis and treatment of psychiatric disorders.

REFERENCES

American Academy of Child and Adolescent Psychiatry (AACAP), 3615 Wisconsin Avenue, NW, Washington, DC 20016-3007. (Phone: 202-966-7300)

American Psychiatric Association. (2022). *Diagnostic and statistical manual of mental disorders* (DSM-5-TR., text rev.). Arlington, VA: Author.

Gadow, K., & Sprafkin, J. (2015). *Child Symptom Inventory manual.* Stony Brook, NY: Checkmate Plus.

Konopasek, D. (2017). *Medication fact sheets: A behavioral medication resource for educators.* Champaign, IL: Research Press.

Konopasek, D., & Forness, S. (2014). Issues and criteria for the effective use of psychopharmacological interventions in schooling. In H. Walker & F. Gresham (Eds.), *Handbook of evidence-based practices for emotional and behavioral disorders: Applications in schools* (pp. 457–474). New York: Guilford Press.

Wilens, T., & Hammerness, P. (2016). *Straight talk about psychiatric medications for kids* (4th ed.). New York: Guilford Press.

Fact Sheet: Psychiatric Disorders and Their Treatments

Disorder (primary symptoms)	Treatments
Oppositional defiant disorder (ODD) (persistent temper tantrums, arguing with adults, noncompliance, etc.). **Conduct disorder (CD)** (overt aggression, destruction, deceitfulness, theft, consistent rule violation, etc.).	**Psychosocial:** Behavioral interventions involving reinforcers for appropriate behavior and ignoring or time-out behavior. Collaboration and consultation with family on behavioral training and problem solving. **Psychopharmacologic:** Mainly for psychiatric disorders that are often comorbid with ODD or CD such as ADHD, depression, or anxiety disorders (see below).
Attention-deficit/hyperactivity disorder (ADHD) (inattention, such as not listening, lack of attention to detail, disorganization, distractibility, forgetfulness, etc.; and/or hyperactivity/impulsivity, such as excessive fidgeting, inability to sit still when expected, excessive running about, difficulty waiting turn, interrupting, etc.).	**Psychosocial:** Behavioral interventions and parent consultation with special emphasis on home–school collaboration for behavior management. **Psychopharmacologic:** Stimulant medications such as Ritalin, Dexedrine, or Adderall. For nonresponders, Strattera (a nonstimulant ADHD medication). Combined medication and behavioral treatment is best.
Depression (for at least 2 weeks, depressed or irritable mood and/or loss of interest/pleasure in most activities; fluctuations in weight, insomnia or sleeping too much, loss of energy, diminished concentration, feelings of worthlessness, suicidality, etc.). **Dysthymia** (for most days over a year, depressed or irritable mood with insomnia or sleeping too much, low energy, low self-esteem, poor concentration, hopelessness, etc.). **Bipolar or manic depressive disorder** (fluctuations in mood from depression, as noted above, to manic episodes with abnormal or persistently elevated or expansive mood along with decreased need for sleep, excessive talkativeness, distractibility, agitation, etc.).	**Psychosocial:** Cognitive-behavioral and/or interpersonal therapies to assist child in monitoring mood and developing coping skills. Few effective programs for bipolar disorder. **Psychopharmacologic:** SSRI medications such as Prozac, Zoloft, or Lexapro. Atypical antidepressants (such as Effexor or Cymbalta) or tricyclic antidepressants (Tofranil) for nonresponders. For bipolar disorder, lithium or Depakote are primary medications. Side effects may limit effective treatment of children with some of these drugs.
Generalized anxiety disorder (excessive worry about events or activities accompanied by restlessness, fatigue, concentration problems, irritability, tension, etc.).	**Psychosocial:** Cognitive-behavioral therapy to assist child in monitoring unrealistic anxieties, learning ways to develop a sense of self-control, and responding in a more adaptive fashion. Some behavior therapies may assist in reinforcing more adaptive responses.

Obsessive-compulsive disorder (obsessions are unrealistic recurrent thoughts or impulses that cannot be ignored or suppressed; compulsions are repetitive behaviors or mental acts that the child seems driven to perform in rigid ways to prevent or reduce imagined distress yet are excessive and unrealistic). **Separation anxiety disorder** (developmentally inappropriate and excessive anxiety concerning separation from home or family with worry about injury/loss to family member, fears about getting lost/kidnapped, persistent refusal to attend school because of separation, fear, etc.). **Posttraumatic stress disorder** (experiencing or witnessing a traumatic event involving intense fear or helplessness and subsequently "re-experiencing" the event persistently in intrusive recollections, dreams, or reminders; avoidance of the event through numbing, detachment, inability to recall details; and symptoms such as sleep disturbance, concentration problems, hypervigilance, etc.).	**Psychopharmacologic:** Some SSRI medications such as Zoloft or Luvox. For nonresponders, atypical antidepressants such as Effexor or possibly anxiolytics such as Ativan or Klonopin.
Schizophrenia or other psychotic disorders (delusions such as thinking one has special powers or that people are out to harm one; hallucinations such as hearing voices; grossly disorganized speech or behaviors; certain symptoms of social withdrawal).	**Psychosocial:** Behavioral and social skills training to assist child in coping, with emphasis on educating family about disorder. **Psychopharmacologic:** Atypical antipsychotics such as Risperdal, Zyprexa, and Abilify, with more traditional neuroleptics, such as Haldol, for nonresponders.
Autism spectrum disorders (social impairment such as lack of eye contact or failure to develop peer relationships or emotional give and take; communicative impairment such as delays in learning to speak, repetitive or odd phrasings; and restrictive or repetitive behaviors such as restricted patterns of interest or motor rituals).	**Psychosocial:** Behavioral and psychoeducational approaches that focus on language development and socialization. Particular emphasis on parent consultation and community support. **Psychopharmacologic:** No medications primarily for autism but some evidence for psychopharmacologic treatment of related overactive, anxious, or aggressive behavior using medications for some of the disorders listed above.

References

American Academy of Child and Adolescent Psychiatry. (2015, December). Violent behavior in children and adolescents (Facts for Families No. 55). Retrieved from *www.aacap.org/AACAP/Families_and_Youth/Facts_for_Families/FFF-Guide/Understanding-Violent-Behavior-In-Children-and-Adolescents-055.aspx.*

American Psychiatric Association. (2013). *Diagnostic and statistical manual of mental disorders* (5th ed., text rev.). Arlington, VA: Author.

American Psychological Association Task Force. (2008). Are zero tolerance policies effective in the schools?: An evidentiary review and recommendations. *American Psychologist, 63,* 852–862.

Anderson, K. P., Ritter, G. W., & Boyd, A. (2015, February). *Do school discipline policies treat students fairly? A second look at school discipline rate disparities.* Paper presented at the Association for Education Finance and Policy Annual Conference, Washington, DC.

Anderson, L., Brubaker, N., Alleman-Brooks, J., & Duffy, G. (1985). A qualitative study of seatwork in first grade classrooms. *The Elementary School Journal, 86*(2), 123–140.

Anderson-Inman, L. (1981). Transenvironmental programming: Promoting success in the regular class by maximizing the effect of resource room assistance. *Journal of Special Education Technology, 4*(4), 3–12.

Anderson-Inman, L., Walker, H., & Purcell, J. (1984). Promoting the transfer of skills across settings: Transenvironmental programming for handicapped students in the mainstream. In W. Heward, T. Heron, P. Hill, & J. Trap-Porter (Eds.), *Focus on behavior analysis in education* (pp. 17–37). Columbus, OH: Merrill.

Ariely, D. (2012). *The honest truth about dishonesty: How we lie to everyone—especially ourselves.* New York: Harper.

Armstrong, M. (2022). *Unpacking the myths: Restorative justice and bullying: A conversation.* [blog post].

Baer, D., & Wolf, M. (1970). The entry into natural communities of reinforcement. In R. Ulrich, T. Stachnik, & J. Mabry (Eds.), *Control of human behavior* (pp. 319–324). Glenview, IL: Scott, Foresman.

Bradley, R., Doolittle, J., & Bartolotta, R. (2008). Building on the data and adding to the discussion: The experiences and outcomes of students with emotional disturbance. *Journal of Behavioral Education, 17*(1), 4–23.

Brooks, A. (2015, September 14). 10 tactics for dealing with tantrums in the classroom. Retrieved from *www.rasmussen.edu/degrees/education/blog/dealing-with-tantrums-in-the-classroom.*

Brooks, D. (2022, January 13). America is falling apart at the seams. Retrieved from *www.nytimes.com/2022/01/13/opinion/america-falling-apart.html.*

Brophy, J., & Evertson, C. (1981). *Student characteristics and teaching.* White Plains, NY: Longman.

Brophy, J., & Good, T. (1970). Teachers' communication of differential expectations for children's classroom performance: Some behavioral data. *Journal of Educational Psychology, 61,* 365–374.

Brophy, J., & Good, T. (1974). *Teacher–student relationships: Causes and consequences.* New York: Holt, Rinehart & Winston.

Brophy, J., & Good, T. (1986). Teacher behavior and student achievement. In M. Wittrock (Ed.), *Handbook of research on teaching* (3rd ed., pp. 328–375). New York: Macmillan.

Brown, E., Low, S., Smith, B., & Haggerty, K. (2011). Outcomes from a randomized controlled trial of Steps to Respect: A bullying prevention program. *School Psychology Review, 40*(3), 423–433.

Brunsting, N., Srechovic, M., & Lane, K. (2014). Special education teacher burnout: A synthesis of research from 1979 to 2013. *Education and Treatment of Children, 37*(4), 681–712.

Chafouleas, S., Johnson, S., & Riley-Tillman, T., & Iovino, E. (2021). *School-based behavioral assessment: Informing prevention and intervention* (2nd ed.). New York: Guilford Press.

Colvin, G., & Scott, R. (2015). *Managing the cycle of acting-out behavior in the classroom.* Thousand Oaks, CA: Corwin Press.

Cook, C., Gresham, F., Kern, L., Barreras, R., Thornton, S., & Crews, D. (2008). Social skills training for secondary students with emotional and/or behavioral disorders: A review and analysis of the meta-analytic literature. *Journal of Emotional and Behavioral Disorders, 16*(3), 131–144.

Cooper, J. (2021, May 11). Texas State psychology professors and students study how and why youngsters lie. Retrieved from *https://news.txstate.edu/research-and-innovation/2021/why-children-lie.html.*

Delaney, A., Frey, A., & Walker, H. (2015). Relational aggression in school settings: Definition, development strategies, and implications. *Children & Schools, 37*(2), 79–89.

Deno, S. (1985). Curriculum-based measurement: The emerging alternative. *Exceptional Children. 52(3),* 219–232.

DiPerna, C. (2005). Academic enablers and student achievement: Implications for assessment and intervention in the schools. *Psychology in the Schools, 43*(1), 7–17.

DiPerna, C., & Elliott, S. (2002). Promoting academic enabler to improve student achievement: An introduction to the mini-series. *School Psychology Review, 31*(3), 293–297.

Doan, S., Greer, L., Schwartz, H., Steiner, E., & Woo, A. (2022). *State of the American teacher and state of the American principal surveys.* Santa Monica, CA: Rand Corporation.

Dougherty, B., Fowler, S., & Paine, S. (1985). The use of peer monitors to reduce negative interactions during recess. *Journal of Applied Behavior Analysis, 18,* 141–153.

DuPaul, G., & Eckert, T. (1994). The effects of social skills curricula: Now you see them, now you don't. *School Psychology Quarterly, 9*(2), 113–132.

Durlak, J., Domitrovitch, C., Weissberg, R., & Gullotta, R. (Eds.). (2015). *Handbook of Social and Emotional Learning.* New York: Guilford Press.

Dynamic indicators of basic early literacy skills (DIBELS) (8th ed.). (2018). Eugene: University of Oregon.

Espelage, D., Anderson, E., Brown, V., Lane, K., McMahon, R., & Reynolds, C. (2013). Understanding and preventing violence directed against teachers: Recommendations for a national research, practice, policy agenda. *American Psychologist, 68*(2), 75–87.

Evertson, C., & Smithey, M. (2000). Research and mentoring effects on proteges' classroom practice: An experimental field study. *Journal of Teacher Education, 93*(5), 294–304.

Fad, K., & Campos, D. (2021). *Lonely kids in a connected world: What teachers can do.* Eugene, OR: Ancora.

Forness, S. R., Walker, H. M., & Kavale, K. A. (1983).

Forness, S. R., Walker, H. M., & Kavale, K. A. (2003). Psychiatric disorders and their treatments: A primer for teachers. *Exceptional Children, 36*(2), 42–49.

Fowler, S., Dougherty, B., Kirby, K., & Kohler, F. (1986). Role reversals: An analysis of therapeutic effects achieved with disruptive boys during their appointments as peer monitors. *Journal of Applied Behavior Analysis, 19*(4), 437–444.

Frey, K., Hirschstein, M., Schoiack Edstrom, L., MacKenzie, E., & Broderick, C. (2005). Reducing playground bullying and supportive beliefs: An experimental trial of the Steps to Respect program. *Developmental Psychology, 41,* 479–490.

Gaffney, H., Farrington, D., Espelage, D., & Ttofi, M. (2019). Are cyberbullying intervention and prevention programs effective?: A systematic meta-analytical review. *Aggressive and Violent Behavior, 45,* 134–153.

Gaffney, H., Farrington, D., & Ttofi, M. (2019). Examining the effectiveness of school bullying intervention program globally: A meta-analysis. *International Journal of Bullying Prevention, 1,* 14–31.

Garrity, C. (1996). *Bully-proofing your school: Working with victims and bullies in elementary school.* Victoria, BC, Canada: Abe Books.

Garrity, C., Jens, K., Porter, W., & Sager, N. (2000). *Bully-proofing your school:*

A comprehensive approach for elementary schools (2nd ed.). Longmont, CO: Sopris West.

Gerber, M., & Semmel, M. (1984). Teacher as imperfect test: Reconceptualizing the referral process. *Educational Psychologist, 19*(3), 137–148.

Gilliam, W. S., & Shahar, G. (2006). Preschool and child care expulsion and suspension: Rates and predictors in one state. *Infants and Young Children, 19*(3), 228–245.

Ginsburg-Block, M., & Rohrbeck, C. (2006). A meta-analytic review of social, self-concept, and behavioral outcomes of peer-assisted learning. *Journal of Educational Psychology, 98*(4), 732–749.

Gion, C., McIntosh, K., & Horner, R. (2014). Patterns of minor office discipline referrals in schools using SWIS. Retrieved from *https://assets-global.website-files.com/5d3725188825e071f1670246/5d7979befedbb681be830b04_final-odr-brief.pdf.*

Golly, A. (1994). *The use and effects of alpha and beta commands in elementary classroom settings.* Unpublished doctoral dissertation, University of Oregon.

Good, T. (1983). *Classroom research: A decade of progress.* Milton Park, UK: Taylor & Francis.

Good, T. (1987). Two decades of research on teacher expectations: Findings and future directions. *Journal of Teacher Education, 38*(4), 32–47.

Gottfredson, G., & Gottfredson, D. (2001). What schools do to prevent problem behavior and promote safe environments. *Journal of Educational and Psychological Consultation, 12*(4), 313–344.

Green, R. (2014). *The explosive child: A new approach for understanding and parenting easily frustrated, chronically inflexible children.* New York: Harper.

Greenwood, C. (1997). *Classwide peer tutoring: Behavior and social issues.* New York: Springer.

Greenwood, C. R., Carta, J., & Hall, R. V. (1988). The use of peer tutoring strategies in classroom management and educational instruction. *School Psychology Review, 17*(2), 258–275.

Greenwood, C. R., Maheady, L., & Delquadri, J. (2002). Class-wide peer tutoring programs. In M. Shinn, H. Walker, & G. Stoner (Eds.), *Interventions for academic and behavior problems: II. Preventive and remedial approaches* (pp. 611–649). Bethesda, MD: National Association of School Psychologists.

Gregory, A., Bell, J., & Pollock, M. (2016). How educators can eradicate disparities in school discipline: Issues in intervention. In R. J. Skiba, K. Mediratta, & M. K. Rausch (Eds.), *Inequality in school discipline: Research and practice to reduce disparities* (pp. 153–170). New York: Palgrave Macmillan.

Gregory, A., Hafen, C., Ruzek, E., Mikami, A., Allen, J., & Pianta, R. (2016). Closing the racial discipline gap in classrooms by changing teacher practice. *School Psychology Review, 45,* 171–191.

Gresham, F., Mai, B., & Cook, C. (2006). Social skills training for teaching replacement behaviors: Remediating acquisition deficits in at risk students. *Behavioral Disorders, 31*(4), 363–377.

Gruener, B. (n.d.). *Top character education programs* [blog post]. Building character in schools. Prosign Design. Retrieved from *https://prodesignsystems.com.*

Hawken, L., Crone, D., Bundock, K., & Horner, R. (2021). *Responding to problem behaviors in schools* (3rd ed.). New York: Guilford Press.

Hawkins, J. D., Catalano, R. F., Kosterman, R., Abbott, R., & Hill, K. G. (1999). Preventing adolescent health risk behaviors by strengthening protection during childhood. *Archives of Pediatric and Adolescent Medicine, 153,* 226–234.

Hersh, R., & Walker, H. (1983). Great expectations: Making schools effective for all students. *Policy Studies Review, 2,* 144–188.

Hollinger, J. (1987). Social skills for behaviorally disordered children as preparation for mainstreaming: Theory, practice, and new directions. *Remedial and Special Education, 8*(4), 17–27.

Homme, L., DeBaca, J., Devine, R., Steinhorst, R., & Rickert, E. (1963). Use of the Premack principle in controlling the behavior of nursery school children. *Journal of the Experimental Analysis of Behavior, 6*(4), 544.

Hops, H., & Walker, H. (1988). CLASS: *Contingencies for learning academic and social skills.* Seattle, WA: Educational Achievement Systems.

Hops, H., Walker, H., Fleischman, D., Nagoshi, J., Omura, R., Skinrud, K., & Taylor, J. (1978). A standardized in-class program for acting-out children: II. Field test evaluations. *Journal of Educational Psychology, 70*(4), 636–644.

Horner, R., Sugai, G., Todd, A., & Lewis-Palmer, T. (2005). Schoolwide positive behavior support: An alternative approach to discipline in schools. In L. Bambara & L. Kern (Eds.), *Individualized supports for students with problem behaviors: Designing positive behavior plans* (pp. 359–390). New York: Guilford Press.

Institute of Medicine. (2009). *Preventing mental, emotional and behavioral disorders among young people: Progress and possibilities.* Washington, DC: National Academy of Sciences.

Irvin, L., & Walker, H. (1993). Improving social skills assessment of children with disabilities: Construct development and applications of technology [Special Issue]. *Journal of Special Education Technology, 12*(1), 63–70.

Irvin, L., Walker, H., Noell, J., Singer, G., Irvine, A., Marquez, K., & Britz, B. (1992). Measuring children's social skills using microcomputer-based videodisc assessment. *Behavior Modification, 16*(4), 475–503.

Johnson, O., Wildy, H., & Shand, J. (2019). A decade of teacher expectations research, 2008–2018: Historical foundations, new developments, and future pathways. *Australian Journal of Education, 63*(1), 44–73.

Josephson Institute. (2014). Character counts—Student engagement project: Research summary. Retrieved from *https://charactercounts.org/research/summary.html.*

Kaimuki Middle School. (2018, August 19). *Independent seatwork is managed and used when needed: Top ten tips for independent seatwork* [blog post]. Retrieved from *https://kaimukimiddle.wordpress.com/2018/08/19/independent-seatwork.*

Kauffman, J., Lloyd, J., & McGee, K. (1989). Adaptive and maladaptive behavior: Teacher attitudes and their technical assistance needs. *Journal of Special Education, 23*(2), 185–200.

Kazdin, A. (1972). Response cost: The removal of conditioned reinforcers for therapeutic change. *Behavior Therapy, 3,* 533–546.

Kazdin, A. (1989). *Behavior modification in applied settings* (4th ed.). Pacific Grove, CA: Brookes/Cole.

Kellam, S., Ling, X., Merisca, R., & Brown, H. (1998). The effect of the level of aggression in the first grade classroom on the course and malleability of aggressive behavior into middle school. *Development and Psychopathology, 10*(2), 165–185.

Kerr, M., & Zigmond, N. (1986). What do high school teachers want?: A study of expectations and standards. *Educational and Treatment of Children, 9,* 239–249.

Kolko, D., & Lindhiem, O. (2014). Introduction to the special series on booster sessions and long-term maintenance of treatment gains. *Journal of Abnormal Child Psychology, 42*(3), 339–342.

Kuczynski, L., Kochanska, G., Radke-Yarrow, M., & Girnius-Brown, O. (1987). A developmental interpretation of young children's noncompliance. *Developmental Psychology, 23,* 276–282.

Kunsch, C., Jitendra, A., & Sood, S. (2007). The effects of peer-mediate instruction in mathematics for students with learning problems: A research synthesis. *Learning Disabilities Research and Practice, 22*(1).

Kyriacou, C. (1987). Teacher stress and burnout: An international review. *Educational Research Journal, 29*(2), 146–152.

LaGreca, A., & Mesibov, G. (1979). Social skills intervention with learning disabled children: Selecting skills and implementing training. *Journal of Clinical Child Psychology, 8*(3), 234–241.

Lane, K., Menzies, H., Oakes, W., & Kalberg, J. (2020). *Developing a schoolwide framework to prevent and manage learning and behavior problems* (2nd ed.). New York: Guilford Press.

Lane, K., Pierson, M., & Givner, C. (2003). Teacher expectations of student behavior: Which skills do elementary and secondary teachers deem necessary for success in the classroom? *Education and Treatment of Children, 26,* 413–430.

Lane, K., Pierson, M., & Givner, C. (2004). Secondary teachers' views on social competence: Skills essential for success. *Journal of Special Education, 38*(3), 174–186.

Levine, T., Serota, K., Carey, F., & Messer, D. (2013). Teenagers lie a lot: A further investigation into the prevalence of lying. *Communication Research Reports, 30,* 211–220.

Linsin, M. (2011). How to respond to a disrespectful student. *Smart Classroom.* Retrieved from *https://smartclassroommanagement.com/2011/02/19/how-to-respond-to-a-disrespectful-student*

Lloyd, J., Landrum, T., & Hallahan, D. (1991). Self-monitoring applications for classroom intervention. In G. Stoner, M. Shinn, & H. Walker (Eds.), *Interventions for achievement and behavior problems* (pp. 201–214). Bethesda, MD: National Association of School Psychologists.

Luby, J. (2013). Treatment of anxiety and depression in the preschool period. *Journal of the American of Child and Adolescent Psychiatry, 52,* 346–358.

May, C. (2012, June 19). When men are less moral than women. Retrieved from *www.scientificamerican.com/article/when-men-are-less-moral-than-woman.*

Mazar, N., On, A., & Ariely, D. (2008). The dishonesty of honest people: A theory of self-concept maintenance. *Journal of Marketing Research, 45*(6), 633–644.

McCabe, D. (2019). Insights into how and why students cheat at high performing schools. *Ethics & Behavior, 22*(5), 378–399.

McClelland, D. C. (1961). *The achieving society.* New York: Free Press.

McClelland, D. C. (1987). *Human motivation.* New York: Cambridge University Press.

McFall, R. (1982). A review and reformulation of the concept of social skills. *Behavioral Assessment, 4*(1), 1–33.

McKibben, S. (2014). *Two minutes to better student behavior.* ASCD guest blog.

McMahon, R., & Forehand, R. (2005). *Helping the noncompliant child* (2nd ed.). New York: Guilford Press

Menard, S., & Gropeter, J. (2014). Evaluation of Bully Proofing Your School: An elementary school bullying intervention. *Journal of School Violence, 13*(2), 188–209.

Mitchell, M., Goodwin, H., Limber, S., Hudson-Fledge, M., Thompson, M., & Sprague, J. (2019). *Testing integrative models to improve school safety: Positive behavior interventions and supports and the Olweus Bullying Prevention Program.* Washington, DC: National Institute of Justice.

Morgan, D., & Jenson, W. (1988). *Teaching behavior disordered students.* Columbus, OH: Merrill.

National Center for Education Statistics. (2018). *Annual report.* Washington, DC: U.S. Department of Education.

Newcomb, A., Bukowski, W., & Patee, L. (1993). Children's peer relations: A meta-analytic review of popular, rejected, neglected, controversial, and average sociometric status. *Psychological Bulletin, 113*(1), 99–128.

Nocera, E., Hillbread, K., & Nocera, G. (2014). Impact of schoolwide positive support on student behavior in the middle school grades. *Research in Middle Level Education, 37*(8), 1–14.

Office of the Surgeon General. (2021). *Protecting youth mental health: The U.S. Surgeon General's Advisory.* Washington, DC: U.S. Department of Health and Human Services. Retrieved from *www.hhs.gov/sites/default/files/surgeon-general-youth-mental-health-advisory.pdf.*

O'Leary, D., & Drabman, R. (1971). Token reinforcement systems in the classroom: A review. *Psychological Bulletin, 75*(6), 379–398.

Oliver, R., Wehby, J., & Reschly, D. (2011). Teacher classroom management practices: Effects on disruptive or aggressive student behavior. *Society for Research on Educational Effectiveness.*

Olweus, D. (1994). Bullying at school: Basic facts and effects of a school-based intervention program. *Journal of Child Psychology and Psychiatry, 35*(7), 1171–1190.

Olweus, D. (2007). *Bullying prevention program: Schoolwide guide.* Davers, MA: Hazelden.

Olweus, D., & Limber, S. P. (2010). Bullying in school:Evaluation and dissemination of the Olweus Prevention Program. *American Journal of Orthopsychiatry, 80*(1), 124–134.

O'Neill, R.,Horner, R., Albin, R.,Storey, K & Sprague. J, (1990). *Functional analysis of problem behavior: A practical assessment guide.* Pacific Grove, CA: Wadsworth.

Ortiz, C. (2018, November 30). *Timeouts get a bad rap but they work—when used correctly* [blog post]. Retrieved November 5, 2021, from *www.washingtonpost.com/lifestyle.*

Paine, S., Hops, H., Walker, H., Greenwood, C., Fleischman, D., & Guild, J. (1982). Repeated treatment effects: A study of maintaining behavior change in socially withdrawn children. *Behavior Modification, 6,* 177–199.

Park, J. (2017). Social skills training for elementary students with behavioral challenges: A review of the literature. *Culminating Projects in Special Education, 43.* Retrieved from *https://repository.stcloud state edu/sped__etds/43.*

Parker, G., & Asher, S. R. (1987). Peer relations and later personal adjustment: Are low accepted children at risk? *Psychological Bulletin, 102*(3), 357–389.

Patterson, G. (1982). *Coercive family process.* Eugene, OR: Castalia Press.

Patterson, G., Reid, J., & Dishion, T. (1992). *Antisocial boys.* Eugene, OR: Castalia Press.

PBIS. (2021). Center on Positive Behavioral Interventions and Supports (*www.pbis.org*). College of Education, University of Oregon, Eugene, OR.

PENT. (n.d.). Debriefing strategies: What is debriefing? Retrieved from *www.pent.ca.gov/pbis/tier1/debriefing-pbis-pent.aspx.*

Peterson, R., O'Connor, A., & Fluke, S. (2014). *Character Counts!: Program brief.* Lincoln: Student Engagement Project, University of Nebraska–Lincoln, and the Nebraska Department of Education. Retrieved from *http://k12engagement.unl.edu/charactercounts.*

Raffaele-Mendez, L., & Knoff, H. (2003). Who gets suspended from school and why: A demographic analysis of schools and disciplinary infractions in a large urban school district. *Education and Treatment of Children, 26*(1), 30–51.

Reid, J. (1993). Prevention of conduct disorder before and after school entry: Relating interventions to developmental findings. *Development and Psychopathology, 5*(1/2), 243–262.

Reinke, W. M., Lewis-Palmer, T., & Merrell, K. (2008). The Classroom Check-Up: A class-wide teacher consultation model for increasing praise and decreasing disruptive behavior. *School Psychology Review, 37*(3), 315–332.

Reynolds, L. K., & Kelley, M. L. (1997). The efficacy of a response cost-based treatment package for managing aggressive behavior in preschoolers. *Behavior Modification, 21*(2), 216–230.

Rhode, G., Morgan, D., & Jenson, W. (1983). Generalization and maintenance of treatment gains of behaviorally handicapped students from resource rooms to regular classrooms. *Journal of Applied Behavior Analysis, 16*(2), 171–188.

Rimm-Kaufman, S., Larsen, R., Curby, T., Baroody, A., Merritt, E., Abry, T., . . . Thomas, J. (2012, September). *Efficacy of the Responsive Classroom Approach: Results from a three-year longitudinal, randomized controlled trial.* Washington, DC: Society for Research in Educational Effectiveness.

Rock, M., & Thread, B. (2009). Promote student success during independent seatwork. *Intervention in School and Clinic, 44*(3), 179–184.

Romer, D., & Heller, T. (1983). Social adaptation of mentally retarded adults in community settings: A social-ecological approach. *Applied Research in Mental Retardation, 4,* 303–314.

Rosenshine, B. (2012). Principles of instruction: Research-based strategies that all teachers should know. *American Educator, 36*(1), 12–19. Retrieved from *www.aft.org/newspubs/periodicals/ae.*

Schoen, S. (1986). Decreasing noncompliance in a severely multi-handicapped child. *Psychology in the Schools, 23,* 88–94.

Serota, K., Levine, R., & Boster, F. (2009). The prevalence of lying in America: Three studies of self-reported lying. *Human Communication Research, 36,* 2–25.

Shore, K. (2003). *Elementary teacher's discipline problem solver: A practical A–Z guide for managing classroom behavior problems.* San Francisco: Jossey-Bass.

Shore, K. (2007, August). *Managing cheating* [blog post]. Education World.

Shore, K. (2018, April). *Lying in the classroom* [blog post]. Education World. Retrieved from *https://.Brianlies.com.*

Shore, K. S. (2021, November). *Classroom problem solver: Completing seatwork* [blog post]. Education World. Retrieved from *www.educationworld.com/a_curr/shore/shore057.shtml.*

Simcha-Fagan, O., Langer, T., Gersten, J., & Eisenberg, J. (1975). *Violent and antisocial behavior: A longitudinal study of urban behavior* (OCD-CB-480). Washington, DC: U.S. Office of Child Development.

Simpson, R. (2004). Inclusion of students with behavior disorders in general education settings: Research and measurement issues. *Behavioral Disorders, 30*(1), 19–31.

Skiba, R., Arredondo, M., & Williams, N. (2014). More than a metaphor?: The contribution of exclusionary discipline to a School-to-Prison Pipeline. *Journal of Equity & Excellence in Education, 47,* 546–564.

Skiba, R., Horner, R., Chung, C., Rausch, M., May, S., & Tobin, R. (2011). Race is not neutral: A national investigation of African-American and Latino disproportionality in school discipline. *School Psychology Review, 40*(1), 85–107.

Skiba, R., & Losen, D. (2015–2016). From reaction to prevention: Turning the page on school discipline. *American Educator, 39,* 4–11.

Skiba, R., Michael, R., Carol-Nardo, A., & Peterson, R. (2002). The color of discipline: Sources of racial and gender disproportionality in school punishment. *The Urban Review, 34,* 317–342.

Smarick, A. (2021). *An encouraging consensus on character education* [blog post]. Education World.

Sprague, J., & Golly, A. (2004). *BEST: Building positive behavior support in schools.* Longmont, CO: Voyager Sopris Learning.

Sprague, J., & Golly, A. (2012). *BEST: Building positive behavior support in schools* (2nd ed.). Longmont, CO: Voyager Sopris Learning.

Sprague, J., & Walker, H. (2005). *Safe and healthy schools.* New York: Guilford Press.

Sprague, J., & Walker, H. (2021). *Safe and healthy schools* (2nd ed.). New York: Guilford Press.

Stokes, T., & Baer, D. (1977). An implicit technology of generalization. *Journal of Applied Behavior Analysis, 10*(2), 349–367.

Stormshak, E., Connell, A., & Dishion, T. (2009). An adaptive approach to family-centered intervention in schools: Linking intervention engagement to academic outcomes in middle and high schools. *Prevention Science, 10*(3), 221–235.

Stormshak, E. A., Connell, A. M., Ve´ronneau, M.-H., Myers, M. W., Dishion, T. J., Kavanagh, K., & Caruthers, A. S. (2011). An ecological approach to promoting early adolescent mental health and social adaptation: Family-centered intervention in public middle schools. *Child Development, 82,* 209–225.

Stormshak, E. A., & Dishion, T. J. (2009). *Intervening in children's lives: An ecological, family-centered approach to mental health care.* Washington, DC: American Psychological Association.

Stouthamer-Loeber, M. (1986). Lying as a problem behavior in children: A review. *Clinical Psychology Review, 6,* 267–289.

Strain, P. (1981). *The utilization of classroom peers as behavior change agents.* New York: Plenum Press.

Strain, P., Lambert, D., Kerr, M., Stagg, V., & Lenkner, D. (1983). Naturalistic assessment of children's compliance to teacher's requests and consequences for compliance. *Journal of Applied Behavior Analysis, 16*(2), 243–249.

Strain, P., & Timm, M. (2001), Remediation and prevention of aggression: An evaluation of the Regional Intervention Program over a quarter century. *Behavioral Disorders, 26*(4), 297–313.

Tanol, G., Johnson, L., McComas, J., & Cote, E. (2010). Responding to rule violations or rule following: A comparison of two versions of the Good Behavior Game with kindergarten students. *Journal of School Psychology, 48*(5), 337–355.

Ttofi, M., & Farrington, D. (2011). Effectiveness of school-based programs to reduce bullying: A systematic and meta-analytic review. *Journal of Experimental Criminology, 7,* 27–56.

U.S. Department of Education and National Institute of Justice. (2014). *Dear colleague letter on discipline in schools.* Washington, DC.

U.S. Department of Education and National Institute of Justice. (2018). *Dear colleague letter on discipline in schools.* Washington, DC.

U.S. National Institute of Justice. (2015, April) *2015 annual report.* Washington, DC.

U.S. Secret Service National Threat Center. (2021). *Averting targeted school violence: A US Secret Service analysis of plots against schools.* Washington, DC: U.S. Secret Service.

Verigin, B., Meijer, E., & Bogaard, G. (2019, December 3). Lie prevalence, lie characteristics, and strategies of self-reported good liars. *PLoS One, 14*(12), e0225566.

Versova, M., & Mala, D. (2016). Attitude toward school and learning and academic achievement among adolescents. Retrieved from *www.researchgate. net/publication/310742651_Attitude_toward_School_and_Learning_and_ Academic_Achievement_of_Adolescents.*

Walker, H. M. (1983). Applications of response cost in school settings: Outcomes, issues, and recommendations. *Exceptional Education Quarterly, 3*(4), 47–55.

Walker, H. (1984). The Social Behavior Survival Program (SBS): A systematic approach to the integration of handicapped children into less restrictive settings. *Education and Treatment of Children, 6*(4), 421–441.

Walker, H. M. (1986). The assessments for integration into mainstream settings (AIMS) assessment system: Rationale, instruments, procedures and outcomes. *Journal of Clinical Child Psychology, 15*(1), 55–63.

Walker, H. M. (1995). *The acting out child: coping with classroom disruption.* Longmont, CO: Sopris West.

Walker, H., & Buckley, N. (1972). Programming generalization and maintenance of treatment effects across time and across settings. *Journal of Applied Behavior Analysis, 5,* 209–224.

Walker, H. M., & Buckley, N. K. (1973). Teacher attention to appropriate and inappropriate classroom behavior. *Focus on Exceptional Children,* 5–12.

Walker, H. M., & Buckley, N. (1974). *Token reinforcement techniques.* Eugene, OR: EB Press.

Walker, H., Colvin, G., & Ramsey, E. (1995). *Antisocial behavior in school—Exhibit 11 (The efficacy of a response cost intervention in increasing positive social interactions in free-play settings among aggressive boys).* Pacific Grove, CA: Brookes/Cole.

Walker, H., Fonseca-Retana, G., & Gersten, R. (1988). Replication of the CLASS program in Costa Rica: Implementation procedures and program outcomes. *Behavior Modification, 12*(1), 133–154.

Walker, H. M., & Hops, H. (1979). The CLASS program for acting-out children: R & D procedures, program outcomes and implementation issues. *School Psychology Digest, 8,* 37–381.

Walker, H. M., Hops, H., & Greenwood, C. (1981). RECESS: Research and development of a behavior management package for remediating social aggression in the school setting. In P. Strain (Ed.), *The utilization of classroom peers as behavior change agents* (pp. 261–303). New York: Plenum Press.

Walker, H. M., Hops, H., & Greenwood, C. (1984). The CORBEH research and development model: Programmatic issues and strategies. In S. Paine, T. Bellamy, & B. Wilcox (Eds.) *Human services that work* (pp. 57–78). Baltimore: Brookes.

Walker, H., Marquez, B., Yeaton, P., Pennefather, J., Forness, S., & Vincent, C. (2015). Teacher judgment in assessing students' social behavior within a response-to-intervention framework: Using what teachers know. *Education and Treatment of Children, 38*(3), 363–383.

Walker, H., McConnell, S., Holmes, D., Todis, B., Walker, J., & Golden, N. (1983). *The Accepts (A curriculum for children's effective peer and teacher skills) program.* Austin, TX: PRO-ED.

Walker, H. M., Ramsey, E., & Gresham, F. M. (2003–2004, Winter). Heading off disruptive behavior: How early intervention can reduce defiant behavior and win back teaching time. *American Educator,* pp. 6–19.

Walker, H. M., Ramsey, E., & Gresham, F. M. (2004). *Antisocial behavior in school* (2nd ed.). Belmont, CA: Wadsworth/Thomson Learning.

Walker, H., & Rankin, R. (1983). Assessing the behavioral expectations and demands of less restrictive settings. *School Psychology Review, 12,* 274–284.

Walker, H. M., Schwarz, I., Nippold, M., Irvin, L., & Noell, J. (1994). Social skills in school-age children and youth: Issues and best practices in assessment and intervention. *Language Disorders, 14*(3), 70–82.

Walker, H., Severson, H., & Feil, E. (2015). *Systematic screening for behavior disorders (SSBD).* Eugene, OR: Ancora.

Walker, H. M., Severson, H. H., Nicholson, F., Kehle, T., Jenson, W. R., & Clark, E. (1994). Replication of the Systematic Screening for Behavior Disorders (SSBD) procedure for the identification of at-risk children. *Journal of Emotional and Behavioral Disorders, 2*(2), 66–77.

Walker, H. M., Severson, H. H., Seeley, J. R., & Feil, E. G. (2014). Multiple gating approaches to the universal screening of students with school related behavior disorders. In R. Kettler, R. Glover, C. Albers, & K. Feeney-Kettler (Eds.), *Universal screening in educational settings: Identification, implementation, and interpretation* (pp. 47–77). Washington DC: Division 16 Practitioners' Series of the American Psychological Association.

Walker, H. M., Sprague, J., & Severson, H. (2016). Antisocial behavior and school violence: Understanding and preventing violence. In R. Haslam (Ed.), *Medical problems in the classroom* (6th ed., pp. 469–518). Austin, TX: PRO-ED.

Walker, H. M., & Sylwester, R. (1998). Refusal and resistance. *Exceptional Children, 30*(6), 52–58.

Walker, H. M., & Walker, J. E. (1991). *Coping with noncompliance in the classroom: A positive approach for teachers.* Austin, TX: PRO-ED.

Weimer, M. (2009, July 20). *Effective teaching strategies: Six keys to classroom excellence* [blog post].

Weiner, H. (1962). Some effects of response cost upon human operant behavior. *Journal of the Experimental Analysis of Behavior, 5,* 210–218.

Weissberg, R., Durlak, J., Domitrovich, C., & Gullotta, T. (2015). *Social and emotional learning.* In J. Durlak, C. Domitrovich, R. Weissberg, & T. Gullota (Eds.), *Handbook of social and emotional learning* (pp. 3–20). New York: Guilford Press.

Wolf, T. L., McLaughlin, T. F., & Williams, R. (2006). Time-out interventions and strategies: A brief review and recommendations. *International Journal of Special Education, 21,* 22–29.

Wong, K., Kauffman, J., & Lloyd, J. (1991). Choices for integration: Selecting teachers for mainstreamed students with emotional or behavioral disorders. *Intervention in School and Clinic, 27*(2), 108–115.

Young, J. (2014). *Encouragement in the classroom.* Alexandria, VA: Association for Supervision and Curriculum Development (ASCD).

Zanette, S., Walsh, M., Augiment, L., & Lee, K. (2020, April). Differences and similarities in lying frequency, moral evaluations, and beliefs about lying among children with and without conduct disorders. *Journal of Experimental Child Psychology, 192,* 104768.

Zelazo, P., Blair, C., & Willoughby, M. (2016). *Executive function: Implications for education* (NCER 2017-2000). Washington, DC: National Center for Education Research, Institute of Education Sciences, U.S. Department of Education. Retrieved from *https://ies.ed.gov/ncer/pubs/20172000/pdf/20172000.pdf.*

Index

229

234 Index

Index

234 Index

Tantrums (*continued*)
  debriefing and follow-up, 82–84
  defined, 78
  management of, 81–82
  oppositional defiant disorder and, 78
  prevention of, 80–81
  RIP and, 82–84
  teacher reactions to, 78–79
Teacher
  dropout rates of, 98–99
  high-expectation students and, 178
  and inadequate preparation for
    challenging behaviors, 98
  match with target student, 178
  violence against, 101
Teacher commands
  alpha *versus* beta, 4–5
  frequency of, 5
  initiating *versus* terminating, 5–7, 6f, 7t
  tone and, 6–7
Teacher defiance/disrespect
  coping and prevention strategies,
    101–102
  defined, 99
  key features of, 99–100
  ODRs and, 67, 69–70
Teacher directives, strategies for
  consequation, 12–15
  effective deliverance guidelines, 11–12
Teacher expectations
  implicit bias and, 68
  types of, 73
  verbal feedback and, 133–134
Teacher implicit bias; *see* Implicit bias
Teacher language, effect on student
  behavior, 149
Teacher praise, examples and guidelines
  for, 120–121
Teacher profiles, SBS Inventory and, 180
Teacher resources, 192–209
  Classroom Check-UP (CCU), 200–201
  Developing a Schoolwide Framework
    to Prevent and Manage Learning and
    Behavior Problems, 207–208
  Dynamic Indicators of Basic Early
    Literacy Skills (DIBELS), 203–205
  The Explosive Child, 208–209
  Family Check-UP (FCU), 198–199
  First Step Next (FSN) Program,
    201–203

Positive Behavioral Interventions and
  Supports (PBIS), 194–196
School-Based Behavioral Assessment:
  Informing Prevention and
  Intervention, 209
Second Step Program, 196–198
Steps to Respect (STR), 193–194
Systematic Screening for Behavior
  Disorders (SSBD), 205–207
Technology, cheating incidence and,
  106
Terminating commands, 5–6, 7t
Time-out, 155–159
  administering, 157–158
  application guidelines, 156–157
  definition and examples, 155–156
  important issues in, 158–159
Transference strategies, 175–185
  from one recess period to another,
    176
  for reintegrating into general
    education classes, 177–185 (*see also*
    Reintegration strategies)
  teacher monitoring/rating in non-
    intervention settings, 175–176, 176f
Triple A strategy, for enhancing executive
  function, 56
2 x 10 strategy, 73–74

U

Undesirable behavior; *see* Decreasing
  undesirable behavior; specific
  behaviors
US National Institute of Justice,
  CrimeSolutions unit of, 92

V

Vandalism; *see also* Damaging behaviors
  case study of, 64–66
  types of, 61–62
Violence
  increase in, 89
  students at risk of, 89
  against teachers, 101 (*see also*
    Insubordination; Teacher defiance/
    disrespect)

Z

Zero tolerance policies, ineffectiveness
  of, 68